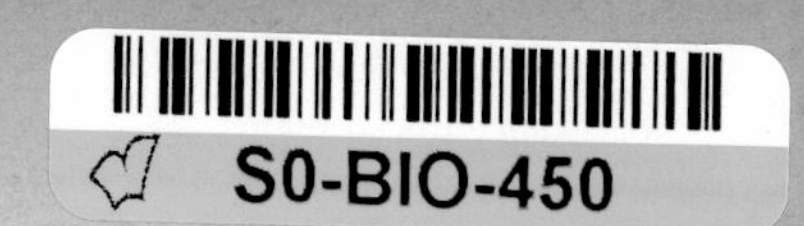

JACK PAAR

likes to refer to himself as being just like any other fellow with a wife and daughter, a pleasant house in the suburbs, a Mercedes convertible, twenty-seven pairs of imported sunglasses and an hour-and-three-quarter TV show.

→ Others are less charitable—he's been referred to as the tallest elf in the world, a wholesome 4-H member just awarded a prize for sowing wild oats, a pugnacious pixie and a number of other things better left out of print.

To find out if you're up to Paar, turn this page and start reading! You won't be sorry you did. →

I KID YOU NOT, Jack Paar's outrageously funny autobiography, was originally published at $3.95 by Little, Brown & Company.

POCKET BOOKS, INC. • NEW YORK

I Kid You Not

Little, Brown edition published April, 1960

GIANT CARDINAL edition published May, 1961
4th printing...May, 1961

This GIANT CARDINAL edition includes every word contained in the original, higher-priced edition. It is printed from brand-new plates made from completely reset, clear, easy-to-read type.

•

GIANT CARDINAL editions are distributed in the U.S. by Affiliated Publishers, Inc., 630 Fifth Avenue, New York 20, N.Y.

•

Notice: GIANT CARDINAL editions are published by Pocket Books, Inc. Trademark registered in the United States and other countries.

L

TO

MIRIAM and RANDY

WHO KNOW WHAT JACK PAAR IS

REALLY LIKE. WITH LOVE

AND GRATITUDE *

* FOR NOT TELLING.

INTRODUCTION

by John Reddy

In 1947 I was an accomplice in a radio program called "Bride and Groom" on which bedazzled couples committed matrimony before the microphone while several million housewives coast-to-coast sighed and sobbed.

One day, while basking in this atmosphere of orange blossoms and chicanery, I received a phone call from my mother. She had recently bought a duplex bungalow in Hollywood and baited her trap for a tenant.

"A very nice couple moved in," she announced happily. "The boy just got out of the Army. His name is Jack Paar. They're both very sweet. He's already fixed the screen door for me."

This was the first of a series of regular bulletins on the new tenants. Mr. Paar, my mother said, was an admirable young man. He repaired the radio for her and mowed the lawn. He said he had a movie contract, but never went to the studio. He had been a radio announcer in the Midwest, and was looking for a job in radio, but didn't know anyone. Would I advise him?

Although Hollywood was overrun with unemployed aspiring announcers, I agreed to counsel the recently unfrocked G.I. on the problems of finding a radio job in the film capital. However, between capturing couples for our air-wave nuptials, and placating the ones who found they were scheduled to honeymoon in Death Valley instead of Paris, several days passed without my getting to meet "the nice young soldier," as my mother called him. She kept bombarding me with calls, describing the sterling qualities of her tenant and urging me to help find him a radio job, but I was so immersed in rigging our show by giving the couples the answers ("I do") that I kept postponing the rendezvous. Again I got a call from my mother.

"You know that nice Mr. Paar," she said triumphantly. "You don't have to worry about him any more. *He was just picked to replace Jack Benny for the summer.* I'm so happy for him. But now who will take care of our lawn?"

Well, the lawn was never the same again, nor were a lot of things. Overnight the young ex-soldier, who didn't know anyone in radio, took over the show with the largest audience on the air. Belatedly I rushed over and fell all over him, and we've been friends ever since. I've known him through thick and thin, usually thin. I've been gladdened by his triumphs and have helped him perpetrate some of his flops. His network career, which began when he replaced Jack Benny on radio, reached its peak with his present nighttime show on NBC which has won virtually every honor in television and has been consistently called "the most talked about program on TV." Now analyzing Jack Paar has become one of America's most popular indoor pastimes, surpassing whist, crossword puzzles and bingo. People all over the country are asking each other what Jack Paar is *really* like. He has now written this book to answer that question and solve the mystery. Since I know more about Jack Paar than Sandburg knows about Lincoln, I was deputized to assist him and write this introduction explaining him so that he doesn't come as too much of a shock to the unprepared reader.

Explaining Jack Paar is not easy. He is the world's tallest elf. He is a paradox and meeting him can be like smoking a filter-tip firecracker. Jack has the natural wholesomeness of a 4-H Club member who won the prize for sowing wild oats. With his winsome smile and cleft chin he could give dimple lessons to Liberace, but he has a sharp wit and is no one to take ad liberties with. This combination of gentle, little-boy manner and barbed wit is as startling as finding Little Lord Fauntleroy with a switch-blade knife.

Jack Paar is like Peter Pan, if Peter Pan had been written by Mickey Spillane. He has a youthful, well-scrubbed appearance which he attributes to reading Little Orphan Annie who has been twelve years old for forty-seven years. His emotions are so supercharged that his nerves may be yo-yo strings, and his blood is not tired but positively exuberant. He has the nervous energy of a man whose tranquilizer has been spiked, and keeping up with him is like trying to dance the mambo with your shoestrings tied together. He is unpredictable and has a tendency to make sudden U-turns in tunnels.

Jack has spent much of his life between the seven ball and the nine ball. He is an honest man who is not afraid of the naked truth. He values integrity and would rather kiss the Rock of Gibraltar than the Blarney Stone. On his program he gives the impression of calm, but off the air he is so shy he would be a wallflower at an orgy. He likes people but not in groups larger than one, and several little old ladies who tried to clutch him on the street were nearly dragged to death in his stampede to escape. Because of this shyness with strangers, the Dale Carnegie Course lists him at the top of its list of the Ten Most Wanted Men.

Jack Paar is proof positive that being difficult can be easy, yet he is so sentimental he cries at basketball scores or laundry lists. At sad movies he sobs so loudly that people for three rows around get up and move. He is sensitive about little things and broods over the fact that the Indians always lose in TV Westerns. He is tense and seems disorganized, but is disciplined and has a passion for neatness. Once *Newsweek* did a cover story on him which he felt did not do justice to such an interesting subject. He deposited it in the garbage can. A little later he decided to check a couple of statements in the story so he could blast the magazine on the air. He went to the kitchen only to find both garbage and magazine had been taken away. "Why is it," he complained to his pretty wife Miriam, "that people never leave things where I put them?"

There is no neutrality on the subject of Jack Paar. People either love him or loathe him. Moreover, his detractors speak with real authority, since they watch him every night. His program defies analysis. It is as unrehearsed as a hiccup. The format consists of a group of people sitting around trying to change the subject. Paar is the first performer to raise interrupting to the status of an art. He is also probably the only entertainer to become a success although his audience is yawning and falling asleep. Most of his viewers watch the show from bed. Several complained about vertical streaks on their screens until they discovered they were seeing the show between their toes.

Jack is critical of his own talents, but can be wildly extravagant in praising others. Performers cower in the wings while he introduces them, afraid to come on because no one could live up to his lavish buildup. He has discovered more fine new talent than anyone in recent show-business history. When young performers appear on the Paar show they frequently become such big hits he can't afford to have them back.

Jack is America's midnight maverick. He is impulsive and inclined to look *after* he leaps. A pugnacious pixie, he has left no stone unthrown in his work. Paper clips make him moody and he shuns the confines of an office. NBC endowed him with a beautiful office but he avoided it so studiously that when he finally had to go to a meeting there he couldn't remember where it was. He dislikes meetings and group suggestions. When he took over his present show he had a covey of network advisers who vetoed many of his suggestions on the grounds that "they" wouldn't like some singer, or that "they" couldn't approve of some act.

"Who is this 'they' that everyone is trying to please?" he finally demanded. "From now on—tell them that I am they."

He assumed full control of the show and it quickly became a hit.

Trapping the Paar torrent of words in a book was a feat comparable to harnessing the Yangtze River. He dictated it in person, on tape recorders and on the telephone. I fielded stories from him on the fly in automobiles, on boats and in planes. Some of our literary conferences took place while floating in the surf just off shore at Key Biscayne, Florida, Nassau in the Bahamas, and Havana, Cuba. Jack thinks best while floating on his back in the ocean, and inevitably had his clearest recollections while we were both paddling to keep afloat and couldn't make notes even with one of those pens that write under water. Some of this he pecked out on a portable typewriter floating around his swimming pool in a rubber raft. Despite doing this literary creation under such marine conditions, he eventually produced this book.

During the course of this close and often damp relationship, I had a rare opportunity to solve the mystery of what Jack Paar is really like. I still don't know! To find out first hand from him, turn the page and start reading.

PREFACE

ALTHOUGH I am a tireless talker, with a larynx as resilient as the thigh muscle of a six-day bicycle racer, I never thought I'd find myself corralling any portion of my awesome output of words in the form of a book.

My activities seem to have a chaotic quality which eludes capture between covers. I sometimes get the feeling that I'm walking up a gangplank with no ship there. I seem to be the kind of person who, if I did the Loretta Young Show, the doorknob would come off in my hand.

As a youngster I was duly impressed by the fable of George Washington and the cherry tree. But I always had a sneaking suspicion that the reason George's father didn't punish him for chopping down the tree was that young Georgie had an ax in his hand.

Nevertheless, I have always tried to be truthful. So far it's gotten me threatened with suit by Jimmy Hoffa and Walter Winchell, nearly mobbed in Cleveland, arrested in the Army, denounced by a U. S. senator, attacked by newspapers, menaced by Mickey Rooney, fired from jobs, dropped by sponsors and cut off the air by censors. To this list of mishaps may now be added becoming an author.

I've always enjoyed words, but the thought of sitting down and putting one word after another until I had a whole book, complete with title, chapters and paragraphs, seemed as unlikely as the prospects of my being named to the diplomatic service. My writing has been confined mostly to jokes for my shows, indignant letters to an assortment of foes and introductions to other people's books, and I never fancied myself as an author. Grammar always seemed to me as mysterious as finger painting, and spelling a baffling science necessary only for crossword puzzle addicts and quiz show contestants.

Although I have never written a book before, I have always been interested in writing and used to wistfully read magazine ads which promised to teach you to write. I never actually answered one of these ads but I had a friend who read one which said: "How do you know you can't write?" Encouraged, he promptly sent in several jokes he had written. They replied with a note that said: "Now you KNOW you can't write."

Despite my lack of formal training as an author, I rashly agreed, under the influence of flattery and money, to write my memoirs. I'd forgotten I have a terrible memory. However, if there are any interludes in my life I can't remember, they're so dull I promise you're not missing a thing. In fact, I can't understand why anyone would want to pay money just to read my life, when they can tune in and watch the unexpurgated edition unfold every weekday night from 11:15 to 1 A.M. on NBC-TV.

However, everyone is writing a book. Rock 'n' roll singers, ladies who disrobe in public, former streetcar conductors and female discus throwers are all penning their lives. "Writing is being taken over," author H. Allen Smith complains, "by strip tease gals who flap it three times at the customers and then dash to their dressing room to finish Chapter Eight."

Where formerly people didn't write their autobiographies until it was time to write their wills, the big trend now is young people writing their life stories before there has been time for anything to happen. Autobiographies are now written in installments. Pat Boone has written his first installment entitled *'Twixt Twelve and Twenty.* This means that if Pat keeps going strong, and he certainly should on his regimen of raw carrots, yoghurt and not kissing girls, his next book will be called *'Twixt Twenty and Twirty.*

The other big trend in books these days is the confession type autobiography in which the author admits to all kinds of failings from alcoholism to Communism. It's gotten so that if you haven't been a Communist, convict or dope addict, your book won't make much of a splash. The Communist confession type of book got so popular for a while that several struggling writers, who couldn't seem to sell anything, even joined the party so they could quit and write a book confessing it.

In view of this demand for sensationalism I was hesitant about writing a book about myself. I've never been a Communist or alcoholic and I've never been psychoanalyzed. Actually, I'm a pretty ordinary guy. I'm just like any other fellow with a wife and daughter, a pleasant suburban home, a Mercedes Benz convertible, twenty-seven pairs of imported sunglasses, and who has an hour and three-quarters TV show every weekday night.

I am a bit of a nonconformist though. I'm the only husband I know who hurriedly says good-by to Zsa Zsa Gabor right after work and rushes home to his wife. My idea of a big time is mowing the lawn or cooking hamburgers on the backyard barbecue for my wife Miriam and our daughter Randy. Miriam is lovely, laughs at my jokes, doesn't complain when I smoke cigars in the bathtub, doesn't chatter when I'm brooding about the next show and cheerfully gets up at any hour to fix me a hamburger, a cup of soup and a bottle of cold beer.

She accepts cheerfully the fact that duty requires that I hobnob on the air with an assortment of glamorous ladies, although she did get a little moody the time Debbie Reynolds partially disrobed me on the program. Randy is a wonderful, bright, blonde little girl who thinks I'm almost as funny as the Lone Ranger.

Another problem about writing a book is that doing a nightly TV show makes it hard for me to find the time to sit down and write. However, I have been abetted in this by a friend named John Reddy who is a writer for the *Reader's Digest*. He is the author of such *Digest* articles as "American Tennis Balls are Underfuzzed," "Are Income Taxes Caused by a Virus?" and "We Go on Honeymoons for Busy People." John has been writing for years, and has the rejection slips to prove it. He holds the *Saturday Evening Post* rejection with six oak-leaf clusters. At one time, he says, his stories were coming back so fast he suspected the mailman was reading them and shoving them back under the door. Together with this impressive literary background, Reddy for years has been patiently harvesting the more sprightly ad libs I have sprinkled around in Chinese restaurants, suburban hardware stores and other fashionable places I frequent. He has also amassed a rare collection of Paarobilia such as canceled radio contracts, enthusiastic letters from several sponsors including Corega Denture Fasteners, an autographed picture of my first sergeant in the Army and the menu from a testimonial box lunch accorded me by a radio station in Youngstown, Ohio. He assisted me by sifting through this literary pay dirt, collecting the anecdotes I relate on the show, correcting my spelling and pointing out the parts that are libelous.

Probably nobody ever had more advice on how to write a book than I had, since for years I've been interviewing authors on radio and television and listening to how they wrote best-sellers. One of the most important things, they told me, was the title. Garson Kanin, an author and director, told me that publisher Bennett Cerf had advised him the way to make any book a best-seller was to have "How to" in the title; that everyone is interested in learning something. "But how about *Gone with the Wind?*" Kanin asked him. "That was very successful." "I know," Cerf conceded, "but it would have been even more successful if it had been *How to Gone with the Wind.*"

Jack Douglas, who turned book author after ten years of writing for me, found a neat way to get "How to" in the title of a book he wrote. He suggested calling it: *How to Make a Million Dollars and Speak Correct English and Be Good Look-*

ing and Sexy and Healthy and Well Read and Perfectly Groomed and What Wines to Order with What Courses and Write Popular Music and Learn Taxidermy in Your Spare Time. "I couldn't use it, though," he told me. "There happened to be another book with the same title."

I had several title suggestions I thought were quite good but which didn't work out for one reason or another. Some of them were *Blood Over the Dam; Where Did You Go? Out, What Did You Do? Plenty; A Rock of Jello,* and *Son of Lady Chatterley's Lover. Blood Over the Dam* the publisher didn't like because it seemed too realistic. *Where Did You Go? Out, What Did You Do? Plenty* was appealing but seemed to fit Porfirio Rubirosa better. *Son of Lady Chatterley's Lover* had obvious commercial advantages, but it impugned the marital status of my parents, something that enough critics were already doing. *A Rock of Jello* was a catchy title, everyone agreed, but it was thought best not to reveal in the title what Jack Paar is really like.

Although I got lots of advice on how to write this book from best-selling authors like Jim Bishop and Alexander King, some of the best advice I got was from George Kirgo who wrote a *worst*-seller. George's book, *Hercules, The Big Greek Story,* had sold fourteen copies at last count. "Word of mouth killed it," he told me. "People heard about it. The publishers were a non-profit organization. They believed that advertising was in bad taste. They didn't print many copies. They used monks with quills instead of printing presses."

Kirgo explained to me the confession type autobiographies such as the story of war hero "Pappy" Boyington who admitted to having been an alcoholic. "He became an alcoholic because he couldn't adjust to peacetime life," Kirgo said. "Some of his friends were trying to start a war to make him feel better." Kirgo added that Christine Jorgenson is writing an autobiography that will probably be made into a movie. "The title role," he told me, "will be played by Susan Hayward *and* Gregory Peck."

Although Kirgo's book originally only sold fourteen copies,

due to the magic of television its sale went up 100 percent after his appearances on our show. It has now sold twenty-eight copies. We might have sold even more but we called off our campaign. We were afraid that success might be too great a shock for his publishers.

My first reaction to writing a book was to get insomnia, so I developed a new sympathy for all the people who have complained to me that my show keeps them awake at night. This insomnia seemed particularly unfortunate since I understand that several famous authors from Sir Walter Scott, who wrote *Ivanhoe,* to Charley Weaver, who wrote *Letters from Mama,* have thought of some of their best lines while asleep. "Some of my best jokes have come to me while I was sleeping," Charley told me.

"How could you remember the jokes if you were asleep?" I asked him.

"I laughed so hard I woke up," he explained.

Rubbing elbows with best-selling authors like Charley I learned some interesting literary facts. One was that the longest sentence in the English language was written in 1675 by Edward Phillips in his preface to a book called *Theatrum Poetarum.* It ran 1,012 words, and most of the readers never got beyond the preface. So enough of this one.

JACK PAAR

CONTENTS

I KID YOU NOT

1. NO ONE IS PURFICT

ALTHOUGH I HAVE probably the largest horizontal audience in television, as most of my viewers write that they watch the show from bed, I seem to be one of the few remaining vertical performers. Many of the actors I know seem to spend a good deal of their time in a reclining position, telling their troubles to a psychiatrist. From Madison Avenue in New York to Beverly Hills's Wilshire Boulevard, psychiatrists' couches are sagging under the weight of actors pouring out their life stories.

I have never felt the necessity to tell my troubles lying down, at least to a psychiatrist. I have no troubles that I can't tell standing up and to several million people at once. Also, even if I felt the need for psychoanalysis, I wouldn't have to pay seventy-five dollars an hour for it. The magazines do it for me free.

If I ever get to wondering what my problem is, I merely seek out the nearest newsstand. There, for a quarter, I can learn all about my psyche. If I'm lucky, and hit a good issue, I may also find out at the same time what's troubling George Jessel, Mrs. Arthur Murray or Dick Clark. In addition to the articles analyzing performers, there are usually several "Letters to the Editor" analyzing the magazine's analyses. All of this volunteer analysis can be very confusing. One article on me quoted one of these amateur psychiatrists as saying that I was very tense, but that there was a good force inside me trying to break out. The same article quoted another amateur as saying I am very tense but that there is a good force outside me trying to break in. No wonder I'm tense, with all that pushing and shoving going on.

I have never understood this recent compulsion on the part of magazines and their readers to psychoanalyze performers. Some former sausage stuffer becomes a singer and makes a hit record and all of a sudden the magazines are probing his soul. Maybe he just likes to sing, but now magazine readers suddenly want to know what makes him tick, and the magazines will never rest until they find out.

Performers can't seem to be accepted simply for what they are. I, for instance, never pretended to be anything but an ordinary guy who talks too much. Yet suddenly there is a concerted movement afoot to find out what I'm *really* like. Although I'm a devout blabbermouth, who has told everything about myself except the size shorts I wear (Jockey, size 34) to millions of television viewers for years, there seems to be some mystery as to my innermost depths.

John Crosby, the television critic, returned from a lecture tour around the country and reported the question he was asked most frequently was: "What is Jack Paar really like?"

Jim Moran, the waggish press agent, reported that while driving through Hollywood he was waved to the curb by a policeman. "Instead of giving me a ticket," Jim said, "he asked me: 'What's that guy Paar really like, anyway?' "

Harry Golden, the best-selling author, whom Groucho Marx calls the "Kosher Mark Twain," had a somewhat similar report. He goes around the country lecturing on Shakespeare and similar weighty subjects. At the end of his speech he asks the audience if they have any questions. "Instead of asking about Hamlet or Lady Macbeth or Polonius," Harry says, "someone always asks what you're really like. I tell them you're like Hamlet. No one has ever figured out what *he's* really like."

Mrs. Miller, the lady who has come to the show nearly

every night since it started, and who even went to California with us, would seem to be an authority on what I'm like. However, when asked that question by an interviewer, she replied: "Your guess is as good as mine."

A researcher who was once paid several thousand dollars by a sponsor to analyze my character reported that I didn't have any, and a writer sent to find out "what makes me tick" finally gave up and ventured the opinion that I'm self-winding.

I can't understand why anyone cares what I'm really like. However, my agent, Marty Kummer, tells me it's important. I asked him why and he said that people's impressions of me are so important because I'm a personality and not a performer.

"What's the difference?" I asked suspiciously.

"A performer is someone with a specific talent like playing the piano or singing," he explained. "A personality is someone like you who really doesn't do anything."

Spurred on by this tactful suggestion I agreed to analyze my character and write a minority report on what I'm really like. Describing yourself is a little like psychoanalysis but without the comfort of the couch. However, since telling my foibles on the air seems only to have confused people, I am now describing myself in writing in an effort to clarify the mystery and make my agent happy. He gets to keep 10 per cent of my faults.

Actually, my character is an open book. I'm complicated, sentimental, lovable, honest, loyal, decent, generous, likable and lonely. My personality is not split; it's shredded. I once had a secretary who left the show to get married and wrote me a note saying: "I loved working for a team like you."

My attitude toward the institutions around us is one of subdued defiance. My battle cry, to paraphrase Admiral Farragut, is: Damn the torpedoes, *half* speed ahead.

Although I make my living talking to millions of people at a time, I'm ill at ease meeting strangers whether it's the man checking the gas meter or a famous celebrity. One night I was having dinner with friends at the Algonquin Hotel when I noticed a man in a red dinner jacket eying me curiously. He was a slim, sharp-faced man with thinning hair and I could sense he was coming over to talk. Dreading meeting a stranger, I immersed myself deeper in conversation with my friends, but the man came over anyway. "I'm Noel Coward," he said. "I just wanted to tell you that I watch your show all the time and I love it."

My dread of meeting people individually is as nothing to my terror at encountering them in groups. This phobia may be traceable to the time I was nearly mobbed by admirers in the gentlemen's room of the Rivoli Theater in New York. I was attending *Around the World in Eighty Days* and as it dragged on I began to suspect it was going to take that long. Soon the suspense over whether Phineas Fogg would make it around the globe in eighty days began to take second place in my mind as to whether I could make it to the gentlemen's room in time. Sensing there might be a rush for these facilities at intermission, I decided to outwit the crowd. I ducked out just before intermission and rushed downstairs where I inquired of an usher the whereabouts of the rest room. He informed me loftily that it was on the mezzanine which I had just come from. I bounded back up the stairs but the intermission had just arrived and a wave of male humanity had engulfed the gentlemen's room and had queued up in line outside. I took my place at the end of the line and hastily counted heads, noting there were nineteen ahead of me. The line inched forward with agonizing slowness. This, I discovered, was because sandwiched in among the nineteen adult heads I had counted were a half-dozen small boys I had missed in my hurried census.

As I shuffled slowly along I felt the hot breath of the elderly gentleman behind me on my neck so close it was ballooning my underwear. Turning, I discovered he was Frank Lloyd Wright, the noted architect. I felt immediately uncomfortable being ahead of such a distinguished gentleman and was debating whether it would be proper to invite him to play through. At that precise moment, however, I was relieved to reach the head of the line. Just then someone in the line yelled, "Hey, there's Jack Paar!" The queue suddenly came to life like a conga line. "Where?" cried another standee. "Right there," yelled another. What touched off this impromptu demonstration I'll never know. I didn't wait to find out. In panic I broke ranks and fled into the night. I never did find out if Phineas Fogg ever completed his mission successfully. I completed mine at last in the bamboo sanctuary of Lum Fong's, a nearby Chinese restaurant.

I once told this story to Joey Bishop, the comedian, explaining how embarrassed I was to be standing in line with a world-famous architect waiting to use the gentlemen's room.

"Why didn't he just build one?" Joey asked.

We have celebrities galore on the program but I rarely see any of them off the air. While the theme music is still playing, I'm out of the studio and headed up the Hudson River Parkway with Jose Melis, my orchestra director, Bronxville neighbor and music lover. One night we were barreling along, the car radio playing softly, when Jose grabbed my arm and shouted: "Stop!" Thinking that some disaster impended I screeched to a stop just short of a bridge we were about to pass under. "They were playing one of my songs," Jose said, "and I didn't want to have it interrupted."

I'm incurably domestic and am happiest at home with my wife and daughter and our dachshund. "If a bomb blew up everyone else on earth you wouldn't know it," Miriam says, "until you went down to the hardware store to get some new tools and there was no one there." I've been inside a night club only a couple of times in my life and my idea of a big time is a buying spree at a hardware store or delicatessen. When it comes to pickles I'm an addict. Sometimes Miriam sends me to the delicatessen for a loaf of rye bread and I come home with a year's supply of pickles: mustard pickles, dill pickles, frozen pickles, instant pickles and pickle sickles. I seem to have a kosher monkey on my back. When the delicatessen man waits on me it's like selling whiskey to the Indians.

My favorite delicatessen is the Stage, in New York's theatrical district, run by Max Asnas whom Fred Allen called the "Corned Beef Confucius." Max, a man of many words, all of them hard to understand, is as round as one of his own bagels and has a heart as big as a slab of pastrami. His small place is so crowded that dining there is not only an adventure in eating but in self-defense. The place seats just seventy people or, as Max puts it, "with mink coats, thirty."

Whenever I stop at the Stage for a bite, Max loads up my car with kosher delicacies. He loves to dispense philosophy with his pastrami and pumpernickel. One night I told him: "You have the best brisket of beef I've ever tasted. But it's hard to enjoy with all this noise and confusion."

"Jeck," he said, "show me a place with brisket like mine and no noise and we'll both go there."

One night I was discussing the joys of Max's food with Harry Golden, who is another kosher food fancier. We spoke ecstatically of the joyous tastes and smells of potato pancakes with sour cream, of chopped liver, of fragrant roast chicken and cheese blintzes.

"Kosher food could put an end to anti-Semitism," Harry philosophized. "Instead of spending money to fight bigotry with speeches and pamphlets, we should send the bigots CARE packages of hot pastrami, potato latkes, knishes and kosher corned beef. We would get to them through their taste buds."

To that I say amen.

Another aspect of my domesticity, besides my penchant for delicatessen binges, is that I'm a do-it-yourself bug. I have a wonderful home workshop, with all kinds of power tools, and love working around the house. I have wired up all the recording and playing apparatus in my home—including a high-fidelity set, a broadcasting setup, a tape recorder and a motion picture sound projector that even plays cinemascope pictures. I also installed a steam room with two vibrating tables and an overhead TV set, which enables me to lie and watch intellectual discussion programs while vibrating vigorously. This gives programs a new and interesting dimension. The last time I watched "Meet the Press" the exceedingly prim and proper May Craig seemed to be undulating like Abbe Lane.

When I got the steam room it was a severe blow to my old friend Ernie Kovacs, the comedian. Ernie and I had always had similar and equally extravagant tastes and a sort of unconscious rivalry grew up between us over our selection in clothes, cars and the like.

When I first met him, some years ago, we talked about cigars which both of us enjoy.

"I get all mine in Havana," I told him. "They're the best. They cost a dollar each."

"Really?" said Ernie, rather condescendingly, I thought. "I only smoke two-dollar cigars. Smoke about twenty a day. It runs me around fifteen thousand dollars a year."

I was consumed with admiration until I tried to buy some two-dollar cigars in the most expensive tobacco shop in New York and found there were none costing more than a dollar.

Not long afterwards we both discovered beautiful, blonde Edie Adams, a talented singer and entertainer. Ernie spotted her first and she sang on his local New York TV show. His show went off the air, I got a network show on CBS and triumphantly hired Edie. She was quite an asset for the show and I felt pretty good about getting her from Ernie. Then one day she came to me after our show. "I hope you won't be mad," she said, "but I have to leave the show. I'm marrying Ernie Kovacs."

The next time I saw Ernie he was lolling in a chauffeur-driven Rolls-Royce limousine on Fifth Avenue, emitting great gusts of cigar smoke. "I'm waiting for Edie," he said, as I stopped to chat. "She's in buying a mink coat." We talked briefly and I admired his car.

"What kind of car are you driving these days?" Ernie asked, engulfing me in a cloud of smoke.

"A Ford Thunderbird," I said. "It's a beautiful little car."

Ernie looked at me pityingly and shook his head. "Gee, I'm sorry," he said. "Nothing like one of these Rolls. They spoil you for anything else."

Some time passed and I ran into Ernie and Edie in a restaurant.

"Where are you living now?" he greeted me expansively.

"Oh, up in Bronxville," I replied. "Miriam and I built a nice little place up there. It's a three-story red barn, with a swimming pool. Maybe you saw it in the *Life* cover story. You can't beat that suburban living."

"The suburbs!" Ernie echoed, in anguish. "Gosh, I feel sorry for you with that commuting grind. Edie and I have a new duplex apartment. Seventeen rooms overlooking Central Park. You must come see us."

The last time I saw Ernie we were both working on a big special TV show at NBC. I'll give it to him this time, I thought to myself, as he came up and shook hands heartily.

"How's that little place in the suburbs?" he asked, with what I swore was a trace of hauteur.

"Just great," I enthused. "I just made a little addition. I put in a steam room."

I could see I'd hit home. Ernie shifted his cigar and his furrowed Hungarian brow got a few more creases than usual. "A steam room," he mused. I could see that in his most luxuriant moments, Ernie had never thought of a private steam room.

"Nothing like a good steam bath to relax you after a show," I told him as we parted. I never felt better; possibly because Ernie looked positively sick with envy. Even his expensive cigar looked limp.

A few days later I got a call from Ernie.

"Guess what I just installed?" he announced. "A steam room, just like you have."

"Gee, that's swell," I said, hollowly.

"Only mine," he added happily, "has stereophonic sound."

Once more I felt underprivileged.

I usually manage to dominate the mechanical monsters with which I have surrounded myself, but on one occasion they rose up to rout me. With summer coming on we installed a complete air-conditioning system for the house with a thermostat set for 70 degrees. However, one sweltering hot day I decided to make it cooler and turned the controls to make the temperature as low as it would go. Then I had to leave for the show. When I got home about eleven that night, our house looked like the set for "Sergeant Preston of the Yukon." Miriam and Randy were huddled under several layers of blankets and our little dachshund looked as cold as an Alaskan malemute. I dived into bed to keep from freezing.

However, our oil burner was not going to take that sort of thing lying down. As the temperature plummeted under the frigid air, it triggered the thermostat controlling the oil furnace and it flared into action. Suddenly the two installations were locked in frenzied combat. The air conditioner loosed blasts of air that felt cold enough to form frost on the rugs. The oil burner exhaled searing gusts that threatened to boil our goldfish in their bowl. We were trapped in a no man's land between heat prostration and frostbite.

In alarm I crawled out of bed, groped my way down to the furnace room and pulled the main electrical switch ending the battle of the elements. It was a draw. The chief result of this struggle of the mechanical monsters was that it ran our electricity bill so high that the electrical company sent an executive over to apologize when they delivered the bill.

Somehow we all escaped either chilblains or third-degree burns. The only real casualty was that when I pulled the switch it cut off the freezer where Randy had stored a bushel of Good Humors of all flavors. The next morning we had half a freezer full of liquid Good Humors in a new flavor: pot luck!

Because of my allergy to meeting strangers I have zealously guarded the privacy of our home in Bronxville. Bronxville is a very conservative community and you aren't allowed to make a left turn anywhere in town. When I finish the show and get home I'm suddenly transformed into a country squire, junior grade, with one third of an acre of rolling estate, mostly in concrete, and one head of dachshund. When we built the house I was so anxious to have a nice lawn that I put it in myself with loving care. Then I had a landscaping expert come to look at it. "The weeds are all right," he said, "but the grass isn't doing so good." Our trouble was crabgrass. I tried everything to stop it but nothing worked. The only thing that would kill it was concrete. I just kept enlarging the driveway. Now we have so much pavement around our house it looks like a frozen custard stand.

The only time the privacy of our home was ever interrupted was by Edward R. Murrow's "Person to Person" TV show . . . an experience comparable to a friendly visit by Attila the Hun. Although the program people are extremely considerate, and even bring their own ash trays, if you are used to privacy there is a certain inevitable commotion when forty strangers drop in.

It all began very gradually. First there was a pleasant telegram from Ed Murrow saying he was looking forward to the show and that it should be fun. Then there was a call from his office. "There will be a few people dropping around to check things," the caller said. "Don't let them bother you." Sure enough, a couple of weeks beforehand, mysterious men began to infiltrate our yard. One phone company man wandered around the lawn and peered through binoculars into the distance. "Looking for the Empire State building," he volunteered. "It's not exactly like looking for a needle in a haystack," I suggested. He didn't laugh; just went on peering.

The man from the telephone company proved to be only the advance guard. Day by day the invading force grew. One man from the network poked around the house shooting pictures with a Polaroid camera. A man from Consolidated Edison appeared to check the electrical outlets. "Gonna need some more power," he grunted. Another man peered into the trees that enclose our yard. All of the men seemed to communicate in grunts. They would look around, shake their heads disgustedly, grunt to each other and then silently disappear. One day several men arrived and went energetically about digging a hole in our azalea bed where they installed a pole and transformer.

This activity reached its climax the day of the show. Cars began coming in and out of the driveway steadily. In midafternoon a truck which looked about as big as the Bronxville A & P Supermarket arrived and squeezed into our yard. Soon our driveway was a jumble of cameras, cables, lights and other equipment.

Late in the afternoon, while technicians grappled with the cameras and cables, Miriam and I were wired for sound. I was given a portable microphone which fitted in a holster under my jacket giving me a slight bulge that made me look like my uncle during prohibition. There was a wire running from the mike down my pants leg and little batteries in my hip pocket. Miriam was similarly outfitted with a mike attached to her bra. "Better not say anything about us," a CBS man said with a grin, "because the whole crew can hear you."

When we had been completely wired and made up, there was nothing to do but wait for the show to go on. We had a walk-through, with a little chitchat for the benefit of Ed Murrow, and occasionally I had to hoist up my jacket and get my batteries changed. Meantime I wandered around, surveying the confusing scene, anxious to be helpful and hopeful of saving a shrub or two from the trampling crew thronging the yard. Amid the sea of masculine faces I spotted a young lady in slacks. She was inspecting things with an authoritative air and seemed to be a script girl or production assistant.

"You probably want to check the house, too," I suggested.

"Oh, yes," she said briskly.

Accordingly I took her around the house, starting with the first floor and going all the way to the third. "Everything is all set on the electrical outlets," I said.

"That's good," she replied.

When we finished our tour of all fourteen rooms, I told her I thought we had covered everything and asked if there was anything else I could do to help.

"Oh, yes," she exclaimed. "Could you show my friends out in the car through your house, too?"

"Your friends?" I asked, blankly. "Aren't you the CBS script girl?"

"Oh, no," she said, blithely. "I was just passing by and we saw all the cars and I came in to see what the commotion was all about. You were so nice to explain it all. Will you tell my friends, too?"

Incidents like these, it seems, are the story of my life. Put them all together and they spell out what Jack Paar is really like. If you're still mystified, think of me. I'm stuck with him.

2. A FUNNY THING HAPPENED TO MY MOTHER

A FUNNY THING happened to my mother one day: Me. I was born in Canton; the one in Ohio, not China. If it had been China and not Ohio, I might still be on television but, considering the history of Orientals in show business, I'd probably be juggling instead of just talking. I wouldn't mind juggling but it might mean that I'd be sandwiched in between acrobats and animal acts on the Ed Sullivan Show and it's not easy following a trained seal.

My childhood was a pretty dull time. The first year I spent mostly in bed and no one has made money writing about that kind of thing since Frank Scully, a friend of mine, wrote *Fun in Bed* which was *not* about his infancy. (It's not about what you're thinking, either, so there's no use rushing out trying to buy it.) When I graduated to a playpen, things didn't liven up much either. My youth brightened up a bit when I learned to thumb my nose, and discovered that the kids with dresses and pigtails were different, but it never did get terribly exciting. Looking back on my childhood, I can remember very little noteworthy. Also, I've always been suspicious of people like Sam Levenson and Gypsy Rose Lee who can remember every little detail that ever happened to them when they were kids. They must have been so busy taking notes I don't see how they had time to do anything to remember.

However, I love to read reminiscences about people's childhood in the past: stories about the little red schoolhouse, and the general store with its warm, potbellied stove, and putting on goggles and duster to drive to Grandmother's house in the spanking new Pierce-Arrow for Thanksgiving. What wonderful days they must have been! Things were different when I was a youngster growing up, but I have wonderful memories, too. I remember the first Kaiser-Frazer. I remember when you could light a cigarette at either end. I remember parking places. I remember when Grandmother used to wear a nightcap, and not take one. I remember drugstores when you could find medicine there without having to fight your way through the appliance department.

I have wonderful memories of show business, too. I've always enjoyed it when Eddie Cantor and Sophie Tucker and George Jessel recalled show business in the old days, with its nostalgic memories of Hammerstein's and Rector's and the Palace, and the wonderful songs of George M. Cohan. My memories don't go back so far, but I like to recall the things I remember best about show business. I remember Gino Prado and Horace Heidt. I recall three-D movies. I remember when movie cowboys were just good guys and bad guys, and not psychological problems. And the wonderful songs of those days! I remember "Mairzy Doats" and "Three Little Fishies." They don't write songs like those any more. I remember when they sang "The Music Goes Round and Round," but the singer stood still.

I was born on May 1st—a date which is observed by parades, speeches and riots around the world. This is because it's a Communist holiday, but I've always felt it was somehow appropriate that my birthday is the occasion for far-flung speechmaking and headcracking.

The name Paar is of Dutch and German extraction. I don't know much about my ancestors except that there is a Thomas Parr buried in Westminster Abbey. He lived to be 152 years old and they named a whiskey "Old Parr" after him. I don't know whether we are related, but the Paars do have a record of longevity and a couple of my uncles always had a special interest in "Old Parr." The one in Westminster Abbey, of course.

As long as I can remember, I've had my nerves jangled by listening to puns on the name Paar. When I was a youngster the teacher used to chuckle that my grades weren't "up to Paar." In the Army, whenever I was demoted from corporal to private, my commanding officer would roar, "Well, I just broke Paar." And in radio and television, whenever I've had a show canceled, the critics would report it was "Paar for the course." After years of this, it's small wonder there are times when I've felt like changing my name to something more inconspicuous like Spangler Arlington Brugh. (That name became available when Spangler Arlington Brugh changed *his* to Robert Taylor.)

My father, Howard Paar, who died in 1956, was a railroad division superintendent. This meant that we could ride free on trains which may be why we moved around so much. From Canton our family—my parents, two brothers and sister and I—moved to Detroit and then to Jackson, Michigan. I was a chubby blond youngster with a Dutch-boy haircut, and my mother used to tell me about the little Dutch boy who saved Holland by sticking his finger in the dike. Ever since, asking me a question is like taking your finger *out* of a dike.

Conversation was the opium of the Paars. My father and mother were both fond of talking. Our family didn't go in for sending chain letters, going to Mae West movies, dancing the Big Apple or any of the other popular pastimes of the 1930s. We just sat around and talked. There was no TV to entertain us, and radio was in its infancy, so instead of turning a dial and listening to Gabriel Heatter or Boake Carter we supplied our own conversation. This didn't necessarily entertain the listeners, but it always seemed to please whichever Paar was talking. I first began to learn the art of conversation by trying to interrupt at the dinner table. I never did succeed, but it was good practice.

My Uncle "Butch" was one of the more vocal of the Paars and the conversation always flowed freely when he and Aunt Frances came to call. He was a railroad man like my Dad, and they would sit by the hour talking railroading, with neither listening to the other. Uncle Butch had a fiery temper and a colorful vocabulary of profanity when aroused. When anything incurred his ire, which was not infrequent, Mother would shoo us children discreetly out of range while Uncle Butch swore a blue streak. I remember once watching from a window while he tried to crank his old Dodge. The balky crank "kicked," hurting his arm. Uncle Butch danced around in pain, holding the injured arm. "Okay," he muttered, glowering at the car. "For that I'm going to blind you." With that he yanked the crank out of the car and bashed out both headlights. Feeling better, he cranked up, got in and drove off happily.

My father's uncle was another gregarious soul. He was a happy-go-lucky man who lived in a model T house but drove a Cadillac. He couldn't always afford gas, but it didn't bother him. If his tank ran dry on the street he'd just sit there happily, as though he were waiting for the traffic light to change. People liked him, and he was elected to the state legislature. He had a unique method of campaigning. He would buttonhole his constituents and say, "Have you heard what my opponent is saying about me?" He would then reel off a list of villainies, which he had invented, and which he claimed his rival was charging him with. Indignant at these charges, the citizens would vote him into office by a thumping majority. This taught me a lesson in human psychology which I later put into effect on radio and television. I would tell my audience, "Have you heard what the critics are saying about me?" and then catalogue a list of insults and reflections on my character and ability. There was only one difference between my granduncle and me: in my case the charges were true!

Grandmother Paar was another favorite of mine. She is a wonderful old lady and when I finally got a successful show, after years of spectacular misses, I made a sentimental journey back to visit her in Saginaw, Michigan, where she lived with Uncle Butch and his wife. She was ninety, silvery-haired and still handsome, although her memory was failing and it was hard to keep the cast of characters straight as we talked about members of the family. I was so pleased because she seemed to remember me. We had a pleasant chat for a couple of hours and as it grew late she thumped her cane on the floor to summon my aunt and uncle to bring a late snack of cheese, crackers and beer.

While they got the snack I asked, proudly, "Grandma, do you ever see my show?"

"What show?" the old lady asked.

"My television show," I said, a bit nonplused.

"What," she asked, "is television?"

While I recovered from that exchange, my aunt and uncle arrived from downstairs with chunks of cheese and cold beer.

"Here," my grandmother said, imperiously. "Give some to what's-his-name."

I grew up during the troubled thirties. It was a deflated decade with all the wind knocked out of it by the depression. Young as I was, I could see that the depression hit the country at a very bad time . . . everyone was out of work. In New York, people were killing themselves jumping out of skyscrapers after the stock market crash. In Jackson, Michigan, where the buildings were much shorter, people were jumping out of windows and spraining their ankles.

We Paars didn't have much money. As a youngster I hardly knew what meat was. When I passed a butcher shop I just thought there had been an accident. We were happy, though, and we managed to get along. We had most of the essentials of life. We had an automatic washer, my mother, and a dryer was a windy day.

There wasn't much to do in Jackson, but we managed to amuse ourselves. In those days the Late Show meant that the neighbors had forgotten to pull down their blinds. People were healthier then, too. We didn't go to a doctor for an allergy. It was called an itch, and you just scratched it. Even the weather reports were simpler. They just told us whether it would rain or snow, or be colder or warmer. I went all through my childhood never realizing that a "high pressure area was moving down from Canada."

I didn't mix much with other children growing up. It seems strange to me now, when I make my living talking, mostly without written material or rehearsal, but I stuttered badly as a child. This made me ill at ease in school and with other kids.

Like many youngsters who stammer I lived a great deal in the world of imagination and books. One day I read about Demosthenes, the great Greek orator, who had cured himself of stammering by putting pebbles in his mouth and declaiming over the roar of the sea. Since we were living in Michigan, with no sea handy, I made do the best I could. Instead of pebbles, I used buttons from my mother's sewing box. And with no seashore nearer than a thousand miles, I used my room at home. On the door I put a sign saying: STAY OUT—THIS MEANS YOU. Then I would stuff some buttons in my mouth and practice speaking. I read papers and magazines, I talked about anything that came into my head. I read books, watching myself in the mirror. Apart from once nearly swallowing a shirt button in a burst of oratorical fevor, the system worked very well. Little by little my speech improved.

About the same time I developed an overpowering desire to go to military school. I was entranced by the ads I saw in magazines for these schools showing boys in uniforms as resplendent as those of the guards at Buckingham Palace. From the time as a youngster that I asked my mother to sew epaulets on my sunsuit, I had been in love with gaudy uniforms. It seemed that destiny had marked me either to save my country or be an usher at the Roxy Theater.

Although my parents could scarcely afford to send me to public school which was free, I started a feverish clandestine correspondence with a number of expensive military academies. Their response was so rapid and wholehearted that soon school catalogues were showering down upon our house in a volume which threatened to collapse the postman. Avidly I thumbed through these catalogues, envisioning myself in uniforms as grand as the leading tenor's in *The Student Prince*. Alas, my dreams of such sartorial glory were not to be.

One day I was sitting on the porch of our home with my father, who was quietly quaffing a bottle of home-brew, when a car pulled up and a man in a uniform as magnificent as those in the catalogues stepped out. It looked like we were being invaded by Graustark and the Field Marshal had arrived to accept our surrender.

"This must be young Mr. Paar," he said, in clipped military accents. "We're happy you're so interested in our military academy."

My father, who had no inkling of my furtive military ambitions, gazed in amazement at the impressively uniformed military man and put down his bottle of home-brew as if he were swearing off forever.

"What's this all about?" he asked.

The man explained that he was there because of the eager tone of my correspondence.

My father said that it was hard enough to get me to go to the nearby public school, and that he had neither the time nor money to train me as a future Pershing or MacArthur. The military man fell back in baffled retreat and my youthful dreams of military glory were over until years later when I heard from my draft board and was misfitted in khaki.

Shortly afterwards a more serious problem developed. I began feeling listless. I had grown into a tall, thin, nervous youngster, and never seemed to have much energy. My mother took me to a doctor who examined me. She came out of the office in tears. "Son," the doctor said, "I'm afraid you've got tuberculosis."

Times were still hard and there was no money for a sanitarium or a warmer climate. I was put to bed at home with my mother caring for me. She looked after our big old house, cooked for her family of five and fussed over me. She filled me with eggnogs and encouragement. Yet I was moody and depressed. I used to read a lot, or just lie on my back and stare at the ceiling. I began to have periods of melancholy which still afflict me occasionally—like several times a day. I grew to like solitude so much I thought of joining a monastery, but I can't stand living in.

It was my father who snapped me out of my depression for the time being. He built a workshop by my bed and taught me about electronics and carpentry and radio. He showed me how to read the diagram of an electrical circuit. It got me away from thinking about myself, and awakened my lifelong interest in working with my hands. To this day, the most wonderful sound in the world to me is that of a nail being hammered in a two-by-four board.

After eight months I got well enough to go back to school, but my heart wasn't in it. I had overcome my shyness to a point where I enjoyed getting up in class to tell stories, and was strong enough to go out for wrestling. I was billed as "Roughhouse" Paar. To look the part I wanted to have a cauliflower ear. To achieve this I used to daub vaseline on my left ear and pound it with my fist until my head rang. To my chagrin at the time, this never actually gave me a cauliflower ear but it did produce a persistent buzzing in my skull and strange hallucinations. I decided that if I couldn't look like a wrestler I'd like to be an actor, little realizing the two callings are nearly identical. In one grappling match I won the school championship from a Negro boy who was dubbed "The Black Panther." Flushed with success, I gave "The Black Panther" a return match and he pinned me in short order. This taught me a valuable lesson in life which, alas, I have not always followed: quit when you're ahead.

Although I enjoyed the student activities, I was not a good student. I daydreamed a lot and couldn't get interested in studying. One day when I was sixteen I was walking to a movie when I passed a radio announcer doing a "Man on the Street" program. Curious, I stood on the fringes of the little group. Finally he poked the hand microphone in front of my face and asked me a question. I still remember the question. It was about Michigan's penal system. I answered it and then some. I wasn't sure what I was talking about, but I rambled on and on as though I knew as much about the penal system as J. Edgar Hoover and "Pretty Boy" Floyd put together. It wasn't easy for the announcer to wrest the mike back.

By the following Monday the station was deluged with letters about the young man who had spoken about the penal system on the "Man on the Street" program. I should explain that in a town like Jackson a dozen letters constitutes a "deluge of mail." Also that the deluge of letters had been written by my mother and me.

The station hired me for three dollars a week. I worked from 9 P.M. until midnight. During the day I was still going to high school, but I used to skip school a lot and hang around the station buying cigars for the news editor to ingratiate myself. The high school principal used to telephone our house to protest my frequent absences, but with frustrating results. My mother would impersonate a colored maid and say, "Ahm sorry, Mrs. Paw is out."

After a few months the station offered me a full-time job at the princely sum of twelve dollars a week. I was in seventh heaven. I dreamed of myself as a famous announcer like Ben Grauer or Harry Von Zell. I was sixteen years old and in my second year of high school.

The next morning I went in to my teacher and said, "I want my dollar deposit on my locker back."

"Why?" the teacher asked in surprise.

"I'm quitting school," I announced.

The teacher was so startled he handed over the dollar. That ended my formal education. When I got home I told my parents I had quit school to be a full-time radio announcer. My father said, "Oh?" My mother said, "Oh, is that right?" That's all there was to it.

3.

PAAR FOR THE COURSE

THE WORDS, "This is station WIBM, Jackson," will probably never go ringing down the corridors of time with such deathless phrases as "I shall return," "Hi-yo, Silver," "Dr. Livingstone, I presume," and "You may fire when ready, Gridley." Yet to me it will always be one of the most beautiful phrases in the English language. It was the first phrase I spoke when I became a full-fledged radio announcer at the age of sixteen in Jackson, Michigan. In fact, for a long time it was the *only* phrase they would let me speak.

They wouldn't let me do commercials because I stuttered, and the station was so small you could walk out of its coverage area by going down the street for a cup of coffee, but I was a real live radio announcer. There was one small catch. In addition to doing the station breaks every quarter-hour, I was expected to dust off the furniture and empty the wastebaskets. I didn't mind the enforced domesticity so much except that sometimes it caused me to lose face with my public. Our glass-enclosed studios were located in a former automobile showroom facing directly on the street, so it was like working in a goldfish bowl. I loved this prominent exposure when my high school friends would come to watch in awe, their noses pressed against the plate glass, as I'd say, "This is station WIBM, Jackson," with all the feeling of John Barrymore doing Hamlet's soliloquy. However, despite my precautions, they also occasionally spotted me as I furtively emptied the trash or hurriedly brushed the dust under the desk blotters.

Gradually, though, I progressed beyond station breaks and emptying wastebaskets. The station began letting me spin records and even do a few commercials. I still stuttered but the sponsors didn't mind because it made their commercials last longer. Then came my chance to be heard on a network.

I was one of the station announcers assigned to broadcast the Michigan Open Golf Tournament over the Michigan State network of several stations. A number of announcers were posted at various vantage points to report the play, and periodically were to give the station cue by giving their name and adding: "This is the Michigan State network." I knew little about golf, and cared even less, but my lack of ad libbing about the finer points of the play was more than offset by the frequency and gusto with which I would announce: "Your announcer is Jack Paar. This is the Michigan State network." This moment of glory on the links ended when some of the listeners suggested they would like to hear more about the progress of the tournament and less about Jack Paar.

Occasionally I got to read the news. Things were more informal in those early radio days, and there was no special news service for radio stations as there is now. We coped with this rather neatly, we thought, by stealing our news from the local paper. Not content with this thievery, we sometimes elaborated on the stolen stories.

On one occasion a story appeared in the paper that a Russian diplomat was visiting Jackson to study its industry. The Russian gentleman's name, the paper said, was Meti Nelots. I wrote and delivered the story about Meti Nelots on the newscast, embroidering it with an imaginary account of the activities of the Soviet visitor. This time I had walked into a trap set by the paper. It promptly printed a story revealing that "Meti Nelots" was imaginary and that spelled backwards it was "stolen item." The paper guffawed in print over our being caught red-handed purloining its news. Fortunately, about this time a news service for radio stations was formed and WIBM hastily subscribed.

While working at the Jackson station I was corresponding avidly with other stations, seeking greener pastures. I was hired by station WIRE, Indianapolis, but grew homesick after a short time and came back to the Jackson station. Although I was only seventeen, and still had little experience, the fact that I had been "clean to Indianapolis" impressed my former colleagues in Jackson and they treated me with a new respect. The station had acquired a news teletype during my absence and, since I had learned in Indianapolis how to change the rolls of paper on a news ticker, I was pressed into service as a regular newscaster.

One of my newscasts was preceded by a program called "The Town Crier" which gave the local news, after which I came on and gave the national and world news. One day the Town Crier got carried away with the sound of his own voice, an occupational hazard among announcers, and not only ran over into my time period but virtually used it all up. At long last, with almost no time left, he announced: "And now, Jack Paar and your national and world news."

"The Town Crier has taken so much time," I grumbled into the microphone, "with his items about Mrs. Howell spraining her ankle, the Reillys' missing fox terrier and next Tuesday's strawberry social at the Methodist church that I won't have time for the news of Mussolini's attack on Ethiopia. Good night."

The manager grabbed me as I came out of the studio and fired me. I began a nomadic career drifting from station to station around the Midwest and East. I went next to station WKBM, Youngstown, Ohio, and then to WCAE, Pittsburgh. One night at WCAE the engineer put on the wrong phonograph record and I burst out laughing. This outburst of mirth had two unfortunate consequences. The engineer rushed up and punched me, and the station fired me. I moved on to station WGAR, Cleveland.

Although Cleveland is more noted for its steel mills and railroads than its romantic atmosphere, and bleak, wind-swept Lake Erie has never been compared with Lake Lucerne or the canals of Venice as a stimulus to the tender passion, I fell in love there. The girl was a beautiful actress in the road company of a play called *Margin for Error*. Our romance was complicated by the fact that she was touring, and I was confined to my WGAR microphone, but I managed to woo her by means of the air waves. These were the days of the big dance bands, and I used to announce some of them from Cleveland over the CBS network. I used to beam romantic messages to my traveling lady love by announcing the band numbers in this fashion. "Now, 'All the Things You Are,' for a certain someone who cares," or "Now, for that special someone who's listening, 'Who's Your Little Whoozis?' " This kilocycle idyll was abruptly terminated when CBS sent WGAR a teletype saying: "Tell Paar to stop making love on our network."

Deprived of this channel of romantic communication, I pursued the young lady to Detroit by train. She had left the road company of *Margin for Error* a few weeks earlier and when that company arrived in Detroit she decided it would be great fun to play a practical joke on her former fellow troupers. Enlisting me in this skulduggery, she led me to a novelty shop where we stocked up on such trick items as exploding matches, glasses that dribble and itching powder. Then we headed for the theater and went backstage well before curtain time. She was warmly welcomed by the stage hands, whom she knew, and had little difficulty surreptitiously substituting her trick glasses, exploding matches and other instruments of torment for the real stage props.

Then, as the curtain rose, we took our places down front to enjoy the proceedings. The Clare Booth Luce play was about a Nazi consul in America and the Jewish policeman assigned to guard him. As the action unfolded, the Nazi consul, played by Kurt Katch, nonchalantly struck a match, only to have it explode with a loud *BANG* startling him so he almost fell into the orchestra pit. He had scarcely recovered from this when he raised a glass to toast *der Führer*. As he touched it to his lips the wine dribbled down his chin splattering the front of his suit. Each of these diabolically inspired mishaps was greeted with howls of laughter by my pretty companion.

As the actors proceeded warily through their lines on the booby-trapped stage, the Jewish policeman, played by Sheldon Leonard, now a prominent Hollywood director, began to twitch like a cooch dancer.

"I put itching powder in his puttees," my friend announced, gasping with laughter, as the harassed actors glared over the footlights at us.

"Come on, let's go back and see them," my young lady said as the final curtain rang down. "You'll love them."

Dubiously I followed her backstage. The cast understandably seemed less than overjoyed to see their nemesis, but her coltish spirits and hearty greeting quickly melted their irritation. "It was all in fun," she bubbled. "Here, have some gum as a peace offering."

Several of the cast took the gum and we said good-by. As we went out the stage entrance I noticed that several of the actors were clutching their throats and otherwise looking apoplectic. "It's hot gum," my fair companion giggled. "Isn't that a riot!"

It may have been little things like that which eventually caused our romance to pall. However, I continued under the romantic spell of Cleveland and not long afterwards I got married. In fact I got married twice—both times to the same girl. Her name was Irene. She was a beautiful girl. She played the piano and we met when she auditioned at the station. We were both too young for marriage, and it didn't work out. The first time we got a divorce it was my fault. The second time it was her fault. We finally decided to quit while we were all even.

While in Cleveland I had the usual misadventures which, my friends suggested, were becoming Paar for the course. One was the case of the missing library book. While under the spell of my actress friend I had obtained the play *Here Come the Clowns* by Philip Barry from the public library. I misplaced the book and for some reason, not entirely clear to me now, ignored the library's cards saying it was overdue. Finally I received a letter from the police demanding that I return the book. This I likewise ignored, for some reason or other. A few nights later two policemen appeared and hustled me rudely off to jail. The next morning I was led before the judge. I thought the best thing was to treat the matter lightly.

"I invoke the magna carta," I told the judge, "but you have the carta before the magna."

The judge didn't even smile at my little joke.

"Ten dollars and costs," he said frostily, "and pay for the book."

It's a good thing I paid for the book. An old friend of mine recently found the book, which it seems I had lent her, and returned it to me. The fine, at the rate of two cents a day for 6570 days, would have been $131.40.

Despite my occasional misadventures, I enjoyed my work at the station. These were the great days of radio: the days of Amos 'n' Andy and Jack Benny, of Bing Crosby and Kate Smith, of Morton Downey and Tony Wons. It was also the era of the bands of Benny Goodman, Glenn Miller, Tommy and Jimmy Dorsey and Guy Lombardo. Frank Sinatra was singing with Tommy Dorsey, and Perry Como with Ted Weems. They were wonderful days and radio then was truly a happy medium. Lawrence Welk was just learning to count, and the horror of rock 'n' roll was far in the future. People used to look at me suspiciously because I liked progressive waltzes.

While working at the station I devoted much of my spare time to trying to learn to be a comedian. I'd appear anywhere for a chance to get up and tell jokes.

I popped up at high school assemblies, Polish weddings, political rallies, grape festivals, bazaars and benefits of every description. For anyone who wanted a few words said, I had a few thousand ready.

One night I was thrilled to get a call from a theater. This was to be an actual professional job for real pay. I arrived at the theater breathless and asked the manager eagerly, "Where are the other acts?"

"There aren't any other acts," he said, sourly.

"But I can only do about a half hour of jokes," I protested.

"Nope, no jokes," the manager said. "If you tell jokes the show runs longer and the projectionist gets overtime. I just want you to raffle off some turkeys."

Deflated, I was led backstage and presented to my supporting cast—a half dozen trussed-up turkeys thrashing about indignantly in protest against their plight.

"Where's my dressing room?" I inquired, by now prepared for anything.

"There isn't any," this manager said. "You just sneak on stage during the newsreel."

So that's how I made my theatrical debut . . . sneaking down the aisle in the darkness while the audience booed Hitler in the newsreel. It was pretty discouraging, following a warm-up by Hitler. But the end of this story is sadder than the beginning.

I'd come back each week and pass out turkeys while the bank-night jackpot cash prize mounted in value. These were recession days and the avarice of the audience mounted each week with the amount of the jackpot.

Finally one night came the drawing for the jackpot. In order to be sure that there were no suspicions, I invited members of the audience to come up and witness the drawing. After much urging, only one lady consented to come on stage. She eyed me suspiciously as I picked a child to draw the winning number. I spun the barrel mixing the thousands of stubs. The moppet then reached in, picked one and handed it to me. With a flourish, I read the winning name. "My God, that's me!" the lady shrieked, nearly collapsing.

I saw several members of the audience coming over the footlights, and didn't wait to see more. I escaped backstage and out a fire escape while the angry crowd milled around the beleaguered manager. That ended my theatrical career in Cleveland. Hazards were also cropping up in my radio job.

One Sunday night in 1939, while I was the announcer on duty, I sneaked out for a sandwich, knowing there was nothing to do for a while, as the network would be carrying Orson Welles's "Mercury Theater." When I returned a few minutes later the switchboard was lit up like Charley Weaver after the cocktail hour at Hurley's Bar. Rushing into the announcer's booth I heard the voice of Bob Trout on the network babbling about an invasion by Martians in New Jersey. For a moment I was baffled that Trout and other actual newscasters were giving the reports, but quickly realized it was part of the Welles drama. I began picking up phones and telling the alarmed listeners that the invasion was fictional. I also broke into the program to announce this, but the calls kept pouring in, many of the panicky callers charging that I was covering up the truth. Finally I phoned the station manager.

"You'd better get down here," I exclaimed. "All hell's breaking loose. Listeners think this Orson Welles program about an invasion from Mars is real."

"Calm down, Jack," he replied. "You're always so emotional. Just take it easy. It's all a tempest in a teapot."

On a similar Sunday night, two years later, I was once more the announcer on duty when again fragmentary reports began coming in on the network about a mysterious attack—this time on a place called Pearl Harbor. The first reports were sketchy and again the station switchboard lit up with listeners asking about the attack.

Once again I called the same station manager. "You'd better get down here," I said. "All hell is breaking loose. The network is broadcasting about an attack on a place called Pearl Harbor."

"Oh, no, Paar," the manager sighed. "Not again. You're always so panicky. What is this—another Man from Mars attack?"

4. HOW TO CHEAT AT WAR

WAR IS HELL, as General Sherman said, and World War II made me simply furious. At first I was going to sit the whole thing out, but I volunteered for the draft in 1942. I'm afraid I was never meant to be a soldier. I never understood the Army and the Army seemed to make no effort to understand me. I had a passion for clean fingernails, said "Good morning" instead of saluting, and liked my first sergeant. Also I liked to be alone, which isn't always easy in a group of eight million men. I was assigned to bolster morale and, despite my best efforts, I'm sure there were times when the Army wondered which side I was on.

I volunteered for the draft in Buffalo, New York, where I had taken refuge at radio station WBEN after leaving Cleveland where I was fired by the station for poking fun at the way the executives' wives jockeyed for position at the annual station picnic.

The Army sent me to a reception center at Camp Custer in Battle Creek, Michigan. There I was classified and dispatched with sealed orders to Indiantown Gap, Pennsylvania. On the train I fell in with some officers and told them I was pleased to be headed for Indiantown Gap, as I'd heard it was a staging area. "I've always been interested in the stage," I confessed. This brought roars of laughter from the officers. "Listen, Mac," one of them said. "A staging area is where you ship out from. That means you're headed overseas fast, buddy. Bon voyage!"

This ominous prospect, as it turned out, was incorrect—at least for the moment. Alarmed, I peeked into my sealed orders. Because of my radio experience, I saw, I had been assigned to the 28th Special Service Company as a camp entertainment director. This was more like it, I thought, heaving a sigh of relief.

Arriving at Indiantown Gap I asked for the 28th Special Service Company. After a confusing search I located the company and was greeted by First Sergeant Gil Hall.

"There are two barracks," he said, indicating two dreary-looking structures. "Which one do you want to be in?"

"Whichever one," I said, with what I felt was becoming modesty, "that the camp entertainment director should be in."

"There are a hundred and twenty men in this company," the sergeant glowered, "and *all hundred and twenty* are classified as camp entertainment directors. Now which barracks do you want to be in?"

Our commanding officer at Indiantown Gap was Captain Sam Booker Carter. Captain Carter was not a career officer. In civilian life he was a sales executive for the Hershey Chocolate Company. He once got his orders balled up, and marched our platoon into a barn, but he was a good officer.

When I met Captain Carter I still didn't quite have the hang of saluting. I stuck out my hand and said: "How do you do, sir. I'm Private Jack Paar." He gave me a look that told me he felt the Army must have reached the bottom of the manpower barrel. We became good friends although he was a real military man and I never could seem to learn the rules of warfare. I had been carefully instructed if anyone approached while I was on guard duty to say "Halt! Who goes there? Advance and be recognized." One night I was on duty when a jeep pulled up. "Halt!" I roared. "Who goes there?" Then I recognized Captain Carter. "Captain Sam," I exclaimed. "How *are* you?" "No, Paar!" he screamed.

"You're not playing by the rules!" Then he shook his head despairingly and drove off.

The function of the 28th Special Service Company was to bolster morale by furnishing entertainment, publishing camp newspapers, providing books and periodicals and the like. Our motley group included everything from a former burlesque comedian to a string quartet. Even though we were a noncombat outfit, we had the same basic training as any other infantry outfit. Our rifles were supposed to be kept in a rack in the barracks, but I formed an attachment for mine and kept it under the mattress on my cot. If anyone had sat down suddenly on my cot I might have killed more people than Audie Murphy.

During our training we were sent out on war games in the rolling Pennsylvania countryside. Two platoons went out at nightfall and dug in, and the two others followed to try and find and "capture" them. Capture was accomplished by tagging a soldier, but rivalry between platoons ran high and tagging often got quite boisterous. I was in the first group of two platoons. As we marched out I realized that the mock battle would provide an excellent opportunity for some of the more warlike G.I.s to practice their commando tactics on the strange new soldier with the dark sunglasses, the clean fingernails and the desire for solitude. This situation, I decided, called for drastic action. As we marched along I plotted my strategy and revealed it to two companions plodding along next to me, a concert violinist and an operatic tenor.

When our two platoons fanned out from Route 22 to dig in, my two buddies and I ducked behind a big signboard while the rest of the platoon plunged into the woods and took evasive action. As soon as they were safely out of sight in the woods, we sneaked down the highway to a diner where I hosted my fellow deserters to hamburgers and chili.

We continued to lie low through the night while the two attacking platoons scrambled through the woods and the mock combat raged. At one point a group of recruits got lost and their lieutenant reassured them: "Don't worry, men. I can find my way out of here blindfolded." From the darkness one of the G.I.s yelled, "Well, blindfold the s.o.b. and let's get out of here."

With dawn breaking we crept back into camp with the weary warriors who had battled through the night. At camp we fell in to hear a critique of the mock battle from Captain Carter. After commending the men for their spirit, he announced: "I want to point out that one new soldier, Private Paar, was never captured. That shows what can be done if you apply yourself."

Captain Carter was always tough on duty, but off duty he was pleasant and sociable. One evening the Hershey Company, for whom he had worked in civilian life, gave a dinner dance in honor of our company. I don't dance but went along on the theory that it couldn't be any worse than marching. At the dance I met a slim, pretty, ash-blonde girl. She had a freckled nose and looked very sexy in a Republican sort of way. Her name was Miriam Wagner and she was related to the Hersheys.

"I don't dance," I told her when we were introduced, "but I'm interesting to talk to."

She eyed me doubtfully, but we sat down to talk. I never talked faster in my life. We met on the 3rd of July. On the 4th of July I surrendered my independence. We became engaged.

Magazines and newspapers are so fond of referring to Miriam as a "Hershey heiress" I'd like to set the record straight. She is a grandniece of Milton Hershey, the founder of the Hershey Chocolate Company. He left an estate of 84 million dollars but, rather thoughtlessly it seemed to me, willed it all to the Hershey Industrial School for Orphaned Boys. If Miriam were wealthy I would retire and devote my energies to fighting crabgrass instead of network executives.

Actually the Wagners are a prosperous, conservative, old-fashioned Dutch family with the thrifty habits of Peter Minuit, the Dutch burgher who hornswoggled the Indians out of Manhattan Island for twenty-four dollars, thus acquiring the future site of the biggest traffic jam in history. Miriam had a sheltered upbringing and her parents took a dim view of the impetuous young private who wanted to get married in such a hurry. Her father was especially concerned over whether I'd had a college education. He was delighted when I assured him I had attended Western Reserve University in Cleveland. This was technically true. As a lark, a friend named Maury Condon and I had once attended two classes in astronomy there. By the time it came to light that my collegiate career was two hours' duration, we were already married and I had set up light housekeeping alone in a tent on Guadalcanal.

Miriam and I were married at the Dutch Reformed Church in Hershey, Pennsylvania, October 9, 1943. Jose Melis, an Army buddy who now is musical director of the show, played the organ, and Mendelssohn's Wedding March never sounded more like the cha cha cha.

Our honeymoon was glorious, or at least as glorious as a honeymoon can be in Hershey, Pennsylvania, on a weekend pass from the Army. Two days after marching down the aisle I was back marching around the parade ground at Indiantown Gap. The only time I got to see my bride was on occasional weekends. Then my feet were so flat from marching that to get me out of the bathtub she'd have to rock me back and forth to break the suction.

Not long afterwards our outfit was shipped overseas. The scuttlebutt was that we were being shipped to Bermuda or Nassau. We sailed south all right, but when our ship made a right-hand turn at the Panama Canal I knew we were in trouble.

We boarded the transport at Staten Island in New York Harbor. When we got aboard we were greeted by Captain Carter who was troop commander of the ship. He had several stitches in his face as a result of bumping into a hatch. We hadn't even left the dock and he was already wounded!

Our trip to the South Pacific took forty-four miserable days.

There were several thousand men on the old transport, packed in like olives in a jar. The only diversion was trying to get something to eat or finding a place in the shade. The boredom was terrible and the food worse. We ate twice a day, standing up. The only interruption in the monotony was an occasional submarine scare. One day, after more than a month at sea, we had one of these alerts. The ship's guns banged away although we couldn't see anything. When the firing ended, I climbed into a lifeboat and yelled: "Men, hear this. I've been asked to make an announcement. There was a Japanese submarine sighted but *unfortunately* the gun crew drove it off. I say unfortunately, because the enemy submarine was trying to bring us food."

The men roared, and the tension and misery were broken for the moment. It may not seem hilarious now, but I still feel fondly it was the biggest joke I ever told. It certainly got the biggest laugh. You could almost feel the boredom and jitters roll away in the big roar of laughter that swept the crowded decks like a wave. It also reminded me of something I was becoming increasingly aware of—that the G.I.s loved humor based on gripes and on poking fun at the brass. Life in the Army was dangerous and tough at worst and dull and lonely at best, and the G.I.s appreciated jokes at the expense of anyone who was a little bit better off than they were.

We landed on Guadalcanal on St. Patrick's Day, March 17, 1944, and that beautiful but battered island looked greener than Ireland. Our Marines and soldiers had captured and secured the island, and it was being used as a staging area for assaults on other Japanese-held islands, but there were still enemy stragglers in the hills and jungles and life on the island was still no picnic. There's something disquieting about a banzai charge if you're allergic to noisy Japanese. After debarking we were taken to a remote section of the island. We pulled up in a clearing, with coarse grass standing higher than our heads, and an officer announced: "This is your bivouac area." Trucks rumbled into the high grass trying to flatten it out and we followed doing sort of a jungle Lindy Hop in an effort to trample down the rank vegetation so we could pitch our tents. To complicate things it was the height of the rainy season.

With our own morale at zero, we set about our morale duties. Army entertainment was crude, but the troops, many of them just back from combat, were starved for any kind of diversion. Our shows usually consisted of an emcee, a few specialty acts like acrobats or jugglers, sometimes three G.I.s with balloons tucked in their shirts lip-syncing to records of the Andrews Sisters singing "Beer Barrel Polka" or "Bei Mir Bist Du Schön" and a small musical group or just a piano. It wasn't much, but, as the old vaudevillians used to say, they loved us in Guadalcanal and Fiji and Suva and Munda. Our role wasn't very heroic, but I can always tell my grandchildren that I played before thousands of armed men and never got shot.

There were times, though, when I thought I might be executed at dawn for insulting the brass. "I suppose I shouldn't talk about officers so much," I'd tell the men. "Some try, a few are sincere—and—what the hell—there's a few who know what they're doing."

The men would roar. I was putting into words their own gripes and frustrations and loneliness. "Soon our day will come, men," I would tell them. "Someday we'll all go home and be free again. We'll join the American Legion and carry on its great and noble traditions. We'll pinch old ladies and throw toilet paper out of hotel windows."

We went from island to island, playing one-day and one-night stands. We used to give one, two, or three shows a day. We played on ships, in hospitals and on the beaches. Once we even gave a little show in a plane over the Fiji Islands. Often we played to war-weary, begrimed men, just back from killing Japs in the jungles, but they always responded to humor. I used to kid ourselves. "The only battle star I have," I would say, "is for being booed at Bougainville. But we, too, sometimes face danger. Just today I reported to our commanding officer: Sir, mission accomplished. Two of our banjos are missing."

I have kept some of my old jokes and am including a few here as historical evidence of some of the dangers our fighting men had to face in the jungle warfare in World War II. In retrospect some of them don't seem as funny as when I first told them. To really enjoy them you had to be there. With bullets, malaria, K-rations and atabrine, they were a riot.

Gentlemen. And any officers who might be present . . . Welcome from the management of World War II. I know you guys are homesick after being out here for two years—but I have good news for you. Last night we took a Jap prisoner—and you all ought to talk to him, because he just came back from a three-week furlough—in Chicago. (He must have lied about his age or something.)

I have some announcements to make: The Captain is censoring the mail again this week—so let's cut down on those big words. . . . Also—I don't care what you think of the colonel—stop using your thumbs when you salute.

The Command is sorry about the foul-up on our Christmas packages from home. We'll get them as soon as they [illegible] breaking them. However, there is an unclaimed package that just arrived for Sergeant York. I don't believe he's in this outfit, or this war. . . .

And we're going to double the guard duty. This morning at the mail tent, seven letters and a package were picked up by Nomoru Hayakawa.

All of you men turn in your helmets tonight—we're taking the rear-view mirrors off the jeeps and putting them on your hats so you can see the lieutenants during combat. . . .

Why is it that on every invasion this outfit makes, the officers in Headquarters Company are so far behind the Japanese lines they may get bombed by the Nazis?

The only way the guys in Headquarters Company are going to get the Purple Heart is if they get caught between two desks coming together. . . .

Now about this blitz that you're to go on next week. The colonel has given orders you are to bring back more prisoners. The reason for this is that he needs a new kimono. . . .

And also try and bring back some girl prisoners. Because last Saturday night in the Officers' Club, they were dancing with each other again. . . . (They're going to give this war a bad name.)

Next week when you go in, you are going to have your top-ranking officers with you on the beach. You'll hear their voices yelling "Geronimo," "Gung Ho," and "This is a recorded announcement."

Now all of us, enlisted men and officers, are anxious to get this war over with and get back home. And after all, there isn't any real difference between us. The main difference between an officer and an enlisted man is that when an officer gets a "Dear John" letter, it's notarized. . . .

Besides, if we all went home now, there's no place for us to live. They can't start putting up new homes for us until they finish building the bowling alleys. . . .

One guy I know got a discharge, got married, and lives in a Quonset hut. Last month I heard his first child was born round-shouldered. . . .

In addition to entertaining the men, I also conducted serious briefing sessions to acquaint them with conditions in the jungles. This is one of my briefings. Please excuse age and jungle mildew.

PAAR: *Some of you men are new out here. There are certain things you should know about this area—certain things you should watch out for. I want to point out a few things you may run across while you're here in the South Pacific—about your own outfit and the enemy. . . .*

← This, of course, is our V for Victory sign.

This means two-to-one they'll never get us back out here again. →

← This sign means "Halt" . . . or "May I leave the war for a minute, Sarge?"

This means the Chow Line starts here. →

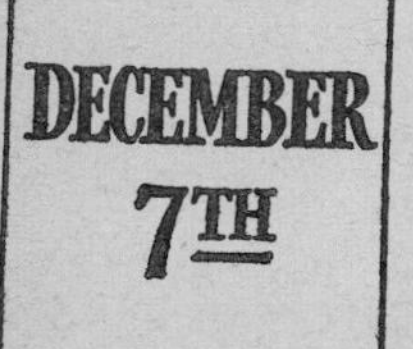

← Don't forget Pearl Harbor.

Don't forget the General's birthday. The officers and the nurses will have candlelight and wine. The enlisted men—warm beer and an old flashlight. →

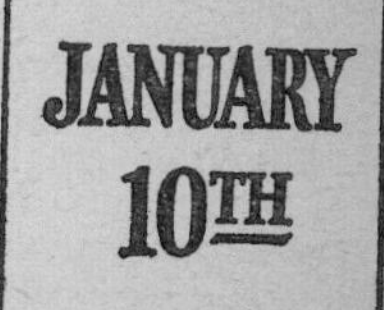

T

← This means Tanks.

This means You're Welcome. →

This means . . . I saw this nurse first—so keep your hands off!

General MacArthur tripped here.

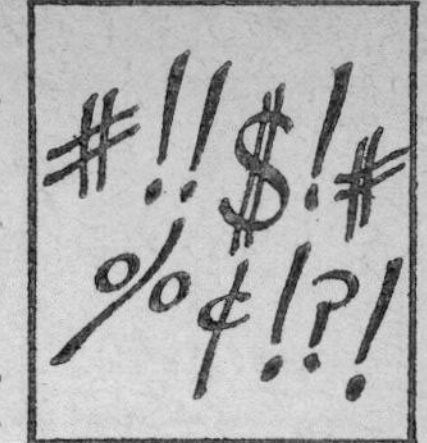

If you see this sign along a Japanese road, it means last chance to get sukiyaki before the parkway.

If you see this sign along the road, you've retreated too far—it's a German cloverleaf.

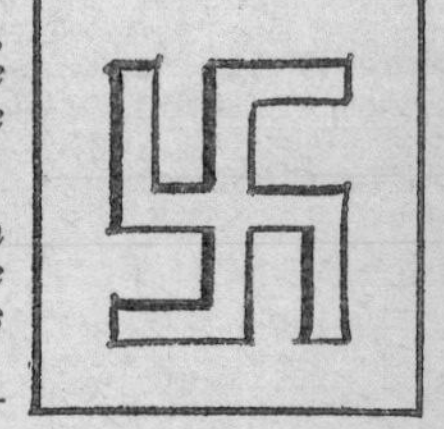

At one time I was assigned to a radio station of the Mosquito network which covered the captured South Pacific islands and even there I succeeded in carrying on my war with the officers. I had with me a phonograph record of Tarzan yells which, incidentally, I still use on my show. I would ask all the men listening to turn their radios up as loud as they'd go. Then I'd put on my Tarzan record, turn the volume up to an ear-splitting pitch, and announce, "Now, men, let's get the officers up."

I got in serious trouble with my needling only once. That was at a Naval hospital in New Caledonia. We were putting on a show for several thousand men, many of them wounded and in wheel chairs or on stretchers. The time came to start but we couldn't begin the show until the Commodore arrived. The men were getting restless and so was I. At last the Commodore appeared, nearly an hour late, with a pretty USO girl on his arm.

"You wouldn't think," I said, as they made their way to

their seats, "that one man and a broad would hold up five thousand men." The men howled, and I felt encouraged.

"The USO girls were supposed to do the Dance of the Virgins for you," I told the chuckling audience, "but they went to the Officers' Club last night and broke their contract."

The men loved it, but the Commodore didn't. After the show I was placed under arrest by a Commander and ordered court-martialed for insulting the commanding officer. But good old Captain Carter came to my rescue. I heard a commotion outside the shower room where I had been locked. "Release this man," Captain Carter demanded. "He's an Army man and you can't hold him in a Navy area." This confused my Navy captors sufficiently for them to free me from the shower room and Captain Carter hustled me off to a friendlier island.

The war ended before there were any further hostilities between me and the Navy. The South Pacific was full of troops, all anxious to get home, and I was assigned to assist in a reenlistment campaign. I wrote and recorded ten oneminute announcements, which were played on the island radio stations, telling the homesick G.I.s all about the joys of re-enlistment. I felt a little hypocritical, since under the redeployment schedule I was slated to leave on the next boat and I knew that the thousands of other troops in the area were just as anxious to get home as I was. However, my smugness was ironically punctured by fate. Suddenly the Army slowed down its redeployment schedule. So I sat around like everyone else listening to the radio to get the latest redeployment news. And to get the news, I had to listen to the honeyed tones of Sergeant Paar pleading with me to re-enlist. I managed to successfully resist his blandishments, as did practically everyone else. But what a miserable six weeks before I finally did embark for home!

5. A BABE IN THE HOLLYWOODS

THE GOLDEN GATE never swung open with a bigger welcome than when my transport steamed into San Francisco Bay in February, 1946. I was eagerly looking forward to shucking my Army uniform and starting out to find an announcing job, but fate had a pleasant surprise in store for me.

During a show one day at a field hospital on New Caledonia, a war correspondent named Sidney Carroll had chatted with me. Later we had corresponded and he had said he was going to do a magazine story about me for *Esquire*. I heard no more about it and my fellow G.I.s took great delight in ribbing me about the supposed article in *Esquire* which never appeared. When we arrived back at Camp Stoneman in California I called my mother in Indianapolis.

"The movie studios have been calling," she said, "and the radio networks."

"The movie studios?" I echoed blankly. "What for?"

"They've read the *Esquire* story," she told me. "They want to sign you up."

I raced frantically out to find a copy of *Esquire* but there was none in camp. To complicate matters just then we were herded aboard a train for Camp Atterbury, Indiana, where we were scheduled to be discharged. There was no chance to get a copy of the precious *Esquire* to read what was causing the excitement. As we rode eastward, my mind was spinning like the wheels of our troop train.

Finally our train stopped in Cheyenne, Wyoming. We weren't allowed off the train but I spotted an Indian dozing near the station. He looked as welcome to me as Pocahontas must have looked to Captain John Smith. I beckoned him over, handed him a dollar and said in my best Apache: "You gettum *Esquire* magazine." The Indian disappeared into the station and when there was no further sign of him I decided my dollar had likewise disappeared for good. The train started to pull out of the station and just then the Indian bolted out of the station waving the copy of *Esquire*. The train was gaining momentum but the faithful redskin put on a burst of speed and tossed the magazine through the train window to me.

Dazed, I sat back in my seat and began reading. . . .

I GIVE YOU JACK PAAR

by Sidney Carroll

I had been hearing stories about him for ten thousand miles. I know it started somewhere in the Solomons. It was at a USO show in the jungle, and I thought the comic was pretty funny and I made the mistake of laughing out loud. The kid sitting next to me, a Marine private, seemed to resent my laughter. He turned and said, "You think this guy's funny? You should hear Jack Paar!" And then the kid sitting next to him turned to me and said, "Yeabo! That's my boy!" That was the first time I ever heard Paar's name. I was to hear it many times in the next few months. All through the Solomons, whenever I'd hear Marines discussing the shows they'd seen, I'd hear the inevitable names of Bob Hope and Jack Benny. But then somebody would bring up Paar's name, and that would be the clincher. Hope and Benny had left some fragrant memories behind them, all right, but this Paar was obviously the favorite of favorites.

This Jack Paar was not a USO entertainer—he was just a G.I. himself. He was part of one of these Special Service units made up exclusively of G.I. talent. They went on month after month, untouted, unheralded, like the foot-slogging infantry itself, doing a job that had to be done, making men laugh in some of the most laugh-proof places in the world.

Jack Paar was a comic in one of those troupes. They told me he was best of them all.

I did a lot of traveling before I caught up with him. His name kept popping up here and there until I felt I was chasing rainbows. He was up and out of the Solomons before I could see him. He passed through Tulagi three weeks before I did. When I got to Fiji they told me he had been there—and they looked at me with pity, and perhaps with contempt, because I had not seen him.

"You never heard Paar? My achin' back—he's got more noive than any bastid I ever seen!"

He was panicking them all over the Pacific Ocean, and he was always just out of my reach. And then I caught up with him.

It was in New Caledonia, and it was an accident. I was out at a field hospital called MOB 107 one day and a Special Service captain named Carter told me there'd be a show for the wounded men that night and would I care to come? "You'll like this one," he told me. "It's got a kid in it named Jack Paar, who'll kill you."

That night at MOB 107 it would have been beautiful beyond words except for the fact that when I looked around at the audience I saw legs in splints, and many wheelchairs, and men with bandaged stumps on their shoulders. At least, I thought, this Paar boy picks himself some audience to make laugh. And while I was figuring his chances of creating general hilarity among these men who'd been torn to pieces and who generally didn't give a damn about laughing at anything any more, the sun went down and the lights went up, and Paar came out and the show was on.

Well, his technique is not like Hope's; it is not exuberant.

It is not like Benny's—he assumes no special character. He plays himself, straight. He is a thin, calm, unhurried, good-looking youngster who just stands up there and talks into the mike.

"I understand there are absolutely no officers present this evening. Pay no attention to those boys in the fifth row. . . . they happen to be a convention of Air Raid wardens."

The officers in the fifth row take that one a little self-consciously, but the men in the other rows are howling. Oh brother—is this good! I ask you to remember the one overwhelming fact about all this: One of the most serious of all offenses is to insult an officer. Keep that in mind.

"The reason I like to have these heart-to-heart talks with the troops is that I want the officers to realize that we're all in the same boat. . . . Only I'm tired of doing all the rowing."

Now I realize that Jack's stuff is not exactly sensational when it's set down this way in print. It's not funny unless you've been an enlisted man overseas for a couple of years, and you're sick and tired, and you're sitting in an improvised theatre hearing him deliver his own lines.

"Colonel Smith here tonight is a great friend of mine . . . there isn't a thing he wouldn't do for me that I wouldn't do for him. And that's the way it's been for the past five years—we haven't done a damn thing for each other."

And thus it goes, on and on, jawing at the same thing with every sentence: Officers, Officers, Officers. He chops them down, tears them apart, chews them up fine. Of course the enlisted men are tickled to death, but the wonder of it is that after a while the officers laugh, too. They sit there and take it, and laugh. Paar is funny, and Paar is likable, and therefore it's impossible to get mad at him, and I know now why he became a demigod among the men he entertained in the Pacific.

He is one of the few G.I.s who spoke out the gripes and groans the men themselves could never express. He did it with humor, and he did it with finesse. When he got up there in front of a bunch of grimy Joes and let himself go, he was suddenly a kind of White Hope. He was Sad Sack suddenly become a Sacred Cow with the special privilege of kicking the general in the pants. In his way, I suppose, he was every unknown soldier's wish fulfillment.

To a lieutenant who kept talking out loud all during one of the shows, Jack turned and said, "Lieutenant, a man with your I.Q. should have a low voice, too." Another time he opened a show by addressing himself directly to the commanding officer: "My dear sir," he said, "and you are none of the three."

The show went on and on, getting warmed up. It went all through the Solomons for twenty months. It touched at places the geography books neglect, but the sand ticks and the heat certainly do not, and Paar made the men laugh.

They followed and preceded stars like Benny and Hope, and the reviews in the Army papers gave them the edge over everything that had ever played out there. The 28th got a Unit Citation, and a Meritorious Service award, and they played to over a million men.

Paar wrote all his own stuff. "All we have is officers and homesickness, so that's what I talk about," Paar said. That was why his little troupe could follow the biggest Hollywood stars the USO had to send, and lay them in the aisles. He was one of them. He said all the things they wanted to say, and the 28th successfully completed its mission: it bolstered the morale in the field.

That story in *Esquire* by Sidney Carroll was the biggest thing that ever happened to me. Here I was back home and broke and ready to start looking for a job as a radio announcer and there was a magazine on the stands calling me a "demigod." I had to look up the word, but the effect was magical. Instead of heading for Cleveland or Buffalo or Detroit to try to get an announcing job, all of a sudden I was getting offers from the big networks and movie studios. I was in a daze. I went to New York and appeared on a big national program with Ethel Merman and the response was so warm I broke down and wept on the air. I signed a contract with RKO and Miriam and I headed for Hollywood.

Hollywood was like Guadalcanal with houses. It had palm trees and strange natives, and there was lots of fighting going on. The big difference was the beautiful homes. Miriam and I drove around for days, just looking at all the lovely houses. Neither of us had ever seen Cape Cod Spanish before. We were amazed to see how many of the houses were perched on hills. Some of the houses on hills were split levels—since the big slide they'd had. We drove through one community called Rolling Hills, which seemed like a new high in honest real estate advertising. Another community we liked is Pacific Palisades, which is on the cliffs overlooking the Pacific. However, the homes there are the kind where one minute you're looking out the window enjoying the view, and the next you're part of it. We also drove through Beverly Hills but we had a hard time finding it because it was unlisted. A service station man told us it is the richest city of its size in America. This apparently is true as it's so swanky that the parking meters didn't even show the price.

Hollywood, we decided, was a nice place to die, but we wouldn't want to live there. Dying seemed to be the biggest industry. The California cemeteries make dying sound so attractive it's a real effort to keep breathing. One cemetery offered everything but green stamps, view lots and ranch style tombstones. It was plain to see the Hollywood undertakers take care of everything. If you die you don't have to lift a finger.

As we ogled the inviting cemeteries, the beautiful homes, including the involuntary split-level dwellings, and the nutburger stands, I was reminded of the old saying that Hollywood is only the glitter of false tinsel. This, I was soon to learn, was false. If you peel away the false tinsel of Hollywood, there is *real* tinsel underneath.

After looking around, we rented a house in Hollywood just a stone's throw from *Variety* and the *Hollywood Reporter*—

in case they ran any derogatory reviews—and I reported at the studio to begin my career as an actor.

I'll never forget my reception when I walked into RKO the first time. The man in charge of talent took a long look at me, jumped up and exclaimed: "A young Alan Ladd." I thought the comparison was flattering, but I knew there was lots of mileage left in the *old* Alan Ladd. A producer sitting with the talent chief shook his head in dissent, a gesture rarely seen in studios. "Nooooo," he mused, looking me up and down critically. "Kay Kyser, but with warmth." Since Kay Kyser, the band leader who is now retired, had an overabundance of warmth, if nothing else, I never did understand *that* comparison.

That was my introduction to Hollywood, and it didn't get any easier to understand as time passed. Being fresh from the South Pacific I thought I knew something about jungle warfare, but not the Hollywood variety. When I first encountered it I thought of the counsel Fred Allen had given me once. "All the sincerity in Hollywood," he said, "you can stuff in a flea's navel and still have room to conceal eight caraway seeds and an agent's heart." However, even though the war was over, as John Paul Jones said, I had just begun to fight.

When I arrived back in New York, and began getting offers, I obtained an agent to handle me since I knew nothing about business. When he got me a contract with RKO for $350 a week I was overjoyed. After several years of K-rations, mosquitoes and jungles, I felt rich. Even so, I was startled after driving to Hollywood in an old car to find my agent ensconced in style in a plush office at the studio. "It's wonderful of you to do all this for me," I said, innocently, taking in his office. "But how can you do it? Your commission on my salary is only $35 a week."

"Don't think a thing of it," he reassured me, paternally. "I'm investing in your future."

I thought this was mighty fine of him. That is, until I discovered that at the same time he negotiated my contract at $350 a week with the studio, he negotiated himself one at $500 a week to "handle" me!

When I confronted him with this he didn't blink an eye. "Don't worry," he said loftily. "I'm earning the money. I'm writing a screen play for you. The studio sees you as sort of a young Jimmy Stewart. This is a story about you, playing the young Jimmy Stewart part, and a goat."

The idea of co-starring with a goat, when I'd been thinking of Jane Russell, came as something of a start and I retired to mull that over. I didn't see my literary flesh peddler for a brief spell and when I did I asked: "How are you coming with the story of me and the goat?"

"Oh, it's turning out great," he enthused. "The studio is crazy about it. In fact, they think it's too good for a young, untried actor like you. They want to do it with Jimmy Stewart."

That ended my association with that agent, and I've been suspicious of agents and goats ever since.

RKO never found many roles for me, with or without goats. I got a sports car, wore dark glasses, posed for still pictures; I did everything an actor does except act. They used to send me on tours to promote pictures I wasn't even in. I can still remember riding through some small town with a police escort while people yelled at me: "Who are you?" They assigned me to a director who began to coach me on such intricacies of the actor's art as shading and tempo. "I haven't got any shading," I told him frankly. "I've got four speeds: fast or slow, loud or soft."

While I was at RKO Dore Schary, a talented producer, was brought in as studio production head and my moribund hopes revived. However, they were quickly dashed. All the contract players, including Jane Russell, Robert Mitchum, Martha Hyer and me, were summoned to appear and perform for Schary and his lieutenants. The purpose of this command performance seemed plain: for the new production chief and his aides to look over the talent under contract and decide which of the actors they wanted to keep. I resented having us all paraded before the brass like pigs at a county fair and saw a chance to express myself when I was nominated to emcee the proceedings.

I began by needling Mr. Schary about the way the studio had treated me. I told him the only part I had played at RKO was so small they should have melted the celluloid back and made a tooth brush handle out of it. The pictures themselves, I observed, were so bad that even the footprints in the forecourt of Grauman's Chinese walked out. I pointed out that I had asked them to loan me out but that they had refused when no other studio would make the five-dollar deposit. I told Schary that we all knew why we were there and that we weren't going to take it lying down. "A few starlets might," I said, "but not all of us." I reminded the gathering that thanks to Howard Hughes, who owned RKO, I was still a new face but that it was rapidly becoming the oldest new face in Hollywood. "RKO did one thing for which I'm grateful," I concluded. "You spent four hundred dollars having my teeth capped. So this is probably the first time you've been insulted with your own teeth."

None of the aides laughed when I began kidding their boss, but Schary was a good sport. He began laughing and all the other executives laughed retroactively. Naturally, because I was obviously honestly willing to leave, the studio thought I must have another offer. It clutched me firmly to its bosom and eventually even gave me a few roles.

Later I made a couple of pictures at Twentieth Century. One was called *Love Nest* and I played opposite a starlet named Marilyn Monroe, then as obscure as I was, and I was as obscure as the country's eleventh best-dressed man. Looking back I guess I should have been excited, but I found her pretty dull. Marilyn spoke in a breathless way which denoted either passion or asthma. She wore dresses with the necklines cut so low it looked as though she had jumped into her dress and caught her feet on the shoulder straps. Despite her obvious physical attributes, Marilyn was interested in culture. At that time she had not yet discovered Dostoevski's *Brothers Karamazov* and, in fact, had only lately discovered Hollywood's Brothers Warner. However, she used to carry around the books of Marcel Proust, with their titles facing out, although I never saw her read any of them. She was always holding up shooting because she was talking with someone on the phone. Judging from what's happened, though, I guess she had the right number.

Another young lady whom I worked with about this time also went on to bigger things. While at RKO I played a small part in a picture with an attractive comedienne named Lucille Ball. One day she and I and the producer, Bob Sparks, were watching some rushes in the projection room. I played a light comedy role in the picture and as we sat in the dark watching it Miss Ball said: "Jack, do you know any young actor who does light comedy like you do in this role who would want to play opposite me in a new TV series?"

I thought hard for a minute and finally suggested Hal March, a good young light comedian I knew, and Hy Averback, another good young actor I had known in the South Pacific.

"I see," Lucille said, without noticeable enthusiasm.

When the rushes ended, and she departed, Bob Sparks came over to me and said: "You dumbbell! Don't you get it? She meant you. Why didn't you suggest yourself?"

"Gosh, I never thought of that," I said truthfully.

Lucille finally settled on an unlikely choice to play opposite her—a Cuban band leader who happened to be her husband, Desi Arnaz.

The last time I was in Hollywood I drove wistfully past RKO which was jumping with television activity. It now belongs to Miss Ball and her husband. They bought it with the money they made from a TV series called "I Love Lucy."

6. MY BIG BREAK—AND HOW I CURED IT

OTHER YOUNG ACTORS' movie careers went up and down in Hollywood, but mine just went sideways. Sometimes it seemed that I was getting nowhere fast, and at other times that I would never get there. However, I got a big break in radio in 1947.

While in the South Pacific during the war I'd met Jack Benny briefly at a hospital on Guadalcanal where he was entertaining the G.I.s. I was tempted to call him when I got to Hollywood but couldn't get up the courage. Although he is known as one of the kindest men in show business, I realized that he had met thousands of soldiers while entertaining during the war and that if they all called him when they got to Hollywood his phone would probably be busy and I wouldn't be able to get him. Also, I didn't know anyone else in radio and it didn't seem right to start at the top.

Eventually I met a comedy writer and together we made an audition record of a radio comedy variety show. I emceed and we had sketches and music. My agent played it for an advertising executive who said: "You haven't got a show there." He then bought it for the American Tobacco Company as the summer replacement for Jack Benny with the provision that it had to get Benny's okay.

We took the audition record to Benny's house where he met us in pajamas. He remembered me from Guadalcanal and greeted me warmly. Then we put the record on to play.

Benny is famed for laughing at almost anything, and is considered by comedians as the best audience in the world, but he listened without smiling throughout the whole record. The supposed comedy show began to take on more suspense than an Alfred Hitchcock mystery. Finally the record ended. "You got a nice show there, kid," Jack said with a smile. "I like it."

I was in! I doubt if any young comedian in history ever got a bigger break than being chosen as Jack Benny's summer replacement at that time. And I doubt if any young comedian ever got tangled up in more turmoil as a result. Just a couple of years away from playing jungles, and just twenty-nine years old, I was suddenly playing to the largest audience of any program on radio. It was a tremendous break, and before long it felt like a compound fracture of the tibia.

The show itself was well received and I was hailed as the "outstanding star of tomorrow." But difficulties cropped up on all sides. By the time the agents finished with me, I was cut up more ways than Poland. In addition, my head writer was getting $1000 a week while I, the supposed star, got $750. I felt like Max Baer who once parceled out 375 percent of himself. When someone explained he only consisted of 100 percent, he protested: "I thought people were like baseball averages—that you figured on a basis of a thousand percent."

Perhaps because of what I felt was the injustice of this situation, and possibly because I was young and insecure in a new and trying situation, I had heated differences with the writers. Their background was Broadway and Hollywood and they loved to write local jokes about LaBrea tar pits or Lindy's restaurant. I told them I was from Detroit and Cleveland and Buffalo and that the people there wouldn't know the LaBrea tar pits if they fell into them, and I didn't want to do jokes people didn't understand. For $4000 a week, I said, the jokes should at least be understandable. One day one of the writers came and asked for a raise. He had been out of work for a year before I hired him, and now was getting $700 a week. He had worked several weeks by this time, and felt he should have a raise. I offered him a $50 a week raise to

$750. "Couldn't you make it $800," he asked, "so that I'd have some *incentive?*" His incentive, I suggested hotly, was that he might become unemployed momentarily, which he did.

Despite the various vicissitudes of my show, my admiration for Jack Benny raged unabated. And this in face of the fact that only once in our association did I ever succeed in making him laugh. I was with him a good deal, and had tossed off a few lines that I thought were fairly hilarious, but Benny always just looked glum. Then came the time I made him laugh—and at something that wasn't even funny.

It happened at a banquet of the Radio Writers' Guild. Ordinarily I shun such ceremonies but on this occasion the request came while I was in the throes of the cocktail hour; an interlude when I am particularly vulnerable. Fortified by a brace of martinis and some lavish flattery, I agreed to emcee the affair which meant ad libbing for an hour or more before an audience of the top comedy writers and performers in Hollywood. Undaunted, I began to indulge in my favorite pastime, talking, getting large laughs from the audience which included such wits as Benny, Groucho Marx and Phil Harris. I felt the laughs must be due to the merry quips I was sprinkling around between the acts, since some of the entertainers were prime suspects in the death of vaudeville.

The feeling that I was never in better fettle was confirmed when I was greeted backstage by Jack Benny with a new respect. "Look, kid," he said, "you've improved a *great deal* since I've *seen* you last. Now I . . . I can follow a *good* act, and if it's *good* I inherit the laughter and rapport they've established, but you're following these *dogs*. They're *terrible. Why* do you *do* it? *How* do you *do* it?"

"I don't know any better," I shrugged.

It wasn't even a joke, but Benny, for the one and only time in the year I knew him, almost fell down laughing.

At the end of the summer, when Jack Benny returned, the sponsor thought well enough of my work to continue me with my own show on ABC into the winter season. The program had a very good Hoover rating. It showed there were more vacuum cleaners turned on when I was on than at any other time. However, the sponsor dispatched a comedy analyst named Ernest Walker to study the show and see how it could be improved. Walker, a genial Southerner whom Maurice Zolotow hailed as "the most dynamic force in comedy since Joe Miller's celebrated joke book," had, it seemed, invented a machine to analyze laughter. This machine, which looked like a Univac designed by Rube Goldberg, measured the volume of laughter on rolls of paper with wavering lines which resembled a seismograph reading of the San Francisco earthquake.

After having his machine record the laughs from my show, and studying his wavering lines, Walker handed down his findings. I got just as many laughs as Bob Hope or Red Skelton, he said, but they were the wrong *kind* of laughs. What I needed, according to Walker, was some identifying characteristic such as Jack Benny's stinginess or Gracie Allen's daffiness. With something like that to joke about, Walker maintained, my laughs would be mellower even if not necessarily longer or louder.

This critique struck a nerve, because if there's anything I didn't and don't believe that is it. I said that I thought that such assumed comedy characteristics, which were a hangover from vaudeville were phony and old hat. I saw no point in howling meaningless catch phrases like "Wanna buy a duck?" or "Vass you dere, Charlie?" I predicted that the comedy of the future would be based on the actual personality of the comedian, and needn't be based on contrived gimmicks such as Ed Wynn's falsetto giggle. Incidentally, I now feel that this prediction has been borne out by the success of people like Arthur Godfrey and Garry Moore, as well as some of the newer comedians like Shelley Berman, Jonathan Winters and Joey Bishop. However, my role of prophet got me about as far as it got Daniel. The American Tobacco Company canceled my show. And my views on comedy, which were picked up by a magazine, involved me in a feud with the comedian I most admired, Fred Allen.

I had always looked up to Allen for his brilliant wit and satire. During the war I had sent him jokes from the South Pacific and he had replied in kind letters offering advice and criticism. After the war I met him at a small gathering in New York. "Mr. Allen," I blurted out, "you've always been my god!"

"What a shame," he rasped. "Five hundred churches in New York and you're an atheist."

When Fred read my remarks on some comedy characterization being old hat because it sprang from vaudeville, he took umbrage at this slur on the medium he loved so well. He began needling me on his program, referring to me as "the young man who made the meteoric disappearance."

Although my admiration for Fred remained undiminished, I plunged boldly into the fray with him. Actually his insults did me a favor. He sent many a witty shaft in my direction, but his jokes died because I wasn't well enough known. But when I struck back the audience howled because everyone knew Fred.

While I was trading barbs with Allen, I found myself involved in another minor breach of the peace. One day, while reading an actors' trade paper, I read an item which said: "H. B. Warner, the star of *King of Kings,* is now starring in the unemployment line." Although I didn't know Mr. Warner, I felt that this jibe at a distinguished actor down on his luck, by a paper for actors, was the unkindest cut sustained by an actor since Macduff skewered Macbeth. I wrote the paper saying so and demanding that they cancel my subscription forthwith. This might have been a grander gesture except my subscription was almost up. They promptly refunded me $1.35 and then began panning my show. I struck back by taking full-page ads in a rival trade paper to say a few slanderous things about the enemy publication. I also wrote indignant letters to the editors denouncing them. It got so whenever I went to the mailbox to get the paper, Miriam would be sneaking around the house finding a new hiding place for the typewriter to disarm me for the day. Looking back on the sound and fury I generated I sometimes wonder about it all. I was young, impetuous, quixotic and sometimes just stupid.

While my feuds flourished my career languished. I replaced Eddie Cantor on "Take It or Leave It," and Don McNeill on the "Breakfast Club," but only as a substitute. RKO, which had carefully preserved my anonymity among moviegoers, dropped me in 1950. Things got so bad that one day an interviewer asked me earnestly: "Could you tell our readers the secret of your failure?" Finally I found myself in the unemployment line. I would stand there, waiting for my $25, and think of my awards. I had been voted the "star of tomorrow" but no one wanted me today. But television was burgeoning.

In 1951 I sold NBC a television quiz show called "Up to Paar." It was something of a landmark in early television—the first fixed TV quiz. Only I wasn't fixing the contestants; some of them were fixing me. When the show had been on a few weeks I began to notice the most unlikely contestants getting the answers to suspiciously difficult questions. You just don't expect some orthodontist from Tarzana to know the date the peace treaty was signed ending the Gran Chaco war. After a little sleuthing I finally decided that some contestants had inveigled someone on our show to feed them answers to the jackpot questions. Since several people on the show generally knew the jackpot question, it was difficult to trap whoever was passing out the payoff questions. However, I figured a way to stop it.

Our jackpot device was one in which all five contestants who had appeared on the show came back at the end to compete for a major cash prize. Setting a trap, I wrote out several different jackpot questions and left them lying on my desk. Then I wrote a new jackpot question, showed it to no one, and stuck it in my pocket. On the air, when time for the jackpot arrived, I pulled the question no one had seen out of my pocket and asked it of the contestants. Immediately a couple of them snapped back with the answer to the *other* questions—the ones I had left lying on the desk in my office. No one got the correct answer.

After that the show was more honest, if no more entertaining. I think its title is what really killed it. The critics couldn't resist saying: "Up to Paar isn't." It wasn't either.

Things got no better after the demise of "Up to Paar," and finally Hollywood's angry young man had become its hungry young man. Television was on the horizon, but it was the Eastern horizon. Eagerly I wired Pat Weaver, then President of NBC: "I am certain that I have a fresh, smart new television comedy show that can be auditioned as well as sold at a very low figure. Or as the agency men say: 'less than X dollars.' I submitted the idea to my agents, Benedict and Arnold, to present to your department. Have not heard from the three of you. Will expect go ahead by return postcard."

Weaver, a far-sighted executive, who has been described as the only man who can reminisce about the future, did reply by postcard. It said: "I hear you and I think. I have turned over your wire to our skulls for mulling." That was the last I got out of *him*.

Undaunted, I decided to try my fortunes in New York. I put Miriam and Randy on a plane for her parents' home in Pennsylvania where they were to wait while I looked for a job. Then I loaded up our station wagon to drive East. A friend, Bob Nye, a radio producer, led me in his car to Highway 66 to get me started on the long drive. "You were a crazy s.o.b.," he said, "but Hollywood will miss you."

7. MY METEORIC DISAPPEARANCE

DID YOU EVER have one of those days where everything seems to go wrong? Well I had several *years* like that. I arrived in New York in the spring of 1953 and soon established myself as a more reliable harbinger of summer than the first mosquito. I was in disorderly retreat from Hollywood where I had run through two movie studios, several network radio shows, one TV show, the unemployment insurance line and an assortment of agents, writers, and sponsors. Trouble just seemed to follow me. When trouble wasn't following me, I was leading it!

I had gotten the biggest break of my life when I was chosen as Jack Benny's summer replacement. However, that seemed to type me as the perennial summer replacement. After Jack Benny I had replaced Eddie Cantor and Don McNeill. I was a substitute so often I became known as the oleomargarine of radio. Whenever the first robin appeared, and people began turning their radios off and heading for the beach or mountains, the sponsors thought of me. "What, I keep asking myself, does Jack Paar do in the winter time?" columnist John Crosby wrote. "Live on the nuts he stores in the summer time? I have learned to tell the season by Jack Paar. When Paar appears it's time to lay away the winter clothes in mothballs and get out the tennis racquet."

Now I had come to New York to see if I could break the

jinx and find a job even in the cool weather. But people still associated me with lemonade, insect repellent and sunburn. The only employment I could find was on a summer replacement quiz show on CBS called "Bank on the Stars." It was an old-fashioned quiz show—it wasn't fixed. The prizes weren't large but the contestants got all the air they could breathe. We didn't lock them up in isolation booths. As always, however, with the coming of autumn, the schools opened, the new plays opened, and I closed.

Then I discovered a program that seemed to offer succor to someone in my precarious straits. It was a CBS show called "This Is Show Business" and its premise was to display the talents of entertainers and to help them find work. There was a panel of four members to analyze the performer's situation and to advise him on show business. I was a little disturbed when I noticed that most of the panel members were out of work themselves, but with my record for nonemployment I felt anybody could advise me.

One of the few employed members of the panel was George S. Kaufman, the eminent playwright. Kaufman took a jaundiced view of some of the problems propounded by entertainers on the program. Since there were several performers on each show, and the problems had to be different, the entertainers sometimes reached pretty far in suggesting dilemmas.

One night one of the performers with a problem was an unknown nineteen-year-old singer from the Copacabana named Eddie Fisher. "My problem," he explained, "is that I work at the Copa with all these beautiful girls."

The panel nodded sagely except for Mr. Kaufman whose nose wrinkled in an expression of polite skepticism.

"I go out with these beautiful girls all the time," Fisher continued, "and we go dancing and flirt and have lots of fun."

Mr. Kaufman buried his expressive face in his hands as though in acute pain.

"I see," said Clifton Fadiman, the show's moderator. "So just what is your problem?"

"My problem," said Eddie Fisher, "is that even if I have

lots of fun with all these beautiful girls they won't take me seriously because I'm only nineteen years old."

"Yes," said Fadiman. "Perhaps Mr. Kaufman has some advice on this problem."

Kaufman paused a moment, running his fingers through his wild shock of hair. "I read in the paper this morning," he said dryly, "that at Mount Wilson out in California, they have just invented a new telescope with which they will be able to see whether there is life on the other planets."

The panel looked somewhat baffled at this, failing to see any connection between the telescope and Eddie Fisher's problem.

"Then if that telescope works," Kaufman continued, "they are going to build another telescope which will be ten times more powerful and with it they expect to be able to see the detail of life on the planets, if any."

Eddie Fisher and the panel nodded blankly.

"When they complete this second telescope," Kaufman snorted, "you will be able to use it to find my interest in Eddie Fisher's problem."

Eddie Fisher has since graduated to bigger and better jobs and problems. My problem was not as alluring as Eddie Fisher's, but it was considerably more genuine and urgent: I just needed a job. I made an appointment with the producer of "This Is Show Business" and then decided I should have an agent to represent me. I called the William Morris agency where I had a friend and asked if he would represent me. He told me to call on him at his office. When I arrived at his fancy office the agent had bad news for me. "I've talked it over with our people," he said, "and we can't see our way clear to handle you right now." As usual, I thought grimly, agents are eager to represent you when you have a job, but not when you are looking for work, which is their supposed task. They are about as helpful, I decided, as an invalid aunt. Dejectedly I left his office and walked to the elevator. As I waited there, the agent came dashing down the hall.

"Do me a favor," he said. "Don't keep that appointment with the show. You look too discouraged. They'll never take you."

Since I had no choice I kept the appointment and did get the show. I did a monologue which critic Jack O'Brian called "the freshest comedy of the season." I listened to the panel's advice but I had no more success getting work than they did. I turned thirty-five years old and it looked as though no one cared but the Serutan people.

Eventually summer rolled around again and, like the crocus, I blossomed once more. This time I replaced Arthur Godfrey. I was determined to take no chances with the rating. I told the viewers that, instead of waiting for the rating service to call them to inquire what program they were watching, they should call the service. To assist them I gave the phone number. Thousands of phone calls, I understand, swamped the A. C. Nielsen Company which actually takes ratings by gadgets attached to TV sets. This naturally didn't make the Nielsen Company very happy, but it must have impressed CBS with the size of my audience.

In any event, CBS gave me a big break. They picked me to handle their big "Morning Show" which was seen nationally each weekday morning from 7 to 9 Eastern time. It had been a news and information show, handled by Walter Cronkite, but the network had decided to change to an entertainment format emceed by me. When I was summoned to discuss this big chance I was shaking. I had been unemployed so consistently even agents were avoiding me.

I went in to meet the CBS business representative, alone and scared, feeling like David going into battle against Goliath. When I saw him the comparison felt even more pointed—he stood six-feet-five inches tall. I introduced myself and he asked, "Where is your agent?"

"I haven't got one," I admitted.

"No agent!" he said, with an expression of horror. He urged me to get an agent since we would be discussing an important and involved contract, with a great deal of money involved, and I should have someone with a thorough knowledge of business and contracts to protect my interests.

"I'm sure you'll be fair," I told him. "Whatever you think is a fair amount of money is fine by me. You just name the figure."

CBS was more than fair. They paid me $200,000 a year—more money than any agent ever got for me before or since.

Excitedly I called my mother in Indianapolis to tell her the news. "What is wrong, son?" she said when she heard my voice on the phone. "Did you get a job?"

"I have a wonderful job," I enthused. "I'm taking over the CBS 'Morning Show.' The one Walter Cronkite does. They've offered me two hundred thousand a year! Think of that!"

"Don't sign it, son," she cautioned me. "There must be something fishy. Anyone who would pay you that much must be crazy."

I took over the "Morning Show" in August, 1954. CBS kept a scoreboard to show how the switch from Cronkite to me was being received by viewers. Under "Cronkite" they put the total of letters expressing regret over his leaving. Under "Paar" they listed letters registering approval of my selection for the show. One day the producer came in sheepishly, handed me a letter, and said: "We don't know how to score this on the board." The letter said, "We enjoyed Walter Cronkite so much and hated to see him leave." And it was signed by my mother!

The "Morning Show" was a tough grind but I enjoyed it because it gave me the chance to do the kind of show I'd always wanted to do—informal, relaxed, with no rigid format or gimmicks—not unlike my present program. I put up a sign on the studio doors which said: "Attention Professional Television Contestants: This show offers no canned goods, cash or Cadillacs." We had a pleasant and talented cast including Betty Clooney, Bil and Cora Baird and their puppets, Pupi Campo and Charles Collingwood. Charles, an erudite commentator and inveterate horse player, broadcast the news on our show and counseled me in betting on a race horse named

Jack Paar. The horse was named for me by my friends the Mackle brothers who own enough of Florida to secede from the Union and start their own state. Jack Paar was fleet of foot and won several races but, like his namesake, had a tendency to trip occasionally and eventually broke his leg.

When I first met Charles Collingwood, my volunteer turf consultant, I remarked on how young he was to have gained such a formidable reputation as a reporter and commentator during World War II.

"I was only twenty-three when I joined CBS," Charles said. "They thought that sounded too young to be a commentator, so a CBS official advised me to list my age as twenty-eight. Shortly afterwards a Washington paper carried a story about me referring to me as the twenty-eight-year-old commentator. On the society page of the same paper was a story about my parents' twenty-fifth anniversary!"

Our efforts to be amusing at daybreak did reasonably well in most respects. The critics were kind and the audience went up to four million viewers daily—an increase of 140 per cent over the previous format—but sponsors proved elusive. The reason for this, the network said, was that I wasn't cooperative with agency and sponsor people. This story started one morning when an agency man handed me some lipstick copy. It said that I had suddenly discovered that my wife was much more attractive than she had been and that after some boudoir sleuthing I discovered it was because she was using the sponsor's lipstick. I refused to read it in that form, saying it wasn't true and wasn't believable. I said I thought my wife was pretty attractive the way she was, and that I didn't think their lipstick would improve her noticeably or turn any other woman into a rose overnight either. The sponsor picked up his lipsticks and quit the show in a huff. They also, I was told, dropped me from consideration as master of ceremonies of a new show then being planned. The show turned out to be the "$64,000 Question." It became a big hit and I was downcast for a time at what I had missed out on. Little did I know, at the time, how much I had missed. I never had the surprise of being grilled by the District Attorney about fixed contestants, the suspense of having my records subpoenaed by the Internal Revenue Bureau and the excitement of being called to Washington to testify before a Congressional committee. I also was deprived of the pleasure of working for the Revson brothers, as doughty a team as ever swashbuckled their way through cold cream and mascara circles.

Not long after the incident of the lipstick, CBS emancipated me from their dawn patrol and gave me a half-hour program each weekday afternoon. It was a pleasant show, with Edie Adams, Martha Wright and Jack Haskell, but it may have had the most minuscule audience in history. There were so few people watching us it would have been cheaper to phone them.

I sensed we were being watched only by other comedians who were stealing my jokes, secure in the knowledge that even after I used them no one would have heard them. My suspicions were confirmed when I noticed that some of the jokes and routines Steve Allen was using on his nighttime show bore a striking resemblance to material I had used. I wrote a friendly letter to Steve mentioning this. I said it was probably being done by his writers and that I was sure he wasn't personally involved. "Please look into this," I kidded him, "or I'll go over your head to Jayne." He replied in a long, ponderous letter giving me a tedious lecture on comedy. Then, a few days later, he used a routine we had originated on my show of wacky book titles, such as *I Married Tommy Manville —Volumes 1 and 2.* Not content with imitating our routine, Steve wound up with this book title: *Death in the Afternoon, by Jack Paar.* Then his wife, Jayne Meadows, began turning up on interview shows to analyze my character. So I bought a microscope and did a little analysis on Steve.

Steve, aided by Jayne, is working on a plan to make him a legend before his time—and before he's done anything. He is the most self-promoted thing since the Tucker automobile. He has done so much public soul-searching he's beginning to sound like a saint. But I still don't think he can walk on the water. He'll have to take the Staten Island ferry like the rest of us. Steve is the greatest living non-authority on comedy. Whenever there is a scholarly discussion of humor, Steve raises his hand. I wish he'd just leave the room.

While I was exchanging broadsides via mailman with Steve, CBS canceled my show because of its anemic rating. There was one consolation about our small audience. When we were canceled, hardly anyone knew but us.

There followed a fallow period during which I entertained at banquets and other miscellaneous affairs. While presiding over a bridge opening in Kansas I met "Professor Backwards," a remarkable gentleman whose act consists of writing and talking backwards at high speed. He had an equally remarkable gift for thrift in telephoning—a secret which intrigued me because of the precarious state of my own finances at the time.

The professor, whose real name is Jimmy Edmundson, had perfected a system by which he was able to call his agent in New York from anywhere in the country and find out where his next billing was without the call costing him a cent.

He would call his agent in New York from, say, Florida, and ask for himself. The agent, schooled in his end of the plot, would tell the phone operator: "I'm sorry, Mr. Edmundson isn't here. But you'll be able to reach him in Indianapolis August 5th at the Claypool Hotel."

(That would mean that the professor's next engagement was at the Claypool Hotel in Indianapolis on August 5th. However, since he hadn't reached the party he had called—himself—the call would not be charged as a completed call.) Even this, though, was not enough for the professor.

"Operator," he would ask. "Could you tell me what room he'll be in?"

"He'll be in room 400," the agent would reply.

(That would mean that the engagement was paying $400. However, even this, relayed by the innocent operator, would not satisfy Edmundson.)

"Are you sure it isn't room 450?" Edmundson would ask.

(Meaning wasn't it possible to get $450 for the engagement?)

"No," the agent would sigh into the phone. "Four hundred was the only room we could get for Mr. Edmundson. He was lucky not to have to take 275 as he did last year."

After the lull in my career, enlightened by the professor's thrifty long-distance phone call system, I did sort of a radio disk jockey show on ABC. It was an underground unspectacular so modest we did it from the basement rumpus room of our house in Bronxville. The cast consisted of Jose Melis, my wife Miriam, our daughter Randy, our dog Schnapps, and me. Then even that was canceled. I was indeed, as Fred Allen said, the young man who made the meteoric disappearance. Now I had run out of networks. I had been served at breakfast time on CBS, lunch time on ABC and dinner time on NBC. Now I had been sent back to the kitchen. Having been fired from movies, radio and television, it looked as though I had run out of mediums. In desperation I suggested a new program for lonely housewives. It wouldn't be on radio or television. I would just go from door to door.

8. BETTER LATE THAN NEVER

THRUST BACK into the ranks of the unemployed I busied myself mowing the lawn—the only other profession I know. I was dejectedly pushing the mower one day when I got a phone call from Earl Wilson, the syndicated columnist who covers the bosom beat. He had narrowly escaped being struck by falling ratings in the collapse of a late night NBC TV show called "America After Dark." Before fleeing the scene of the accident, Earl told me, he had recommended to NBC that I replace the departed program. "Don't call them," he cautioned me. "Let them call you."

Stifling the urge to grab the phone, I waited impatiently. Finally it rang. Sure enough, it was NBC. A vice-president invited me to lunch at 21, a restaurant so chic that they put seersucker sleeves on the banisters in the summer. Although I had been doing network radio and television shows for ten years, including two on his own network, he opened the conversation by saying: "Now tell me, Jack, just what is it you do?" Despite this inauspicious start to the conversation, he wound up by offering me a show. When I heard what it was I was underwhelmed. Being selected for it was a signal honor, like being chosen as a kamikaze pilot. The show was to run from 11:15 P.M. to 1 A.M. nightly and to be called "Tonight!" —the title of a program that had previously occupied that troubled late night hour. Expectations were high but the budget was low. The previous debacle had scattered the audience, and even "Mr. Keen, Tracer of Lost Persons" couldn't find a surviving sponsor. NBC was tempted to give the time back to the Indians and cowboys, but flushed with failure recklessly decided to give live programming one last try with me.

I felt like the young flier in those old World War I movies where the officer, tapping his puttees with his swagger stick, says: "They're not going to send the kid up in *that!*" Friends warned me that doing an hour and three-quarters of program nightly I would suffer from "overexposure," but with me it was a question of overexposure or undernourishment.

Also I had a cherished theory I was anxious to test. I had always believed there was a place somewhere on TV for non-accordion players. Although the airwaves were clogged with quiz shows and Westerns, I felt sure that people would enjoy good, frank and amusing talk and pleasant entertainment minus isolation booths or other gimmicks. After a few skirmishes NBC agreed to let me do the show my way with a free and easy format which one columnist described as "as predictable as the Christmas office party."

I started doing the "Tonight" show July 29, 1957. Our debut wasn't very conspicuous. I told the viewers frankly that they didn't have much choice at that late hour; they could watch Milton Sills and Laura La Plante on the old movie or watch live boners on our show. "Why trade a headache for an upset stomach?" I asked. We didn't have enough of a budget for dancing girls or jugglers so we had to fill the time mostly with conversation. There was not much written, and no holds barred. "It's Russian roulette with commercials," one writer said. On the show I grappled with a heavyweight wrestler, threw vegetables at the audience and fed catnip to a lion.

However, none of these incidents were as dangerous as the conversation on the show. The talk is sort of a verbal barroom brawl with the cast using words instead of pool cues and beer mugs. We don't perform; we just defend ourselves. At times it feels like defending the Alamo every night. "Jack Paar," one paper observed, "is the only bull with his own china shop."

Our debut was a disaster, and the reviews were terrible, but the show soon caught on. When we started we had 62 stations, a small audience and two groggy sponsors. Before long we had 154 stations, an estimated thirty million viewers weekly and so many sponsors I feel guilty when I interrupt the commercials with the program. My belief in people and conversation had paid off. Soon Jack Paar was more popular than jackpots. Our show became a success and most of the quiz shows folded their isolation booths and silently stole away—one jump ahead of the District Attorney. Informality was suddenly so popular that one show hired Goodman Ace at $9000 a week just to write interruptions.

We don't have a terribly high rating, but we do have the largest audience watching from bed. In fact, we have so many viewers watching in pajamas and underwear that when NBC changed the show's title from "Tonight" to "The Jack Paar Show" we thought of calling it "Jack Paar and Selected Shorts." For years I couldn't get a sponsor and now I have so many commercials I'm afraid to take a bow for fear NBC will sell an ad on top of my head. It's not easy ad libbing through 105 minutes of show without a script, but I have a motto which has stood me in good stead: when in doubt do a commercial.

Someone once defined a filmed television show as a program where anything can happen but never does. Our show, on the other hand, is one of the few free-wheeling, live, video-in-the-raw programs where anything can happen and sometimes we wish it wouldn't—at least so often. There was the time with Zsa Zsa Gabor and the commercial. I was demonstrating a Norelco shaver when Zsa Zsa shrieked, "Be careful, darling, you'll cut yourself!"

This so confused me that I blurted out, "It won't cut *anything*."

Presiding over these goings-on requires the balance of an adagio dancer, the control of Clyde Beatty, the lion tamer, and a good lawyer. Never before, I'm sure, have so few talked so much for so many. Or for so little money.

One of the wildest nights we ever had was when the cameramen went on strike and were replaced by executives of the network. When I come out I usually ask the audience: "How many of you are seeing the show for the first time?" This night when I asked the question two cameramen put up their hands!

Then there was the time in Hollywood when I sat down in a breakaway chair and it collapsed on me. I was nearly knocked out and might have been even more seriously hurt but my fall was broken by the smog.

The unpredictable course of conversation and the unplanned turn of event have provided the show's wildest and most memorable moments.

Once, while doing a commercial for Bufferin, I actually had a headache so I decided to take two tablets. I took the top off the bottle but couldn't get out the wad of cotton to get the tablets. Trying ingenuity, I poured a little water into the bottle and took a sip. Then I corked up the bottle. Little did I know that the action of the water on the tablets in the capped bottle would have a detonating effect. A few seconds later the bottle exploded, showering me and our guests with enough soggy Bufferin to cure headaches for the whole studio audience.

Flying blind through the midnight air, so to speak, calls for people who can talk amusingly and nearly endlessly, and I think we have had some of the best talkers since Dr. Johnson was holding forth in London coffeehouses. Conversing with them is like playing straight man to a knife thrower: exciting but dangerous. "Trying to talk on a show like this," Joey Bishop said, "is like trying to get into an elevator that's gone up."

The secret ingredient in our show is people. I'm a people jockey, and what people! Charley Weaver, the one-man slum, has the baggiest pants but the best-pressed wit in show business. It's seldom he can be topped with a joke, or even bottomed. Genevieve, our delightful French gamine, with the scrambled hairdo and vocabulary to match, is the best thing we've got from France since Vichyssoise. Alexander King, a delinquent angel with a bent halo, has given conversation a bigger impetus than anything since the invention of the martini. Peggy Cass has a voice like a tugboat in mating season, and what she says comes out funny. Hugh Downs is our science editor and my faithful Tonto. Whenever Hugh says "Kemo Sabe" I know it's time to do a commercial.

Hans Conreid, the actor who played so many Nazis in the movies that it was felt his career would end with the fall of Hitler, is another of our favorite guests. One night he and I were reminiscing about the war in which he served in the tank corps and I was with that Special Service Company which included opera singers, a string quartet and cello players. "Democracy," I observed, "was never meant to be saved by cello players."

"No," Hans replied, "and anyway they should be serving in the cavalry."

Sometimes the free-wheeling conversation on the show erupts into verbal scuffles among the guests. One such occurred one night when Elsa Maxwell lashed out at Elvis Presley because, she said, the swivel-hipped singer had signed his autograph on the bosoms of some of his more impulsive young lady admirers.

"I don't see why Elsa is so upset," Hermione Gingold said. "After all, you could write a three-act play on *her* bosom!"

This caused considerable coolness between the two ladies, but they eventually made up. "I admire anyone," Hermione said, "who can go so far on so little."

Another always welcome guest on my program is Reverend Billy Graham, the famous evangelist, who became a good friend as a result of his appearance. In chatting on the show I told him that my mother had always wanted me to be a minister. He said it was too bad I hadn't.

"I'm afraid I'm too mixed up," I laughed, "to make a good minister."

"I know someone who can straighten you out," the famous clergyman said.

"Not even my boss, Robert Sarnoff, can straighten me out," I kidded.

"No," said Dr. Graham softly, "but *my* boss can."

After appearing on our program, Dr. Graham wrote inviting me to join in his crusade. I told him I would always have a silent prayer for the wonderful work he is doing, but that I would not be able to actively join his crusade because we had a sponsor conflict. "While your life is dedicated to beautifying the soul," I wrote, "mine is committed, with options, to tidying up the body via shampoo, denture fasteners, electric shavers and an oil for aches and pains. I'm sure that in the long run you will attain a higher rating than I. However, for the time being at least, I must continue with my little commercials while you continue with your Big One."

The thing that has pleased me most about the success of the show is that it is a triumph of honesty. Whenever I say something and add, "I kid you not," I'm not kidding. It's a modest show, of light conversation and pleasant entertainment, but it's live and real and true. When you tune in you may see a star born or a joke die. We don't pretend to be anything we're not. "Since you don't sing, dance or play a musical instrument," someone in the audience once asked me, "just what is your talent?" "My talent," I replied frankly, "is that I admit it." I don't feign surprise when a guest I know is coming shows up. When Elsa Maxwell or Zsa Zsa Gabor take out after someone my terror is real. When I've wept on the air, as I sometimes have, the tears were real and not applied by the makeup man. And when there is laughter on the show it's real and spontaneous.

Once while doing the show from Hollywood, I noticed during rehearsal some technicians moving a strange-looking machine into our studio. I asked what it was and was told that it was a machine to record laughter.

"You mean they're going to record the laughter for our little, live, ad-libbed show?" I asked a network man in wonderment. "What will they do with the laughs after they're recorded?"

"Oh, they'll dub them into some of the big comedy shows," the man said.

How strange, I thought, that our program, with its modest budget, scanty written material and little rehearsal, is furnishing laughter for expensive shows which are on only once a week and which are carefully rehearsed and written by staffs of expensive writers.

What worries me about this is that there is no longer any standard of excellence. When Jefferson wrote in the Declaration of Independence that all men are created equal, he didn't mean equally funny. Laughter is the comedian's criterion of talent. With a live audience, if a joke is funny they laugh; if it isn't they don't. Today when you watch a filmed show and hear laughter and applause you don't know whether the audience likes the comedian or he just has a good sound man. At this rate engineers will be the stars of the future. I won't be surprised one of these nights at the end of a show if the one who comes out to take a bow is not the star but the sound engineer. It depresses me to think our little live laughs may turn up someday, volume turned up as loud as Ethel Merman, on some show like "Lassie."

There is also the matter of tears. I'm a sentimental soul, easily moved by emotions, and have been known to weep on the air at some touching story or thrilling moment when a new talent has been recognized by an audience. I cry so easily, in fact, that since childhood people have called me "Leaky Jack."

So if television is to have canned laughter, how about canned tears? Since I seem to be the dampest exponent of this phase of the emotional gamut, perhaps I could clean up a tidy sum recording my sobs, sighs and tears. There might be a wonderful market selling canned tears to programs like "This Is Your Life" and "Queen for a Day" for emergencies when they get some unfeeling guest who refuses to cry on cue when reunited by surprise on camera with a great-aunt he's been studiously avoiding for years.

9. THE TROUBLE WITH ME

For someone who loves his family and quiet suburban life, shuns drinking and night clubs, and who is not mad at anything but crabgrass, I guess I'm Exhibit A that clean living is no guarantee of peace. I've been in hot water so often that instead of an Emmy I've been awarded a gold thermometer. My midnight utterances seem to have occasioned more uproar than any similar nocturnal outcries since Paul Revere.

This seeming paradox appears to result from an unfortunate habit I have of saying frankly what's on my mind. Speaking honestly has been hazardous ever since Socrates drank the hemlock, and doing so with several million people watching hasn't reduced the risk noticeably. When the bloodshot eye of the TV camera is on you, a little frankness goes a long, long way.

There have been times when I have been tempted to be less outspoken, or at least to take obtuse lessons at Berlitz. My wife has begged me to be less candid, my friends have reasoned with me, and around the corridors of NBC, where I understand I am known as "The Defiant One," I get the feeling that the network people would be happier if I were less uninhibited on the air. However, I can't seem to resist saying what I think in a way not exactly conducive to winning a Dale Carnegie medal for tact. This has not only kept my existence from getting humdrum but has done a lot to keep the legal profession going full swing. If all the people who were threatening to sue me were laid end to end I'm sure my attorneys would be very happy.

One of these is Jimmy Hoffa who parlayed a long record and a short memory into the leadership of the Teamsters Union. I seem to have aroused the ire of Hoffa when I had Robert Kennedy, the counsel for the Senate Anti-Rackets Committee, as a guest on the program, as he has announced he is suing Kennedy, NBC and me. Kennedy came on to explain the Fifth Amendment which many of Hoffa's officials had been ducking behind when called to testify before the Committee. The young lawyer explained the amendment and urged people to write their congressmen to pass legislation aimed at labor racketeering.

"Unless something is done," Kennedy said, "this country is going to be controlled by people like Johnny Dioguardi and Jimmy Hoffa and Tony "Ducks" Corrallo who are gangsters and hoodlums."

"We may be in court together, you and I," I said. "I hope you know what you're doing. Have you ever spoken so frankly before in public?"

"I don't think I've ever been asked questions like this before," he said.

"You're with big mouth now," I warned him.

Kennedy concluded his appearance by asking viewers again to urge their congressmen to press for legislation to end labor-management racketeering. His appearance brought the greatest mail response our program ever had. Capitol Hill was similarly inundated by mail and Kennedy told me later it was the greatest flood of mail on a public issue since President Truman relieved General MacArthur of his command. "It may be," the *St. Louis Post-Dispatch* editorialized, "that Jack Paar will exert a deeper direct effect on Congress than President Eisenhower, who has come out again for a strong labor reform bill." Papers across the country said the mail generated by Kennedy's appearance on our show prompted the President to take to the air himself and appeal for labor reform legislation.

Our appeal for mail also created great confusion on Capitol Hill. Many viewers, it turned out, didn't realize that the Senate had already passed a labor reform bill, and it was in the House that the legislation was pending. I managed to add my bit to the confusion. Feeling that having urged viewers to write to their representatives I should do likewise, I wrote a letter to my Senator, Jacob Javits of New York, strongly urging him to vote for labor reform legislation He not only had already voted for such legislation, the Senator replied, but was one of the sponsors of the legislation.

Bob Kennedy laughingly told me that his brother, Senator John Kennedy, co-sponsor of the Senate bill, was also the recipient of a flood of mail sternly demanding that he vote for the legislation which he had authored. Adding insult to injury, some of the letter writers insisted that he vote for "Senator Bob Kennedy's bill."

By this time, fortunately, both Kennedys were inured to confusion. About the same time Senator John Kennedy was on a plane when a lady fellow passenger came up to him and asked, "Aren't you Mr. Kennedy?" He smiled and said that he was.

"I'm so delighted to meet you," the lady said. "I watched you on TV at those labor hearings. I think it's wonderful what you are doing to get Jimmy Hoffa."

"Thank you, ma'am," Kennedy said, "but that's not me. That's my brother Bobby."

"Oh, I'm sorry," the lady said. "I realize now. But I've seen you, too, in the papers and magazines. And I know how happy you must be with your wife and those lovely children on the farm in Virginia."

"Thanks again," the Senator grinned, "but that's Bobby too."

Thoroughly confused by this time, the woman said apologetically; "I'm terribly sorry to have mistaken you. But will you be seeing your brother?"

"Certainly," the Senator said.

"Well, tell him for me that I sure hope he wins the Democratic nomination for President."

"That isn't my brother," Kennedy said. "That's *me!*"

Despite all the confusion we created for the Kennedys and Congress, it's nice to think that the blizzard of mail we helped stir up had something to do with the labor reform legislation which Congress subsequently passed. The only problem now is that Hoffa says he's going to sue me. Well, I don't care how dangerous and powerful Jimmy Hoffa is. If he wants to sue me he'll have to stand in line like everyone else.

Another altercation that started on the program was my well-publicized hassle with Mickey Rooney, the world's oldest adolescent. It all began quite innocently one night in Hollywood when Mickey was a guest on the show. We were having an amiable enough interview when Mickey began to get so tangled up in his sentences I thought he might accidentally hang himself on a dangling participle. At first I wasn't sure whether he was pulling my leg or had had a few too many, but, as the interview progressed, if that's the word, it became increasingly evident he was stoned, or at least marbled. He slumped over the desk, broke into song and frequently contradicted himself.

He mentioned he had come from celebrating his first wedding anniversary with his fifth wife, and it was becoming more and more apparent the celebration had included copious doses of fire water. Mickey began to develop a list to port, and the way the interview was bogging down I felt like the captain of the *Andrea Doria* during the second chorus of "Nearer My God to Thee." Soon the alcohol fumes were so thick I was afraid I'd get a hangover just from listening. I suggested to Mickey that he might have had a few too many at his celebration.

This seemed to antagonize him, and he announced he didn't like the show.

"I'm not a fan," he mumbled. "I don't care to watch your show."

"Would you care to leave?" I asked.

At that, the audience applauded. Annoyed, Mickey drew himself up to his full five feet three inches and departed, tilting to starboard with all the dignity of Lord Calvert.

The next morning I was floating around the pool of the Beverly Hilton, pondering the strange ways of Hollywood, when I got a call from Mickey. He was indignant at my allusions on the air to his drinking and announced he was coming over to the hotel to punch me in the nose. This possibility of getting punched in the knee alarmed me, and I quickly reconnoitered. Not wishing to be part of a naval engagement, I got out of the pool and decided to confront the aroused former Andy Hardy in my suite. Mickey was reputed to have a bodyguard of husky former football players, so I hurriedly took stock of my own forces. The best I could muster up was my producer, two writers and a unit manager, and a sorry-looking group of prospective combatants they were. Rallying to my alert in their dripping swimming trunks, they were as unwarlike a party as you'd be apt to find this side of a girls' basketball team. I doubt if any of them had ever struck anything more dangerous than a typewriter, and their legs looked as spindly as ostrich necks. At the head of this motley patrol I led the way to my suite to await the enemy assault.

We didn't have long to wait. The phone rang and Mickey announced he was on his way up from the lobby to commence the bloodletting. Although he is not tall, Rooney is husky and has a fiery temper, and the notion of a battle with the aroused actor, and possibly a platoon of muscular former gridiron stars, seemed fraught with peril.

The doorbell rang and Mickey burst into the suite. He was flanked by four men and was wearing gym shoes and a sweater, seeming indications he had indeed come bent on action.

His supporting cast, I was relieved to note, while a beefy

lot, did not give the appearance of having been recruited from the University of Southern California football team.

"What are you so mad about?" I asked, as he rushed in.

"I want to talk with you," he said, "*alone.*"

I asked my four stalwarts to adjourn to the corridor, and his quartet likewise slouched out to await developments.

Then Mickey and I began talking. After some preliminary verbal sparring, which at times verged on violence, the atmosphere began to thaw. I told Mickey I had always admired his talents and was sorry if anything I had said had offended him. He admitted he had been drunk on the show, and said he was sorry about it. I also told him how much I liked his little boy Teddy whom I'd had on the show. Before long we were boon companions, and were talking earnestly about religion.

Suddenly from the corridor we heard muffled sounds of impending combat. My head writer, Paul Keyes, and Mickey's manager, Red Doff, carried away by partisan zeal, were threatening to dismember each other. This rumpus had started when Doff asked Paul scornfully why I needed writers if I was such a good ad libber. "I suppose," Paul had snarled back, "that Mickey ad libbed all those Andy Hardy pictures."

Mickey and I rushed out and succeeded in calming our respective cohorts. Having come to punch me in the nose, Mickey had wound up as peacemaker! In a wave of good fellowship, he and I retired to my suite and shook hands heartily. I told him how much I admired him and that I wanted to have him as a friend. Carried away by good will I said, "What do you say, Mickey, that we have a drink on it?"

Then I remembered. That was what started it all.

The last individual whom I managed to outrage, all with the best intentions, was a doctor. I was visiting him, not, as might be imagined, to have my foot extricated from my mouth, but to have an examination for an insurance policy.

I got a very pleasant doctor except that he spent an interminable time asking me questions that could have been answered by a seven-year-old boy. For this he went ten years to medical school, I mused, as he had me say "Ahhh" and elicited from me the information that I had measles when I was five, and that there was no record of leprosy in my family. He also tapped my knees with a hammer, noting that I have overactive reflexes—something that any of my sponsors could have told him.

"Do you spend all your time doing this?" I asked with my usual tact. "Is all you do just tap people's knees and fill out forms?"

Puzzled, he admitted that much of an insurance doctor's time is taken up with routine physical examinations and filling in forms.

"If you're going to be a doctor why don't you be one?" I asked. "You study for years to be a surgeon and then spend your time tapping people's knees with a little hammer, or having them say 'Ahhh.' Why don't you be like Dr. Dooley and really get out and help people?"

As I held forth it suddenly occurred to me that I had no right to be talking like that. After all, if the doctor wanted to be an insurance doctor that was his business, and I could tell by the grim look he gave me that he thought so too.

"Let's test your lungs now," he said. "Just take a deep breath, and hold it."

I inhaled and held it . . . and held it . . . and held it. My eyes were popping and the room began swimming before my eyes but the doctor was smiling happily as he listened to his stethoscope. My whole life seemed to pass before my eyes, and I didn't want to go through *that* again. Dimly I could hear the doctor saying: "Hold it." But I could hold it no longer. The air exploded from my aching lungs with such force that it blew some of the forms off his desk.

"Very good," he said, removing the stethoscope. "Now we'll test the old blood pressure. I wonder if you'd just jog a bit, standing there in one place."

Somewhat skeptically, I began to jog vigorously.

"I'll be back in just a moment," the doctor said. "Just keep jogging."

I kept jogging. My heart began thumping and my lungs started aching. I began wondering what happened to the doctor. I finally jogged out to the nurse. "I don't see his hat," she said. "He may have gone out to lunch."

At last he appeared and I fell into a chair, feeling as if I'd just broken the four-minute mile. The doctor seemed terribly happy as he took my blood pressure.

"Did you pass the medical exam all right?" Miriam asked as she met me at the door that night.

"I'm not sure," I told her, "but I won a silver cup for running the mile."

I didn't really win a silver cup but the doctor did give me a small bottle. I never did fill it as I can't ad lib if I'm not in the mood.

Among the rather formidable forces with which I have found myself in conflict is the U.S. Army.

My differences with the Army, which I caused some discomfiture during World War II, and vice versa, have been recounted earlier, but hostilities broke out again in 1959. I was scheduled to do an Army routine on a big television show for the Ford Company. The special color program, with Rosalind Russell as hostess, was a cavalcade of show business, and I was to re-create one of the Army routines I had done during the war in the South Pacific.

An audience is vitally important in doing a comedy monologue, of course, and for an Army routine it was particularly important that the audience be soldiers. Hubbell Robinson, the producer, had been promised Army cooperation and had assured me that the military would have several hundred G.I.s on hand when I did my bit.

The show was being taped in NBC's color studio in Brooklyn, a vast and cheerless gymnasium-like building more suitable for calisthenics than comedy. I was scheduled to tape my monologue in the morning—a time when no one, particularly me, feels very funny. Moreover, on my arrival there was no soldier audience to be seen. The Army, it turned out, had read my old script, poking fun at the officers, and had turned thumbs down. Not only were they not sending any G.I.s, I was told, but they had forbidden any to show up. I was stranded with my jokes and no one to laugh at them.

In desperation the director rounded up some stray stage hands, a few bored technicians and some tired musicians who had been working on other sets. With this motley group impersonating G.I.s, I stood on the back of a truck and told my jungle jokes.

Even fifteen years later, the audience thought the jokes at the expense of the brass were funny, even if the Army didn't. My material, which had helped my outfit win a Presidential Unit Citation during war, had gotten me declared off limits in peacetime. But I got the last laugh and, thank heavens, it was a hearty one, from the audience.

In another skirmish of rather far-flung dimensions I once found myself pitted against the sovereign state of Pennsylvania. This was brought about by rushing to the assistance of Peggy Cass, the actress with the voice which sounds as if she's wound too tight.

Peggy was emoting one night in *Born Yesterday* at the Bristol, Pennsylvania, Playhouse when a Justice of the Peace named Earl Dougherty swooped down and arrested her for violating Pennsylvania's 1794 blue laws by working on Sunday. He trapped her backstage during the intermission after the first act and announced: "I'm Squire Dougherty."

"Oh," said Peggy, "you sound so old English."

Dougherty then handed her a "conviction on view" notice.

"I don't want that," Peggy said, recoiling. "I never won a thing in my life."

Not amused by Peggy's sally, the Justice of the Peace told her that she'd get six days at hard labor in the Bucks County Prison if she didn't appear in court in response to his summons.

"I'm entitled to a trial by a jury of my peers," Peggy insisted. "I read that in *Ivanhoe*."

Peggy, it turned out, was bagged along with 158 other citizens when Squire Dougherty swept across Bucks County like Sherman en route to the sea. The stern guardian of the law hauled in cab drivers and golfing instructors, pounced on a radio announcer in mid-broadcast and even nabbed some toll-takers on the Pennsylvania Turnpike. He attracted a covey of reporters as he swept along, and promptly arrested all of them. He suffered a measure of retaliation, while arresting Peggy, when Bristol police tagged his car for illegal parking while he was inside the Playhouse making the pinch.

Peggy reported all this, with full sound and fury, in her next appearance on our show. Rather than pay the $13 fine, and perhaps face six days at hard labor, she confessed, she had taken it on the lam from Pennsylvania.

"I was in Philadelphia once," I said sympathetically, "but it was closed."

"Someone said Philadelphia is a national shrine," she retorted. "Well, so is Arlington National Cemetery. Anyway Squire Dougherty was working on Sunday himself arresting all of us."

"You should pay the fine," I advised her. "It's part of a plan to keep Pennsylvania green."

After Peggy's recitation of the reign of terror in Bucks County, she showed me the summons Squire Dougherty had given her.

"You know we have a good deal of influence on this program," I told her. With that I took the notice, scribbled on it "null and void," and handed it back to her. "You can just ignore it," I assured her.

However, the Commonwealth of Pennsylvania took no such light view of these goings-on. The next day I got a wire saying: "Saw your show where Peggy Cass appeared mocking and ridiculing this judicial officer and the laws of the Commonwealth of Pennsylvania. I deem it necessary to demand equal time on your TV show immediately to state my position for the people of Pennsylvania regarding her recent conviction notice for violation of the Pennsylvania blue laws. Earl B. Dougherty, Justice of the Peace."

Peggy also got a call that the Pennsylvania State Commission wanted to see her.

"I hung up the phone and cried," she said. "I'm a coward to the core. I didn't call them and I wouldn't answer my phone for days. My answering service sure got a workout."

We never did grant Dougherty his request for equal time, figuring that giving anyone equal time with the irrepressible Peggy still isn't being fair to them. She is still, as far as I know, a fugitive from the Bucks County Prison and if the Commonwealth of Pennsylvania is still on her trail I have a tip for them on how they can identify her. Her voice sounds as if she gargles with peanut butter.

Another state which I ran afoul of was Wyoming, and, take it from me, there *is* a Wyoming. This scuffle started when comic Milt Kamen did an amusing routine on our show maintaining with great persuasiveness that there is no Wyoming. "Wyoming is just a hoax on the people of the East," he said. "It's really not there. What they call Wyoming is just a wide expanse of nothingness. The only reason it's on the map is that it fills out the U.S. But when you drive through what they call Wyoming, and look out your car window, there's nothing. It's just closet space that never got to New York."

Although the audience and I got quite a kick out of Milt's amusing contention, it was no laughing matter to the veteran Senator from Wyoming, Joseph O'Mahoney. The following morning we got a long, angry telegram from O'Mahoney upbraiding Kamen and me for suggesting the nonexistence of Wyoming. Wyoming, he hastened to assure the skeptical, is real. The irate Senator's two-page wire fumed at what he described as our misplaced sense of humor and lack of responsibility. He went on, at rather tedious lengths I thought, listing the wonders of Wyoming including such well-known real estate as a chunk of the Rocky Mountains, Yellowstone Park, the Grand Teton Range and the Jackson Hole country.

He also threw in its resources in agriculture, mining and oil, and mentioned such bustling communities as Laramie and Cheyenne. Wyoming had everything, it was apparent from the Senator's wire, except a sense of humor.

While wading through the Senator's verbal travelogue, somewhere between Laramie and Old Faithful, my eye spotted two interesting things. One was that Senator O'Mahoney, while proclaiming the glories of Wyoming, was at the moment in Florida. The other was an unusual code designation on the telegram. I checked Western Union on this code number and they told me that the wire had been sent at government expense.

The next night on the show I apologized to the people of Wyoming for helping to foment the idea that there was no such place. "There obviously is a Wyoming," I admitted, "with people in it paying taxes, or how else could Senator O'Mahoney send such long wires at the government's expense? However, if Wyoming is as wonderful as Senator O'Mahoney says, I wonder what he's doing in Miami Beach."

That brought another hot wire from the Wyoming Senator, denying that he charged the government for the first telegram, explaining what he was doing in Miami Beach and again excoriating me for having raised doubt in the public mind as to the existence of the fair state of Wyoming.

I'd like to take this opportunity to answer that second wire from the Senator. However, my lawyer, who is looking over my shoulder, suggests this would be an ideal place to end this chapter. He says the chapter has dramatic continuity the way it is, and, also, he's busy enough right now.

10. RANDY

Almost every comedian has a charity these days, and I have one of which I'm very proud: overprivileged children.

Believe me, it's not always easy for a comedian to find a cause. When I first began looking, I found out all the really interesting diseases had been snapped up long since by other comedians. Jerry Lewis was working for muscular dystrophy. Milton Berle had cerebral palsy. Danny Kaye had underprivileged children. Bob Hope had everything else that wasn't nailed down. Oh, there were a few obscure diseases left over, like sinus trouble; what can you do with one like that? I thought jealously of Danny Kaye and his work with underprivileged children. Think of the job of helping all those poor misguided kids who have nothing to do all day but steal hubcaps and fight with switchblade knives. Then in a flash it came to me—*over*privileged children! There are more of them and they're more miserable. Well, I've been surveying the field and it's amazing what I've learned.

The biggest cause of overprivilege, I discovered, is the television set. It hands the kids learning on a silver platter, and in such exotic subjects. When I was a youngster we all had to walk or ride the bus to school to study prosaic subjects like arithmetic and spelling. Now, thanks to the magic of television, all you have to do is park Junior in front of the set and turn the knob. In an instant the little tyke is absorbing basket weaving from Miss Frances on "Ding Dong School" or how to care for a marmoset from Captain Kangaroo. It's a magnificent advance in educational methods. Of course there's the danger of forgetting and leaving your child overparked in front of the TV set, in which case he may learn how to blackjack you from Mike Hammer or skewer you with the breadknife from Zorro. It's things like that which lead to overprivilege.

I've had a wonderful opportunity to study firsthand the tendency of TV to promote overprivilege in raising our daughter Randy who is ten. Randy can scarcely remember when there was no television, a time she refers to as "the olden days." She even first learned to count to ten from watching TV, but she counted backwards as she picked it up from watching missile countdowns on science-fiction shows.

When Randy was born I was delighted. I had always wanted a daughter. I never cared much for little boys. Perhaps it's because I can't stand the smell of wet corduroy.

Randy was born in a Hollywood hospital. When they wheeled Miriam out of the delivery room unconscious I fainted and keeled over into a passing laundry cart. The doctor told me it was a psychosomatic reaction. He said that as they helped me away for first-aid treatment I said: "It's all right—put it on my tab."

When we learned the baby was coming, I began building a nursery on the garage of our home overlooking the Sunset Strip. My desire to be domestic was well intentioned, but it turned the last three months of Miriam's pregnancy into a nightmare in stereophonic sound. However, when we brought little Randy home from the hospital, a beautiful new nursery awaited her. There was just one problem. Our garage roof slanted slightly, with the result that the nursery had a noticeable tilt. Consequently, we'd tuck the baby into bed at night only to find that by morning she would have rolled to the lower side of the slanting bed and be trapped there in the clutches of gravity.

We left Hollywood when Randy was four years old. One reason we were glad to leave was that we were not anxious to bring our daughter up there. She might have gone through life thinking that all restaurants were shaped like brown derbies, that most ladies wore slacks and dark glasses and that Chevrolets were foreign cars.

New York, we felt, was a much more sensible place to raise a child, free from the make-believe of Hollywood. Our first Christmas in New York was a great thrill for Randy. There was real snow. I'll never forget the excitement of walking down Fifth Avenue in the snow, showing her the beautiful Christmas windows and listening to the carols. You could tell the shoppers with the true spirit of Christmas. They were the ones who hummed carols while they shoved you. Miriam and I had told her all about Santa Claus, so I took her down town to meet him. One problem about telling your child about Santa Claus in New York is how to pick one. There are about three to every block. You have to explain: "Yes, Virginia, there *are* Santa Clauses. How can you doubt it, when you can see dozens of them with your own eyes?"

We pushed our way through a sea of Santa Clauses and went in to Sak's Fifth Avenue where children could meet Santa. He was a fine specimen, plump and jolly, shaking with merry "ho ho's" as the children filed past to meet him. We got in line and shuffled along for quite a time before we got to Santa. It was worth it, though, to see the sparkle in Randy's eyes when Santa tweaked her cheek and whispered something to her.

"What did he say to you?" I asked as we left.

"He just told me to keep the line moving," she said.

This streak of the practical in the phony St. Nick did nothing to shatter Randy's illusions, as she had always had a strong sense of the fanciful. Once after driving home with her mother along the Hudson River Drive she confided in me that she had seen a fairy.

"Really," I said. "What do fairies look like?"

"Like boats," she assured me gravely.

Randy also is extremely sentimental, particularly about animals. She once had two little turtles who became quite a nuisance to us because whenever we went away on vacation we had to leave them with someone, and turtle sitters are notoriously difficult to find. Then one of the turtles died. We buried him with full honors in a match box in our garden after I had rejected Randy's proposal that he be buried at sea in our swimming pool, since he was amphibious.

Shortly afterwards, when we were leaving for a vacation in Florida, I suggested to Randy that we take the surviving turtle to the neighboring creek and turn him free. At this she protested strenuously that the turtle would catch cold. Patiently I explained that turtles don't catch cold. She then complained that the turtle would be lonely if turned loose in the creek without his late companion. I remained adamant and decreed that the turtle must go. With long faces, Miriam and Randy drove away on their sad mission. When they returned they reported the turtle had been dutifully deposited in the creek. However, they had first gone to the Fifteen Cent Store and bought two other turtles. They then released all three together, so our erstwhile turtle would not feel rejected.

When any pet or wild creature dies Randy is disconsolate, and I am ordained by Miriam to assuage her grief by conducting last rites for the departed. On one occasion I was pressed into service for a double funeral. Her friend Michael Melis's goldfish had died, and Randy had found a dead robin in our yard. I built two little white crosses and Randy tenderly wrapped the bodies in Saran Wrap and aluminum wrap and then placed them lovingly in an envelope. "That's so the ants won't get them before they arise," she said. I then spoke a few words of eulogy, we joined in a little prayer, and the deceased were laid to rest near the swimming pool. This cheered Randy up immeasurably and I have since been expected several times to deliver these eulogies. I've become sort of the George Jessel of the animal kingdom. Randy's concern for birds extends even to those being prepared for the table, as we discovered once when she found Miriam stuffing a turkey and sewing it up. That night, while we were in bed, Randy slipped downstairs and cut the strings with a scissors evidently to ease the bird's discomfort. The next day, when we were eating the turkey, I offered Randy some stuffing. "I don't want any," she said, "and I don't see how the turkey stands it, either."

When Randy reached school age we discovered we had to take a stand on her method of upbringing. There are two schools of thought, we learned, on how to raise children these days. There is the Jean Kerr or treat 'em firmly school. Jean, a Westchester neighbor of ours, believes in the old adage of whap 'em first and argue afterwards. On the other hand, there is the progressive or let 'em do what they want school, typified by James and Pamela Mason, who are also good friends of ours. Their six-year-old son, whom they call Charley Poo, smokes cigars, wears a straw hat and loves to listen to old Harry Richman records. Their daughter Portland, who is a friend of Randy's, learned to swim when she was six months old and has been learning other things at a correspondingly early age. Now, at a ripe old ten, she wears Zsa Zsa Gabor's old dresses and goes out to night clubs.

Portland once came to visit us and Randy showed her through our house.

"How many bathrooms does it have?" Portland asked casually.

"Four," replied Randy.

"Oh," said young Portland, in a voice dripping with disdain. "We have six."

There was a long silence.

"I think we have two more in the attic," Randy said, "but I've never bothered to go up there."

In raising Randy, Miriam and I have tried to steer a middle course, somewhere between the airy abandon of the progressive Masons, who have Portland's childish crayon drawings hung in gold frames in their magnificent Hollywood home, and the ironhanded rule of Jean Kerr and her distinguished drama critic husband, Walter.

Miriam and I reached a very practical compromise on discipline: she does it all. Since I have always thumbed my nose at authority, I approached the role of parent with trepidation. The idea of telling anyone, even a five-year-old, how to shape his destiny, when my own seemed to have been sculpted by Salvador Dali, seemed inconsistent. I recoil at any disciplinary measure stronger than cutting off Randy's Popsicles, and the idea of using force on a child reduces me to absolute jelly. I feel that spanking a child can result in serious misunderstanding, a feeling that is borne out by a story told me by Gerald Peters, a Canadian entertainer.

Peters has a daughter named Sally who is quite a handful. On one occasion, when she was five years old, she was particularly naughty. She was soundly paddled with a hairbrush and ran crying upstairs to her room. Her sobs gave way to silence and Peters became worried. Going quietly upstairs he opened the door to her room. Sally was standing in front of the mirror, her little skirt held up, looking back over her shoulder to inspect the damage from the spanking.

"Well, I hope you're satisfied," she said bitterly. "You've cracked it."

Fortunately discipline has never been a real problem with us. Randy has always been a well-behaved youngster and has never been apprehended in anything more sinister than digging a hole under the welcome mat.

Although Miriam is the family disciplinarian, she and Randy are extremely close. As mentioned earlier in this chronicle, I was married twice briefly to the same girl before my present marriage to Miriam. Randy did not know this and we were waiting to tell her until she was a little older and would understand better. One day, however, while coming home with a schoolmate, she spotted a fan magazine that had emblazoned on the cover: "The Three Marriages of Jack Paar." When she got home, Randy pulled Miriam aside, handed her the magazine and whispered: "I didn't get to finish it, but I think you're the third."

One thing we have always tried to do is to teach Randy the value of money. Little by little, since Randy was born, we have been putting little sums of money in the bank for her. One day we noticed that her account had reached seventy-three dollars.

"Why don't we make it an even hundred dollars and then buy her some stock with it?" I suggested to Miriam.

"No, let her earn it by doing little things," Miriam said firmly. "That way she'll appreciate the value of money."

I agreed that this made sense. However, for some reason Miriam got upset a few nights later, when we were going to a movie, and I told Randy, "Honey, if you'll help Mama with the dishes I'll give you twenty-seven dollars."

In trying to make her practical about money, I sometimes read to Randy from the financial page and explain the story to her as it applies to our family. Once I read her a story saying that it might be necessary to devalue the dollar. "That means the dollar will be worth less money," I explained. "What will you do about your dollars?"

"Just change them to quarters," she said, airily.

When we told Randy that she had a hundred dollars and could buy herself something useful she gave us quite a start by getting a copy of *Yachting* magazine and perusing the ads. However, our alarm was unfounded as it developed she was not planning to order a yacht or a 60-foot cabin cruiser. She simply wanted to get prices of some of the things she saw advertised in the magazine. Miriam composed a letter of inquiry and Randy sat down to type copies of it to send to the various companies whose ads caught her eye. A little while later Miriam found her in tears. She was trying to type out eight carbon copies at a time and had put her carbon paper in backwards causing a monumental snarl. I had explained to her devaluation of the dollar, but had forgotten to tell her how to put carbon paper in a typewriter. The confusion was finally ironed out and she became a faithful pen pal of a score of marine companies, all of whom addressed her as "Mr. Randy Paar." A sample of one of their letters follows:

> Dear Sir:
> We are pleased to comply with your recent request for further information on Maxim silencers for wet marine engine exhaust, as advertised in YACHTING magazine, and we are enclosing the following literature.
> Schedule "D" Price List.
> Schedule "H" Price List for WMI, WM2 and TR3 silencers.
> A bulletin entitled "Maxim Wet-type Marine Exhaust Silencers: Their Installation and Application."
> If you have further questions, please call upon us.
> Sincerely yours,
> Assistant Sales Manager

She has been unable to think of any further questions.

Although Randy had problems with the typewriter, she is an accomplished hand with the telephone, and uses it with a consistency and length generally only achieved by teen-agers in the boy-struck stage. We have an upstairs and downstairs phone in our house, and she uses them with impartiality and frequency. Once Bill Anderson, a friend of ours, called, and she picked up the phone and said hello. A moment later I picked up the upstairs phone and also said hello. Bill did not hear me but heard Randy's voice and said, "Hello, is that you, Randy?" Randy, having heard me pick up the phone, replied: "Partly."

In our catch-as-catch-can manner of bringing up our daughter, I have come to the conclusion that being a television performer is no help at all. In reading Gesell, Spock, Art Linkletter and other authorities on children, I learned it is a great help in raising a child if the child admires and respects the parent. Well, Randy has always been respectful enough, but I can't say as much for the admiration department. Other people clutch me by the lapels and tell me that I'm responsible for their insomnia, but Randy sleeps like a log. The critics have flung posies, the ratings have soared, the sponsors have congregated, but Randy remains unimpressed. In fact, when I was named TV's "Man of the Year" I sensed a distinct coolness. She thought Bret Maverick should have had it hands down. She even tells time by TV shows. She says she'll be home by Mickey Mouse, she wants to eat by a quarter of Dick Clark, but she promises to go to bed by half past Pat Boone.

At first I was secretly quite hurt by my daughter's seeming indifference. Then I began to rationalize. I consoled myself that the reason that Randy didn't appreciate me more is that she rarely sees my show because it's on so late. She was an avid viewer of all my former shows, all of which were canceled. Now, when I come home after a good show with famous guests, she's fast asleep. I spend twenty years becoming a success and she sleeps right through it.

After much thought I think I've figured it out. I suspect she thinks of me more as a television performer than a father and the competition is strictly unfair. First she was in love with Kukla, Fran and Ollie. As she got older it was the Mickey Mouse Club. Now it's Maverick. There's nothing to look forward to but Ricky Nelson and then Omnibus.

It's no picnic, being in direct competition with your child's idols. The ordinary father is a great guy to his children if he reads his little girl the funny paper or plays a spavined game of catch with his son in the backyard. But I'm a bum because I can't fence like Zorro, draw as fast as Wyatt Earp, or fly like Superman, and I don't have ears like a Mouseketeer.

I finally realized what I looked like as a performer from a child's-eye view when one of Randy's friends, a boy of eleven, came to the show with her and wrote this report on it for his class in composition:

The other night Randy Paar and I went to her father's television program. We were supposed to go to a movie but there was a big crowd there and we wanted to go someplace to get away from the people.

Before the show they make you wait outside in line so you'll think it's good when they let you in.

Jack Paar is a nice man who introduces commercials. At the start of the show Hugh Downs said, "It's the Jack Paar Show!" Then a commercial came on. Then there was another commercial. Then Jack Paar came on. Then there was another commercial.

Jack Paar doesn't look much like the other comedians I've seen on television. He's taller than Mickey Rooney and straighter than Jayne Mansfield.

Jack Paar is very funny. Some of the things he said were so funny I couldn't help laughing. But a lot of people could.

Jack Paar said: "We'll have a lot of fun tonight." Then he told a story that made himself cry.

The guests on the show were Genevieve, Hermione Gingold, Zsa Zsa Gabor and Charley Weaver. Charley Weaver spoke English.

He read a letter from his Mama. I think she's funnier than he is.

Jack kissed all the ladies when they came on. Randy says her mother doesn't mind. Jack explained to her that kissing Zsa Zsa is all just part of the day's work.

The show kept starting and stopping. The band would play and a sign on the screen would say: "More to come." Then there would be another commercial.

It's a very nice show, though. It was a lot like a radio show, only you couldn't see as well.

When the show ended lots of people asked Jack Paar for his autograph. I was going to ask him but Randy said she would get me one. She said she had more than she needs.

After the show we had a hot dog and went home. The hot dog was very good.

11.

A BULL IN HIS OWN CHINA SHOP

GARSON KANIN, the author of *Born Yesterday* and assorted other hits and misses, tells of the time he went to visit some people who were watching our show and enjoying the free-wheeling conversation.

"Why are we watching *other* people talk?" someone finally asked. "Why aren't *we* talking?"

With that they turned off their TV set and talked for hours. "We never had a better time," Garson recalled. "We'd forgotten how much fun it is to talk."

I hope this notion of turning off our show in order to talk doesn't get out of hand, but it's nice to know that our little midnight talkathon has stimulated some good conversation. I've always been partial to good talk myself and have often wondered why some other people would rather collect stamps, build Japanese rock gardens or play gin rummy. I was always convinced that people would just as soon listen to good conversation as watch dog acts or sword swallowers, and yet television had seemed to make the strangest use of good conversationalists. For a long time most of the best talkers I knew were doing something else. Charley Weaver was wielding a hammer and saw on a do-it-yourself show. Alexander King, one of the most brilliant conversationalists around, was writing a book. Gypsy Rose Lee was taking her clothes off. I just wanted to hear Charley Weaver talk, instead of watching him put up awnings. I even preferred hearing Gypsy Rose Lee converse to watching her undress. Now I have my wish and I think that some of the liveliest talk going on these days crackles along the davenport where guests sit on our show.

It's wonderful more or less refereeing these conversational bouts, and, apart from the feeling that at times I should have a chair and a whip, I enjoy it. The guests we've had on the show include some of the fastest verbal guns alive, and there's a temptation to duck when they start shooting with live conversational ammunition.

One of the most deceptive ad libbers around is Charley Weaver, whose benign expression, glasses and droopy pants disguise one of the fastest wits who ever squelched a heckler.

Charley once tangled with Jack E. Leonard, the hefty comic who can overwhelm a whole table full of fellow comics at Lindy's with his endless cascade of insult jokes.

I once had Leonard on the show. As always, he came out with a bombardment of insult jokes. "I've followed your career with great interest," he said. "First in radio and now television. I think you'll make a great telegraph operator." Eyeing his hefty, 300-pound figure, I fired back: "What a hernia you'll give your pallbearers." Jack kept right on talking through my efforts to start a conversation with him. Finally I reached behind my desk, whipped out a large pruning shears I had hidden there, and clipped his microphone cord leaving him talking to himself instead of America. It was probably one of the few times in his life that Jack was speechless.

Another time was when he tangled with Charley. As usual, Jackie came out with a rush. Looking at Charley's old-man get-up he snapped: "Hello, Grandpa. Whatta ya hear from General Grant?"

Gazing innocently through his glasses, Charley rifled back: "Jest heard from him. He wants to know why you deserted."

I don't think I've ever heard Charley at a loss for a word,

or even a few thousand words, and they're always well chosen. One night, when we had the Reverend Billy Graham as a guest, our studio audience was jammed with members of the Lions Club in New York for an international convention. They seemed to enjoy the show and there were many references to their presence, all of which they applauded vociferously. During the conversation with Billy Graham I mentioned that he had gotten me to go to church.

"I tried to go to church once in Buffalo," Charley said, "but I couldn't. It was Sunday and the churches were closed."

"Your churches are also closed on Election Day," I kidded him. "Anyway, I'm a good Christian."

"Be careful," growled Charley, "or I'll throw you to the Lions." The Lions roared, along with the rest of the audience.

Although Charley is seldom topped on a joke, I think I succeeded in that rarity one night. Charley has scores of enterprises going and one night he told me of one of his new ones: manufacturing Toby jugs in the form of his own face.

"But what do you use them for?" I inquired, looking at the small, circular mug with Charley's beaming features on the outside.

"It looks like a small pottie," Hugh Downs suggested.

"I never thought when I was aboard ship in the service and went to the head," I told Charley, "that someday it would be yours."

For once Charley had no comeback.

Another agile ad libber is Gypsy Rose Lee, who of course originally gained fame as a strip tease artist. Author H. L. Mencken coined the word "ecydist" to cover her as at the time she was covered by little else except a few beads in strategic areas and goose flesh on chilly nights.

Gypsy has come far since those days, and can now converse on many subjects, something she will do at the drop of a garment. One night I was doing a commercial for Postum and advised the viewers: "Don't be overcoffeed."

"That's the story of my life," Gypsy sighed. "Overcoffeed and underdressed."

Trying to ride herd over my conversational mavericks I often find myself feeling like a loser in the bucking horse competition at the Pendleton Roundup.

I'll never forget the night in Hollywood when Groucho Marx came storming out on the stage, unannounced, and began to belabor me with insults. I decided to parry his wrath with sweetness.

"Just think, Groucho," I said, pleasantly. "Two years ago you wouldn't even take me as a contestant on your show, and here you are coming on mine."

Groucho flicked the ashes off his cigar and shot back: "I wouldn't take you as a contestant *today* either."

Another guest who gave me a hard time was Adolphe Menjou, the veteran actor who is famed for his perfection in dress. Although I felt particularly well turned out that night, in sports jacket and slacks, Menjou reeled as if struck when he saw me.

"Your jacket and trousers don't match," he cried in dismay, "and in the evening that is unthinkable."

"A gentleman *always* wears suspenders," he continued, surveying me with mingled horror and disbelief, "and you have on a belt. Your shirt doesn't show enough cuff, and you're wearing brown shoes at night."

I gazed at him speechless through this sudden sartorial critique, and noted that he himself was indeed a model of proper dress. He was turned out to the teeth, from his burnished black shoes to the jaunty carnation in his lapel, and looked as proper as the merchandise director at Forest Lawn Cemetery. The only flaw I noted in his otherwise impeccable ensemble was that he had evidently forgotten to button the fly on his trousers!

Oblivious to this small oversight, Menjou continued with his criticism of my attire. "Your slacks don't taper and they have pleats," he sighed, his carefully waxed mustache twitching furiously. "The shoulders of your jacket are too wide, and it doesn't fall properly. The whole ensemble is dreadful . . . dreadful."

Hy Averback, our announcer, looked from my casual sports outfit to Mr. Menjou's clothes of dark, old-fashioned elegance.

"Mr. Menjou," Hy remarked, "dresses like a Pierce-Arrow."

One of my favorite guests is Hans Conreid, the tall, flowing-maned actor, whose Shakespearean flair and gentle wit make him sort of an Elizabethan Good Humor man. Hans has an accent which defies analysis and which he describes as "natural affectation." He is well informed on many things, particularly the Orient, having served in Japan in the Army and seen *Flower Drum Song* and *The World of Suzie Wong* several times. Moreover, he has a gift of improvisation, and whatever he doesn't know he is always glad to make up. Once Hans was walking down a Los Angeles street with Jesse Oppenheimer, the creator of "I Love Lucy," and they passed the Temple Baptist Church. They were engrossed in conversation but Oppenheimer noticed that several of the neon lights spelling out the church's name had been knocked out in a storm. As a result the sign read: "Temple Ba Chu." Whimsically he asked Hans: "Have you ever heard of Temple Ba Chu?"

Hans furrowed his brow for a moment as they paced along. "Oh, of course," he said. "Temple Ba Chu is one of the more beautiful but obscure of the Oriental temples. It's somewhere in Southeast Asia. In Laos, I believe, or is it South Viet Nam? It's a Shinto Temple, I think, or perhaps Buddhist."

Hans then happened to glance up and see the broken sign spelling out "Temple Ba Chu."

"He began chasing me down the street," Oppenheimer recalled.

One night when Hans was on the show a fellow guest was Billy Pearson, the jockey and art connoisseur. Billy showed us a beautiful Roman vase, from about 200 A.D. which, he said, was as good as the day it was made.

I said it was hard to believe that it didn't have some cracks. To test it I filled the vase with water and handed it to Hans to inspect. He put the exquisite blue vessel to his lips and took a long swallow. He pursed his lips and rolled the liquid around in his mouth as though testing a fine wine. Finally he said: "You know, 200 A.D. was a very good year for water."

On another occasion, when Hans was a guest, I was talking with Virginia DeLuce, a voluptuous actress noted for her interest in astrology and her vital measurements, not necessarily in that order. We spoke of astrology and she said that I was a Taurus and she was a Venus. "I've been checking my horoscope," she said, "and your Taurus touched my Venus."

Hans raised an eyebrow, looked from the curvesome Virginia to me, and beamed: "Congratulations."

Some of our liveliest ad libbing has been provided by guests from outside show business. One such guest was Eleanor Harris, an attractive young lady who had visited Elizabeth Arden's Maine Chance Farm for the $500-a-week beauty course and had written a magazine article about it. She told of the beautiful surroundings, and the days of being oiled, rubbed, steamed, exercised, kneaded, rollered and buried in hot wax.

"At the end of two weeks," she said, "I had lost nine pounds. I also lost inches everywhere, including one place where I didn't want to lose anything."

"Where do you suppose that weight went?" I mused. "Have you ever thought of that? When you lose nine pounds, what happens to it?"

"It's back," said Eleanor.

Another lively lady is Hermione Gingold, whose accent is so British that Queen Elizabeth gets an inferiority complex when she hears it. Hermione was a guest one night when we had a rather eccentric gentleman who explained that he owned outer space. "But if you claim outer space," Hermione asked in her best *grande dame* manner, "where are you going to plawnt the flawg?"

Joey Bishop, another of our irregular regular guests on the

show, is a dead-pan comedian who knows his way around an ad lib. One night Joey was on with Jimmy Cannon, the sports writer. It was just after Ingemar Johansson had won the heavyweight boxing championship from Floyd Patterson. Because the handsome Swedish heavyweight had won after doing considerable training on the dance floor with his beautiful fiancée, Jimmy suggested his victory might revolutionize boxing training.

"They're going to close gyms and boxers will train at Arthur Murray's," Cannon cracked. "Ingo looks like the tenors who used to sing in *The Student Prince*. I thought he'd come out swinging a stein and challenge Patterson to a duel."

Jimmy concluded his amusing analysis of Johansson by saying, "He's a new kind of fighter. He's an original."

"Somebody is going to find out he's an original," cracked Joey Bishop, "and put him on canvas."

Another time when Joey was on the show he and I went into the studio audience to chat with some of the people. We were going up one aisle when a woman in a far corner of the studio yelled: "Come over and interview us. We're from Texas."

"Our mike cord won't reach that far," I said. "You're too far away."

"If you're really from Texas," Joey shouted, "just lean over and you can reach us."

Speaking of leaning over, I've had to do considerable conversational tightrope walking on the show with some of our opulently endowed lady guests who have appeared with necklines which plunged a little farther than the NBC censor thinks is proper.

One such young lady is Joyce Jameson who appeared with a low-dipping neckline and all the trimmings. "I have a feeling that dress is trying to tell us something," I said when I saw her backstage before the show. "Bend up. It isn't the dress, it's the fallout."

I summoned the wardrobe mistress and suggested that she do something to camouflage Joyce's décolletage so that it wouldn't short-circuit the network. When she came out on the air I saw that the wardrobe mistress had indeed tucked some net into her plunging neckline, but not enough to really break the plunge.

"My dear," I said as she sat down, "I'm afraid your net doesn't quite cover your gross."

Earl Wilson, the columnist who is something of a student of such matters as the above, once told on the show of his experience covering a nudist convention. "All I wore was a hat and shoes," he explained.

"Where did you keep your things?" I asked.

"I kept my keys and press pass in my hat," Earl said. "I put on pajamas to go to bed but took them off when I got up in the morning. To get dressed I'd just put a little powder on my vaccination and be ready to go."

Ed Reimers, our announcer, asked Earl if it wasn't embarrassing interviewing people who had no clothes on. "Where do you look when you talk to them?" he asked.

"I look straight ahead," Earl explained. "That way I'm looking at their forehead."

"But what if you're a midget?" I inquired.

Pat Bright, an attractive comedienne who had a frustrating experience with our show, poured all her frustration into one wonderful line. Pat appeared several times and each time it seemed her act would have to be cut because of some major news event. One night part of our show was pre-empted by a special program on the death of the Pope. Another night it was some other event of world importance. After this had happened several times she finally appeared and got to do her whole act. I thanked her and said I was sorry that on previous occasions some happening of world interest had cut into our program and her act.

"That's okay," she said blithely. "Call me again when World War Three starts."

One of the hardest times I ever had conversationally on the show was with Gloria Swanson who showed up one night bringing more commercials than we already had. Gloria, who is sort of the General Motors of actresses, has more side enterprises than Walt Disney. When she appeared this night, she was carrying two suitcases. For a minute I thought she was confused and thought she was playing Willy Lohman in *Death of a Salesman.* After greeting me she reached down to open her suitcases and I began hoping they were full of jokes. Instead she began hauling out dresses and other merchandise bearing her name, hawking them as shamelessly as a streetcorner pitchman. Minutes flew by while I tried to interrupt the flow of sales talk with a little light conversation. Gloria careened on, oblivious to interruption. Finally I was getting as tired as the audience of her unabashed commercialism.

"May I interrupt your commercial," I asked, "to do a commercial?"

Trying to ad lib with guests, and at the same time remember what the next commercial is and when I have to do it, requires sort of an endless mental adagio. One of the most exciting nights we ever had on the show was the time I mentioned before when Robert Kennedy, counsel for the Senate Anti-Rackets Committee, appeared as a guest to explain the controversial Fifth Amendment. In the course of our interview he strongly criticized Jimmy Hoffa and other labor leaders for using the amendment to avoid testifying before Senate committees. I asked him what could actually be done to correct such abuses, and then realized that it was time to do a commercial.

"Before I ask you how we can save our country," I said, "first a word from our sponsor."

One night Carmel Quinn, the Irish singer, was explaining to me what the word "romancing" means in Ireland. "Romancin'," she said in her soft brogue, "means sweet talk. It's when old friends get together and just sit around and talk about old times. That's what we call romancin' in Ireland."

"Over here," Arlene Francis said, "we just call that old age."

One of the funniest ad libs on the show was uttered by

Tonto, the Indian actor who is usually confined to saying "Kemo Sabe" on "The Lone Ranger". I asked him about his wife and he said she was an Italian girl.

"How did you happen to marry an Italian girl?" I inquired.

"As an Indian," he said with a wide smile, "I'd been looking all my life for a way to get even with Columbus."

A disarmingly innocent-looking ad libber is Wally Cox, the mild, bespectacled little actor best known for his role of Mr. Peepers on television. One night I asked Wally if he ever watched our show.

"Oh, yes," he said, in his wispy voice. "I watch you more than other shows."

I beamed at this compliment from a witty and accomplished actor.

"I should point out," he added quietly, "that there is a syntactical pitfall in that sentence. Other shows may not watch your show very much."

The only way my family
could get me to stop talking
was to buy me ice cream cones.

War is hell and World War II made me simply furious.

In Cleveland radio days I interviewed visiting celebrities. This one is Simone Simon, the stone-age Brigitte Bardot.

I had a narrow escape in the South Pacific. I was nearly shot—by **our** officers.

Guadalcanal was never like this. The pretty singer with me in this bogus jungle is Jane Greer.

In Hollywood I played opposite Marilyn Monroe in **Love Nest.** She invited me to pose for a calendar with her but I forgot the date.

Cornell Capa, LIFE Magazin

Randy thinks I'm almost as funny as the Lone Ranger.

LOOK Magazine Photo

The Paar
mixed quartet.

Two of my favorite guests are Charley Weaver, the wild old man, and Genevieve, the Parisian pixie with the scalloped hairdo.

This is what we laughingly call preparing the show.

Cornell Capa, LIFE Magazine

Our show is not terribly formal. The young lady mugging me is Debbie Reynolds.

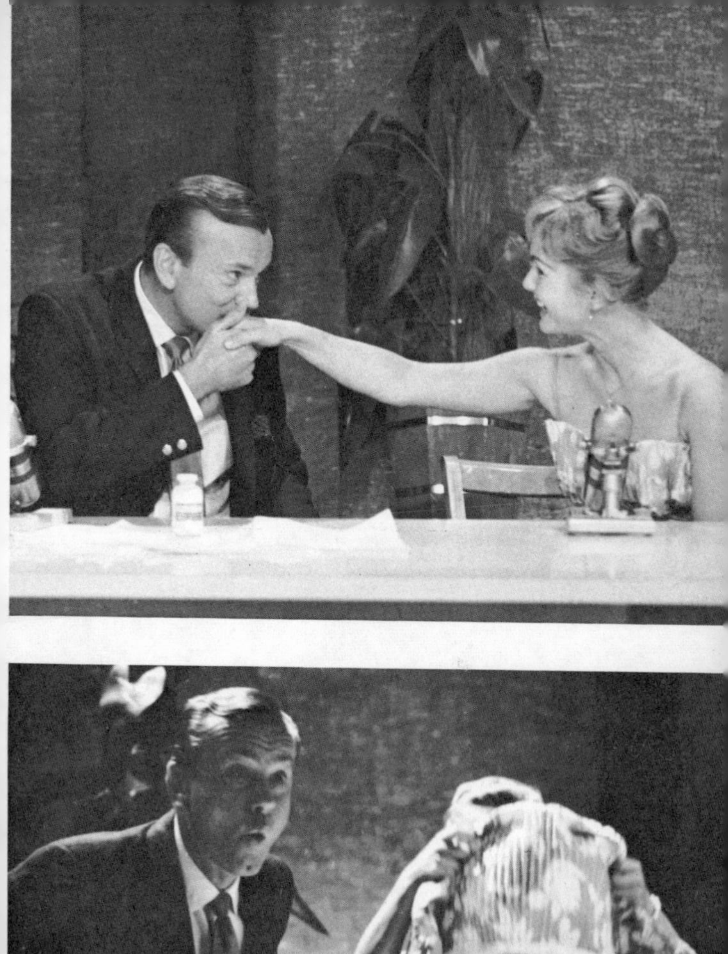

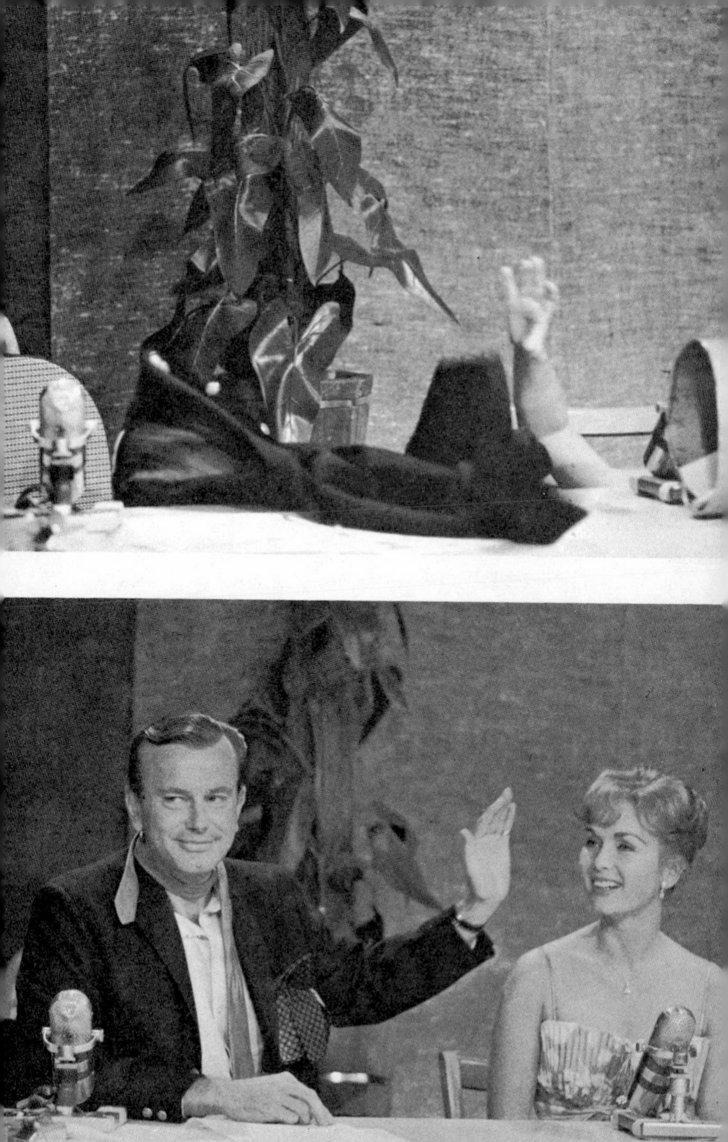

It's hard to tell which end of Zsa Zsa Gabor's dog is which. Sharing the mystery are Pat Harrington, Jr. (Guido Panzini) and Hugh Downs.

Hermione Gingold is the Den Mother of the British Empire.

This is
my idea
of bliss.

Cornell Capa,
LIFE Magazine

I won the Purple Heart for my do-it-yourself achievements.

Cornell Capa, LIFE Magazine

Cornell Capa, LIFE Magazin

I tape the show earlier the same evening so Miriam and I can watch it from bed like other people.

12. A CINDER IN THE PUBLIC EYE

THE PUBLIC is extremely fickle, as Marie Antoinette, the Betty Crocker of France, discovered the time she lost her head over that ill-advised kitchen hint: "Let 'em eat cake."

The public doesn't seem quite as impulsive these days, and no actors that I know of have been guillotined lately for their ad libs, although I have a short list of nominations if the tumbrels start rolling again. However, despite the decline in head-loppings, performers still live and die by public favor —a perilous fate at best.

I enjoy performing for people, but I must confess I don't always understand the public. I appreciate the public en masse, but am often baffled by the individuals who accost you and want to talk, usually when you're trying to help a lady in a bouffant skirt into a sports car, or ordering a dinner for eight from a French menu.

I have always tried to be nice to people I met on the way up (elevator boys) because I didn't want to have to walk back down. I have always been respectful of the pretty girl in a tight-fitting sweater sitting next to me at the soda fountain. This is because I realize that she may be the next Lana Turner. It is also because I'm just naturally respectful of pretty girls in tight-fitting sweaters.

However, people still confuse me. One day you're the apple of the public eye, and the next you're the cinder in it. One minute they're running after you for your autograph, and the next they're chasing you for your scalp.

One evening shortly after I had taken over the "Tonight" show, I was waiting for an elevator in a Miami Beach hotel when an amply upholstered lady accosted me.

"Look at these," she said, indicating circles under her eyes which made her look like a loser on "Queen for a Day." "Thanks a lot."

I must say I was flattered, although I couldn't think of any really nifty reply. I still don't have a good answer and I'm no longer flattered that I induce insomnia. I now feel that if ladies have circles under their eyes they should complain to Helena Rubinstein and not me.

There is one variant to the crack about circles under the eyes. Just when I least expect it, some hefty housewife will slap me heartily on the back, causing my vertebrae to click like castanets, and howl genially: "Hey, Jack, my husband hates you. I never go to bed now. All I do at night is watch your show."

It seems so strange, my becoming sort of an electronic bundling board. I haven't been out with anyone but my wife since our marriage, and now I'm a home wrecker by remote control.

The persistent autograph seeker and the uninhibited greeting caller are strange birds indeed, and their peculiar habits have never ceased to amaze me. I have never understood what these people do with autographs when they get them—a mystery which so far as I know has never been solved by anyone else.

This mystery was best illustrated, I think, by something that happened to Hugh Downs. He went to pick up his little daughter Deedee at school and several of her little schoolmates crowded around and got his autograph. One awed little girl said to Deedee: "Gosh, you're lucky. You can get his autograph any time you want." "Yes," Deedee said, doubtfully. "But I wouldn't know what to do with it when I got it."

Although I have never figured out why people want autographs, I at least had the morbid satisfaction of finding who originated the daffy practice of asking for them. A friend of mine, Leonard Sillman, a reformed dancer turned Broadway producer, has confessed to starting the whole ugly trend when he was a moppet years ago in Hollywood. Leonard turned from dancing to producing after his terpsichorean efforts were described by Fred Allen in these words: "Leonard trod the heavy fantastic, and his dancing sounded like a log jam in a dry river. If he had pursued his iron-footed career he would have beaten holes in every stage from coast to coast, and ruptured the acoustics of every theater in the land."

Long before launching this assault on the eardrums of theater goers, Leonard has confessed to me, he began the odious practice of autograph seeking by obtaining the signature of Wallace Reid, the silent screen star. "He was flabbergasted," Leonard recalls. "No one had ever asked for such a thing before." Young Leonard had learned that Reid, Mary Pickford, Charlie Chaplin and other silent stars gathered at a Hollywood hotel.

Having tasted blood, he closed in at the head of a phalanx of small fry. "In no time at all," he says, "the lobby was densely populated by howling mobs of kids tearing the lobby apart for autographs. Mary Pickford finally complained to the management. She made particular mention of a skinny little monster who seemed to be leading the pack." That skinny little monster, Leonard blandly admits, was he. Even though he invented the practice of autograph seeking, even *he* doesn't know why he wanted the autographs.

Getting an autograph, it seems to me, is much like shooting a lion. You can't eat it, and it's not essential for the house if you've already got a bath mat. Collecting autographs seems just as senseless as shooting lions, yet people go right on doing it. Seeing a recognizable face seems to affect many people the same way a mountain affects Sir Edmund Hillary who has to climb it "because it's there." They seem to feel they have to get an autograph just because the recognizable face "is there." Fortunately, I usually succeed in making myself less conspicuous than Anapurna or Mt. Everest.

The autograph-seeking odd balls get some strange kick out of suddenly encountering a familiar face, even when they don't know who it is. George Gobel was once walking out of the Hampshire House in New York when he was buttonholed by two women. "Why, Mabel!" one exclaimed to her friend. "Look who it is! Why it's . . . er . . . ah . . . What's your name again, sir?"

Gypsy Rose Lee, whose charms are not easily disguised, and who for years made absolutely no effort to disguise them, told on our program of the night she and her sister June Havoc decided to have a quiet dinner. Wanting not to be disturbed they went to an out-of-the-way Chinese restaurant where they were sure they would not be recognized. They were quietly attacking their moo goo gai pan with a flourish of chopsticks when Gypsy heard a patron whisper: "Oh, look, there's what's her name!"

The same lady then recognized Miss Havoc and exclaimed: "And there's the *other* one."

In addition to the people who recognize you but can't place you are the ones who spot you but think you're someone else.

Dave Garroway was once hurrying through Radio City when a man rushed up and said: "It's you! It's really you!"

Flattered by the man's obvious admiration, Dave nodded that he was indeed himself.

"And how is *Mrs.* Goldberg?" the man asked happily.

Hermione Gingold, one of our favorite guests, who is so British that she wears tweed nightgowns, returned to our program on one occasion after a trip to Hollywood looking ravishing. I complimented her on her wonderful appearance and she explained that the transformation had been wrought by a Hollywood studio. They had put caps on her teeth, her hair was lightened and she had shed a few pounds in strategic areas. The renovated Hermione was in a Fifth Avenue shop one day when a puzzled lady came up and asked politely: "Didn't you use to be Hermione Gingold?"

The autograph seekers that I have come to loathe are of the species who, not content with asking for an autograph, specify in detail a message longer than the Dead Sea Scrolls.

I encountered one of this type once in an elevator in the British Colonial Hotel in Nassau. "Hey, Jack," she burbled, thrusting a postcard into my hand. "I want you to write a card for me. Just take this down: 'Dear Maud: Guess who is writing this—' "

"I'm sorry," I said, handing back the card, "but I don't do custom work."

Cary Grant is particularly vehement on the subject of rude autograph seekers who demand custom work. "A type I've had to deal with," he says, "is the man who comes up to your table, shoves a menu in your face, and says: 'Put your John Hancock there.' I tell him that my name is not John Hancock and I have no intention of putting it anywhere. The inevitable reply is: 'Who the hell do you think you are?' To that I reply: 'I know who I am. You obviously know who I am. But who the hell are *you?*' "

Politicians by nature are better disposed than actors toward autograph seekers, as Vice-President Nixon once demonstrated when he attended a performance of *Two for the Seesaw* at a New York theater. A little girl somehow managed to squirm through the Vice-President's party as he entered the theater, and asked him for his autograph. Mr. Nixon graciously signed his autograph and handed it to the girl. "You'll like the show," she beamed to the Vice-President. "It's doity."

Kindred souls to the autograph seeker are the pests who call out to you on the streets or in public places.

One of my favorite stories of this kind was told me by Gypsy Rose Lee. She was shopping in a department store when a woman came up and inquired hesitantly: "Aren't you . . . aren't you Gypsy Rose Lee?"

"Yes, I am," Gypsy admitted. "But why did you hesitate?"

"Well," the woman answered politely. "Imagine how terrible it would have been if I'd been mistaken."

Groucho Marx had the perfect squelch for the rude approach. He was once walking along Rodeo Drive in Beverly Hills when a haughty matron demanded brusquely: "Oh, you there. Are you Groucho Marx?"

Groucho took his cigar out of his mouth, scrutinized her balefully through his spectacles, and snapped, "No, are you?"

I used to give autographs whenever possible but became disillusioned after an experience with a youngster in Hollywood. When I was replacing Jack Benny a little girl came up to me in the parking lot after the show and asked me to sign her autograph book. I asked her name and wrote some nice things in the book and signed my name. She took the book and ran to join a little group of friends nearby. As I climbed into my car I saw her tear the page out of the book and throw it away. As she did, I could hear her say: "See, kids, *I* was right. He spells it P-a-*a*-r."

13. SOME VIEWS ON VIEWERS

As SOMEONE who gets tired just signing his name, it follows naturally, I suppose, that I'm not a very good correspondent. I've never been very conscientious, I must confess, about answering mail, even from friends and family. Since I've been getting an average of four thousand letters a week for the past few years, I'm afraid I've fallen a bit behind in my correspondence.

When I first began doing national network shows on radio I used to try to answer people who wrote to me about programs. However, as I moved from radio to TV, and the mail piled up, I could see it was a losing battle. If I tried to keep up with my mail it was plain I would turn into a permanent pen pal, instead of a performer, and would be so worn out from writer's cramp that I'd be unable to drag myself before the TV cameras. My role in life, I decided, would have to be only on the receiving end of correspondence, like Lord Chesterfield's son or the Corinthians who, as far as I can tell, never did answer those epistles St. Paul kept writing them.

Some television performers, however, rejoice in fan mail and go to extremes to whip their adherents into frenzies of letter-writing by forming fan clubs and sending out barrages of autographed photos and other badges of undying loyalty. I have never encouraged this sort of carrying on and, in fact, have done my best to discourage it. A group of misguided zealots in Nutley, New Jersey, once formed a Jack Paar Fan Club but I refused to extend diplomatic recognition. They were a determined lot, though, and the last I heard were still functioning as a Jack Paar Fan Club in Exile.

Despite my apathy about answering fan mail, I do read some of it when I get the chance. You learn so much about what people are thinking about you. I've had letters calling me an idiot, a creep, a square, a bum and a schnook. One lady addressed me as "son" and another as an s.o.b. Some of the correspondents complain that I keep them up at night and others that I put them to sleep. A lady in Oregon threatened to kick me in the shins, a man in Wisconsin to kick me in the pants and a woman in Chicago to kick me in the face. (She must have been more limber than the others.)

The thing I like about the mail is you're never bored with consistency. People complain that I interrupt too much, and that I let the guests ramble on too long. I've been accused of being a homebody and a home wrecker. One man wrote that I made him feel better, and a lady said I made her sick. I've been called an old fogy and a young punk. I've been called pro-labor and anti-labor, an egghead and a fathead, a wit, and a nitwit. I've been labeled as egocentric and excessively humble. So there are days, after reading the mail, that I'm a trifle confused.

A puzzling thing to me is that so many of the people who write to me have the same last name—Viewer. Judging from my mail, there are more Viewers than Joneses in this country. I hear constantly from Angry Viewer, Outraged Viewer, Indignant Viewer and Ex Viewer. Ex Viewer is a particularly faithful correspondent.

I never try to answer abusive letters, although Garry Moore told me a good way of handling them. When he gets an insulting letter he mails it right back to the sender with this note: "The enclosed letter arrived on my desk a few days ago. I am sending it back to you in the belief that as a responsible citizen you should know that some idiot is sending out letters over your signature."

Although I don't answer poison pen letters, I have figured out a good reply for insulting phone calls. Once while I was walking through my office I saw one of the secretaries in tears on the phone. It was clear from the conversation that she was being berated by someone. I picked up the phone and found it was a woman heaping criticism on the show and on me.

"Madam," I cut in, "could you please give me your address and the serial number of your set?"

"Certainly," she huffed, "but why?"

"Because we'll have the show disconnected at this end," I said. "That way you won't have to be bothered with it any longer."

In addition to the regular mail and phone calls that a television show gets, there are the bizarre forms that some correspondence and gifts take. One man sent a homing pigeon with a message attached to its leg. All I had to do, the message said, was to fill in the date and time when the sender could audition for our show, and then turn the pigeon loose to wing its way home with the news. We released the pigeon, all right, from the top of Radio City, but without any reply for the sender. I was afraid that if word got around that we were booking acts by homing pigeon, it wouldn't be long before our waiting room would be filled by St. Bernard dogs, ponies and other forms of message-bearing animal life.

One playful soul, in fact, sent me a poison pen letter in the form of a live rattlesnake. This was a joke, I presume, and not an assassination attempt, as the snake was enclosed in a screened box and couldn't strike. However, the secretaries who opened a cardboard box and were suddenly confronted with a coiled and hissing rattler in a screened box inside didn't think it was very funny. Neither, I suspect from its expression, did the snake. He was the unhappiest looking rattlesnake I'd ever seen, and I never did see one that looked particularly happy.

The letters I get are full of personal advice. I have been advised not to wear Argyle socks, to get lost, to move to

Cuba, go jump in the lake and to not be so friendly with my lady guests. Some suspicious wives have accused me of being a philanderer for calling Genevieve or Betty Johnson "honey," or kissing Betty White or Peggy Cass, little realizing that kissing among actors is as common as hypocrisy, and that in show business any casual friend, or even enemy, is automatically called "honey," "darling," "sweetie" or "baby." Although I am fond of all of my gabby and glamorous lady guests, and usually greet all of them with as much warmth as if they had just escaped from Devil's Island, if I have any hanky-panky afoot I do not plan to advertise it in front of seven million viewers. It's when I *stop* greeting any of my lady guests with my customary effusiveness that it will be time for the letter-writing guardians of my morals to start worrying.

One thing I've noticed from the mail is that there is a considerable degree of intolerance among the letter-writing public, and no dearth of correspondents willing to cast the first stone. In fact, there are people willing to cast the second, third and fourth stones, and to keep on pegging indefinitely at people or occurrences which incur their wrath. "These cases of arrested development," my toy terrier friend Alexander King once said, "seem to be watching their TV screens with ballpoint pens poised in their twitching fingers ready to send off an illiterate barrage of protest every time a full-grown adult appears before them and doesn't bother buttering them up." I have learned, in the course of dodging some of these verbal brickbats, that almost everyone or every group is intolerant of something or someone.

I frequently get letters from unthinking people of the South asking why I have Negroes on the program. My answer is simple: because many of them are extremely talented and some of them are my good friends. Then I get letters from the North asking why we have Southerners on the program. Apparently some Northerners, in their dislike for intolerance, become intolerant themselves. They assume that almost any Southerner is biased against Negroes which, of course, is not true.

I've had complaints from Protestants when I mentioned my admiration for Bishop Sheen. Catholics have written in to ask why I use so many Jewish performers. And, finally, I have had letters from Jewish people protesting my having had Billy Graham as a guest. So the wheel of intolerance has turned full circle in my mail.

Show business people, I have found, are the most tolerant of all. It is a field where, despite any other shortcomings its practitioners may have, the only requirement for acceptance is talent. The attitude of entertainers toward intolerance was aptly summed up by Jack Benny when the son of Dr. Ralph Bunche, the distinguished Negro who won the Nobel Prize for peace, was barred from a tennis club because of his race. "If they let him in," Benny said, "the first thing you know the club would be overrun with Nobel Prize winners." My own feelings on tolerance are those of Jimmy Durante who once asked: "Why doesn't everyone leave everyone else the hell alone?"

Many of the letters I get offer suggestions on how to improve the program. Although I appreciate the thoughtfulness of the writers, I have never followed any of the advice. For one thing, even if I wanted to follow suggestions from viewers, they are so numerous and contradictory that I would lose my mind in short order. Also, since I have a staff of scores of talented people, who devote all their time to working on the show, it would be unlikely that we would get a suggestion of something that hadn't already been thought of from, say, a veterinarian in Ishpeming, Michigan.

Yet the letters of advice come in by the bushel. People who would never think of telling a tree surgeon how to operate, or a plumber how to plumb, think nothing of blithely informing us how to conduct an enterprise which costs millions of dollars a year to produce. Many even volunteer to take over and demonstrate personally how to improve things. I spent twenty years as a performer *ending up* with our present show. Now I get a dozen letters a day from youngsters with no experience telling me they have picked our show as the one on which they are willing to *start.*

Many youngsters hopeful of a career in show business, but with little or no experience, say that if they could get on the show they are sure it would lead to their being discovered, as the program proved the path to stardom for people like Pat Suzuki, Elaine May and Mike Nichols, Genevieve, Shelley Berman, and Dody Goodman. Although it is true that our show was the springboard to stardom for those people and others, all of them had had years of experience, not to mention talent, before getting the kind of exposure that led to their success.

Almost all the advice we get about the show is something we already know. We make mistakes, of course, but when we do we are usually the first to know and be upset. In fact, we are usually more upset than the most indignant letter writer, even my old friend Ex Viewer. If anyone, including me, in the confusion of conversational crossfire, says something risqué or in bad taste, or unwittingly offends someone, we are always quickly aware of it and genuinely sorry.

However, if I turn a calloused ear toward the advice of the public, the television industry as a whole welcomes it in a smothering embrace. In fact, TV can't even wait for the public to write and express its views. It lays siege to the citizenry in their homes, assaulting them by telephone, doorbell and gadgets attached to their sets, to find out what they think of programs. Television researchers yank hapless citizens off the streets into theaters to watch TV shows and commercials even *before* they go on the air. The captives are placed in seats with more contrivances than an electric chair and instructed to push a set of buttons to indicate the degree to which they like or dislike a show. If a citizen can escape his phone, and elude the scouts for program testing services, he may still be clutched by the lapels by one of a myriad of poll takers, soliciting his opinion on anything from Karl Marx to Groucho Marx.

Hollywood is nearly as bad about testing pictures in advance. There they issue cards at sneak previews for the audience to jot down what they think of the picture they have just seen. Some movie mogul, who has spent thirty years making pictures, and three million dollars making the epic in question, cowers in a cold sweat in the rear of the theater while some delinquent who has just been bounced out of junior high school for flunking reading dismisses the movie by scrawling "It stinks!" on his preview card. For this, the producer then rushes to his psychiatrist.

The broadcasting industry has gone much further than the movies in studying the public scientifically, and can reduce the listener or viewer to mathematical terms. One station, after an exhaustive study, figured out that its typical listener is married and lives with 2.61 other people, of whom 1.46 are high school age or below. He is 29.7 years old, has 10.8 years of schooling and earns $4478 a year. He owns 2.79 radios.

Inspired by this study, and with the aid of NBC's far-flung research facilities and a gypsy fortuneteller, I have scientifically worked out this composite picture of the typical family which watches "The Jack Paar Show."

He is 33.4 years old, married 2.1 times, owes $754 at a loan company, lives with 3.2 other people (it's sort of a Noel Coward arrangement), has an IQ of 76 and is wearing ½ of his pajamas (the bottoms). His wife is 29.8, her measurements are 28-36-40, she went to 7.2 schools (that's seven years in the second grade) and is also wearing ½ a pair of pajamas (his tops).

His feet are size 9½, hers are size 7, and they have a 21 inch screen. Since they watch the show lying down, with the TV set at the foot of the bed, they can't see very well, although they have 20-20 vision. (She has 35 and he has 5.)

Although I now have this impressive mathematical data on what the typical family viewing our show is like, I don't know what to do with it. I don't want to understand our viewers. I just want to leave them the hell alone.

14. WHAT'S MY LION?

THE AFRICAN SAFARI has made its way to television, and you can now get a charging rhinoceros or a maddened bull elephant in your living room as easily as Mickey Mouse or Rin Tin Tin.

I've always liked animals, although for the life of me I've never been able to get very excited about watching a giraffe or hippopotamus reduced to the dimensions of a mouse by the limitations of a 21-inch screen. However, I seem to be in a minority on this question. It's been getting so the average TV studio has more wild life around than a Nairobi water hole.

Maybe I'm prejudiced against our animal friends, from once having had to compete with a chimpanzee named J. Fred Muggs when I was doing a morning show on CBS, but for a long time I was afraid that animals were going to take over television completely. J. Fred Muggs was so successful opposite me that he went on a triumphant world tour. Lassie and Rin Tin Tin were clobbering human opposition in the ratings. Ed Sullivan seemed to be using more animals than actors on his show, and Fred Allen even suggested that Sullivan himself could be replaced by a pointer dog, if he rubbed his guests with meat, since all Ed did was point at his acts in introducing them. In desperation I appealed to my viewers: "People, be loyal to your own kind. Watch people. Animals are taking over TV!"

Finally I decided there was no use fighting our four-footed friends; I'd better join 'em. Although my only experience with animals was persuading our dachshund, Schnapps, to get off my bed at night so I could get in, I was soon surrounded by more animals than Clyde Beatty.

Now years of trekking with camera and microphone through the darkest TV networks has taught me one thing: the perils of stalking hungry crocodiles and prowling leopards in the jungles must be child's play compared with the hazard of braving nervous parrots, recalcitrant llamas and fun-loving chimpanzees on live television. There's something about the beady red eye of the TV camera that brings out the beast in the most domesticated animal. A seal that bounces balls on its nose and plays "The Stars and Stripes Forever" on horns in rehearsal will turn as phlegmatic as Perry Como once the show starts and a few million people are watching coast to coast.

When I first decided to use animals on TV I secured a native beater named John Dougherty who had established a reputation for bringing animals back alive for television shows. John had acquired custody of a hen named "Winnie the Wonder Bird" which he introduced to the press at a conference in the presidential suite of the Roosevelt Hotel in New York. Winnie, a fowl with a high IQ, won immediate fame by correctly predicting the outcome of the nip and tuck National League baseball race.

I promptly signed the erudite hen for her TV debut. In rehearsal we worked out a gag for Winnie. We set up pictures of Liberace, Harry Truman and Vladimir Horowitz. The hen was led out and I explained: "One of these pianists is known for his gleaming smile, his sequined tuxedos, his candelabra and his brother George. Which one is he?"

Winnie waddled over and pecked at the picture of Liberace.

"No!" I protested. "She's got to peck Truman to make it funny!"

"Winnie can't do that even for a joke," Dougherty protested. "This bird has integrity. We can't do anything to shake the public trust in Winnie."

That ended Winnie's career as a comedienne. Her timing wasn't any good anyway. The last I heard of Winnie she was scratching around a pen on Long Island, her integrity unimpaired.

Dougherty found it frustrating acting as a white hunter for animals, even such domestic animals as the cow. In pursuit of a cow for my show, he called the Borden Company in an effort to get Elsie, the cow made famous in their advertising.

"How would Elsie be used?" an expert in cow advertising demanded.

"She would just appear and be milked on TV," Dougherty explained.

"I'm afraid that would never do," the cow man said flatly. "We have established Elsie in a boudoir setting in our ads, and we can't let her appear out of character."

One day Dougherty produced a wombat named Wimpy, a small, piglike marsupial. Wimpy was to be introduced on the CBS "Morning Show" to a goat. "Wombats are highly emotional," John explained, "and will die of loneliness unless they have another wombat." In lieu of another wombat, some TV genius had arranged this public blind date between the wombat and a goat. However, the emotionally unstrung wombat reacted to its TV debut by revealing publicly that it was not exactly housebroken.

This mishap caused momentary consternation among the crew but order was quickly restored and the show proceeded as scheduled. However, when it was learned that John was bringing a cow to the program later in the week, a jurisdictional battle broke out between two unions. The stagehands' union said that if the cow did what the wombat did, the result would be a special effect and hence the concern of the special effects' union. The special effects' union retorted that if such mishap should come to pass it would be an Act of God and therefore come under the jurisdiction of the stagehands. Fortunately, nothing untoward happened during the cow's appearance, so this delicate matter of jurisdiction remains to be settled.

I have also encountered problems with the larger jungle animals, filming them for my show at Africa USA, a several-hundred-acre compound near Boca Raton, Florida, where lions and other wild beasts roam freely together. However, no problem of mine with animals ever reached the monumental peak of frustration achieved by my friend Jack Peterson, the owner of Africa USA, when he imported two baby giraffes from Africa for his ersatz jungle.

The two young giraffes, which stood about ten feet high, had scarcely teetered down the gangplank on their spindly legs when government inspectors pounced on them. The inspectors said there was an Agriculture Department ruling against importing giraffes because they might infect other animals. Peterson's two animals were hustled off to New Jersey and held there.

Fuming, Peterson filed suit against the government contesting the legality of snatching his giraffes. His lawyers demanded that the imprisoned giraffes be handed back forthwith. Oblivious to the legal battle raging around their long necks, the young giraffes sprouted rapidly. By the time their case reached the highest court in the land, they were just about the highest giraffes in the land. By this time, too, the bizarre case had attracted a tremendous amount of attention.

At last the court found in Peterson's favor. The two animals were freed amid the applause of giraffe lovers. But in handing over the two giraffes, the government also handed Peterson a whopping bill for their feed during the time they were held.

By this time Peterson was as wild as one of his own animals. Again he dispatched his lawyers into court contending the government had no right to charge him for feed his giraffes ate while being held against his will. The legal battle was resumed while the giraffes kept growing. Finally Peterson triumphed again. The court ruled that he did not have to pay the giraffes' board bill while they were languishing in the embrace of the Agriculture Department.

Flushed with victory, Peterson instructed the railroad to haul his two emancipated giraffes to Florida. "Those giraffes are too tall for a train," a railroad man announced, after surveying the two towering animals. "They wouldn't go through a tunnel."

Peterson then sent for a truck man. He studied the two lofty beasts and grunted an equally discouraging report. "Them giraffes are too tall to go under bridges," he said.

It was evident that Peterson had a large problem on his hands. However, a man who hobnobs with lions and tigers for a living, and had routed the U.S. government in court, was not to be daunted even by the fact that his giraffes, which now stood seventeen feet high, couldn't be squeezed through a railroad tunnel or under a highway bridge.

He got a special truck outfitted with twin slings that could be attached to the long necks of the two giraffes. Thus equipped, the truck set out for Florida with the two animals. As it approached an underpass, the attendant would operate the slings, hauling down the necks of the giraffes like a submarine commander lowering his periscope. The two unhappy giraffes finally reached Florida where they were installed as the animals with not only the longest but the limpest necks in Africa USA.

And you think you have troubles.

Another friend of mine, Ace Williams, a veteran director and cameraman, also has experienced the tribulations of filming animals for movies and television. In Williams's case, however, it was people and not animals who furnished the frustration.

Ace went to Africa to shoot a jungle picture and organized a safari deep into the Belgian Congo. Filming in the jungle is a difficult and complex undertaking, and Ace had a party of natives to assist him and transport his various cameras and equipment. Money meant nothing in that remote jungle region and he had learned on previous expeditions that the best medium of exchange was sour balls—the round, hard chunks of lemon candy which the natives loved to devour. Soon Williams had established a whole sour ball economy in the region where he was filming. He paid so many sour balls for a day's march, so many for hunting, so many for acting in his picture, and so on.

Finally his script called for a scene involving a native boy. The customary fee for a day's acting, as negotiated between Ace and the natives, was ten sour balls. Ace picked one of the dusky youngsters and his native interpreter explained to the boy that the white Bwana wanted him to act as if he were dying. For this, the interpreter told the boy, he would get ten sour balls.

The lad sputtered something in Swahili. The interpreter told Ace that the boy was willing to play the scene, but he wanted twenty sour balls.

"What's he mean, twenty sour balls?" Williams demanded angrily. "It's always been ten sour balls for one day's shooting."

There was more mysterious conversation between the interpreter and the boy.

"He says ten sour balls for playing alive," the interpreter informed Ace. "Pay for playing dead should be twenty sour balls. Harder to play dead than play living."

Ace had visions of inflation gripping his sour ball economy. He protested that the boy only had to act as if he were dying; he didn't actually have to die. The other natives joined in the argument and finally the exasperated Williams referred the matter to the tribal chief for arbitration. "I'll abide by what he says," he told the interpreter.

There was much excited argument in Swahili as the boy and the interpreter explained the issue and the chief listened gravely. Then he handed down his decision. The boy was to get the twenty sour balls he demanded for his scene.

"Okay," grumbled Ace, as he handed over the candy. "Here are his twenty sour balls. But tell him he'll never work in pictures again."

One thing I have discovered, from sad experience, is that no matter how frustrating an animal is on TV, the sympathy of the audience is invariably with the animal and not the harassed human who is trying to get him to perform. Critics also seem to share in this preference for animals over people when they appear together on television.

I made this discovery when I appeared with three basset hounds on "The Polly Bergen Show." The trio of dogs were supposed to register affection for me which they did in abundance, even to licking my face. A couple of reviews made no comment on my performance, but mentioned the dramatic talent of the dogs in showing their liking for me so lavishly. What the reviewers didn't know was that the reason for the dogs' slobbering display of affection for me was that I had thoughtfully smeared liverwurst behind my ears!

15. THE WILD OLD MAN

ONE NIGHT on the show I was reminiscing with Fran Allison about the good old radio days in Chicago, and some of the wonderful performers who came from there. "I wonder," I asked her, "whatever became of Cliff Arquette?"

Three thousand miles away, happily retired after thirty-four busy but relatively anonymous years in show business, Cliff Arquette happened to be sitting in his San Fernando Valley, California, home watching the show. "I was so surprised," he told me later, "I almost dropped my Scotch."

The next day I got a wire which said: "Have old man suit. Will travel."

A few nights later he came slouching out on our stage, crumpled hat rolled up in front, his stomach lopping over his drooping pants, glassless spectacles perched on his nose. He fished a piece of paper from his pocket and announced in exuberant bucolic accents: "Hiya there, Johnny! I've got a letter from Mama."

That night Cliff Arquette was eclipsed by Charley Weaver, certainly the most disreputable but lovable Frankenstein's monster ever to tread the boards. The character of the wily but endearing old codger from Mt. Idy, a community which exists only in his own wild imagination, has become a national favorite, upstaging Cliff Arquette, a wily, not so old actor from Hollywood.

"People all call me Charley now," Cliff admits. "I don't mind because I'm growing into Charley. Some mornings I'm afraid to look in the mirror for fear he'll be there."

Charley gave Cliff a second wind in the entertainment business at the age of fifty-three, and the wind soon reached gale proportions. In addition to appearing on our show, he got his own program on ABC-TV which reached a very high rating: 90 proof. His book, *Letters from Mama,* became a best-seller. He made a Columbia record album called *Charley Weaver Sings for His People* which features his own compositions including such sentimental numbers as "They're Draining Snyder's Swamp in the Morning." He has a flourishing Civil War museum in Gettysburg, Pennsylvania. He has made Mt. Idy almost as famous as Mt. Vernon, and "his people," including Elsie Krack, Grandma Ogg, Wallace Swine and Ludlow Bean, seem as real to millions of Americans as their own neighbors. His sidelines are too numerous to mention, but include Elsie Krack's Kashew Krunch, Wallace Swine's Pecan Waffles, a beer mug in the form of Charley's head, a similarly designed Popsicle and even a cologne and after-shave lotion which carries the dubious guarantee to make you smell like "a wild old man."

Charley is living life to the full, which he often is. His success as a wild old man who pinches pretty girls, insults people and loves to nip is probably the worst body blow suffered by the temperance movement since the repeal of the Eighteenth Amendment. It's hard to dramatize the evils of drink when Charley is cheerfully getting rich talking about how he thrives on an occasional belt. He makes no secret of the fact that he likes a shot now and again and is a walking, or at least reeling, ad for the advantages of drinking. If Charley gets any more successful, Alcoholics Anonymous will have to go underground.

One night in fun I called him a "crazy, alcoholic old man."

"I am not *crazy,*" Charley snapped.

Although Charley has turned Hurley's Bar in Radio City, which he uses as sort of a secret entrance to the studio, into a more popular tourist attraction than the Hayden Planetarium, and delights in his role of a rube, both his drinking and rustic qualities are vastly exaggerated. He is the kind of hayseed that the traveling salesman couldn't trust *his* daughter with, and a drinker like General Grant, whom he greatly admires, and who found a good snort before battle a stimulus to victory. Charley says that a couple of snorts before the show increase his mental agility, and he remains as sharp as the verbal needle he enjoys pricking people with on the air. However, his reputation as a drinker clings to him like the essence of Haig and Haig Pinchbottle.

Once he was flying from New York to Los Angeles and a pretty stewardess was wheeling a cart of liquor down the aisle of the plane. Suddenly the plane lurched, tipping the cart and dousing Charley in liquor. The startled stewardess looked down, inhaled the fumes from the spilled liquor, and then recognized the soaking passenger. "Wouldn't you know," she cried. "Charley Weaver!"

Actually, Cliff Arquette is not frequently recognized when in mufti and out of his old man costume. He is a chunky, pink-cheeked, amiable man with a white crew-cut and blue eyes, and might be a small-town mayor which he was a few years ago in Sherman Oaks, California. Once he pulls on his old clothes, however, a transformation creeps over him and he becomes the outrageous old duffer who looks like a hick but acts like a city slicker. Charley has a mind like a mousetrap and is the only man I know who indulges in *triple* entendres. One time on the show, Charley clobbered the formidable Jack E. Leonard in an exchange. After being winged by one of Charley's barbs, Leonard snorted: "You must have a better writer than I do."

"Nope," said Charley. "Just a better memory."

On another occasion I asked Charley who wrote his material.

"I remember it myself," he declared.

Charley does compose, or remember, his own letters from Mama, and his remarkable memory helps make him the dangerous conversational opponent he is. He has thousands of old jokes stored away under his crumpled hat and shaggy wig, and when you bandy words with him there is always the chance of getting speared by some hoary jest originally uttered by Gallagher and Shean or Petroleum V. Nasby. However, he also has a wild imagination which has given birth to such outlandish products as Swanson's Ointment, the only known antidote for creeping nussman.

Some of Charley's jokes may be older than his Civil War museum, but he also thinks in terms of picture jokes of outsize proportions. An example of one of these is the one about Charley meeting the man who had nine broken bones, two black eyes and fourteen contusions. "He took a full swing at a golf ball in a tile bathroom," Charley explains.

Another example of his picture jokes is the one about Grandpa Ogg driving into town from his farm in his new Rolls-Royce limousine. "The reason he bought a Rolls-Royce," he explains, "is because of the partition between the driver and the rear seat. He likes that. It keeps the sheep from licking the back of his neck."

When Charley comes on to read one of his letters, he hoists himself up on my desk with an arthritic grunt. As he reads, he mugs, squints, scratches and resorts to a hundred other tricks envied by accomplished scene stealers. "Don't shoot that scene over Charley's shoulder," Dennis Day once warned during a filming. "That guy can get laughs with his ears."

Cliff's real Mama, a sprightly, witty lady of eighty-plus, who lives in San Francisco and not Mt. Idy, is a veteran of show business herself. She and Cliff's father once formed a vaudeville act known as "The Funny Hebrew and the Singing Soubrette."

"That title was misleading," Cliff says. "Dad wasn't Hebrew, and he wasn't very funny either. Their act was terrible. He finally settled in Toledo and became a barber."

Cliff began impersonating old men while still, as he puts it, "an evil little boy." At six he won a Charlie Chaplin contest from a host of other Toledo small fry. Intoxicated with triumph, he resolved to learn to play the piano.

"Papa played the fiddle," he recalls, "but there was no one to accompany him. He bought himself an old player piano and played the fiddle while pumping the piano with his feet. When he wasn't playing the piano I learned to play by pumping with my feet and watching which keys went down. Then I got different colored paper to mark the keys to play. I learned to play that way, but I sound like a player piano."

The young human player piano organized a jazz band at fourteen called the Purple Derbies because someone had given him a crate of them. Before long he became part of a vaudeville act called "The Nuts of Harmony," and when vaudeville expired he fled to radio where he specialized in playing old men and even old ladies. Cliff also worked for Walt Disney and did the voice of "Doc" in *Snow White and the Seven Dwarfs*. He played on many of the big radio shows including "Fibber McGee and Molly" on which he coined the catch phrase, "That wasn't the way I heerd it." With the advent of TV, and the disappearance of many of the big radio shows, Cliff decided to devise a picturesque character for the new visual medium.

Appropriately the character of Charley Weaver sprang from a bottle, although in this instance it was ink. Cliff, a one-time cartoonist, doodled Charley into life on the drawing board, and then placed him in the imaginary home town of Mt. Idy which he peopled with a bizarre set of rustics like himself. When the newborn Charley took his first unsteady steps, no one liked him, Cliff recalls. "All the advertising men reacted more like tailors," he says. "They wanted to shave off Charley's mustache, change his hat or pull up his pants. No one liked him the way he was."

Despite this cool reception, Cliff finally managed to introduce Charley on a local show in Hollywood. "I wrote the show, produced it and got fired," he chuckles. Next he did a show with Dennis Day and a do-it-yourself show with Dave Willock. Charley Weaver made no splash at all, but he was fondly remembered by various Hollywood people including me, which is what occasioned my on-the-air inquiry about his whereabouts.

Introduced on our show, however, with nothing to inhibit his wild behavior, Charley got a new lease on life, and ever since he's been cutting up like someone trying to break the lease. Our show has almost no format, and what little it has he manages to dissipate. He insults the guests, leads the orchestra like a senile Lawrence Welk and ad libs outrageously with all comers.

One night we were talking about husbands paying little romantic attentions to their wives, like suddenly kissing them or hugging them by surprise. "Did you ever go up behind your wife when she's working at the kitchen sink," I asked the panel, "and surprise her with a little hug or a tickle from behind?"

"I did that once," Charley said innocently. "Don't ever do it when she's cleaning a turkey."

Despite his wild antics, people love Charley. If he were a building he would be condemned, and it costs a lot of money to keep him looking that disreputable. His baggy Charley Weaver clothes cost more than the fashionable suits of Cliff Arquette. He wears no face makeup as he acquires a ruddy glow from the internal makeup he applies at Hurley's Bar.

With his success, Charley left Hollywood for the East. A long-time Civil War buff, he settled in Gettysburg, Pennsylvania, where he bought a 140-year-old former Union prison and turned it into a museum featuring miniature soldiers which he carves himself. In addition to his soldiers, he sells everything but splints for broken legs. He also likes to compose songs about the Civil War period and has one soulful melody called "The Bottle Hymn of the Republic." Jim Bishop, who wrote *The Day Lincoln Was Shot*, is now writing a book titled *The Day Charley Weaver Was Loaded.*

Charley's museum has made him the second citizen of Gettysburg, and he sometimes manages to steal the spotlight from the first, President Eisenhower. Any Sunday that the President and Mrs. Eisenhower go to church in Gettysburg, a crowd gathers to see them leave the services promptly at 10:30 A.M. Charley frequently manages to drive by just a minute or two earlier, drawing friendly greetings from the gathering. "I don't envy Ike his job, though," Charley observes. "I'd rather be tight than President."

Although he is a shrewd businessman, Charley can be as funny off the air as on, and often talks in the same outsize picture jokes that he does in his letters from Mama.

Once an elevator broke down in his hotel when he was hurrying to catch a plane. "I had to run down twelve flights of circular stairs," he told me. "I was running so fast in circles I nearly screwed myself into the basement."

Another time in Florida I got on an elevator with him and he said to the operator: "Four, if it's not out of your way."

Success hasn't changed Charley and he remains completely maladjusted—he's always happy. Nothing disturbs his equanimity, even the fact that he is a two-time matrimonial loser. One night on the show he was complaining about how much alimony he had to pay under California's community property law which rules that half of all property belongs to the wife.

"Oh, you're so rich," I needled him. "I understand you own Lake Tahoe. How did you divide that up?"

"I waited until it froze over," he shot back, "and gave my wife her half in ice cubes."

Charley is quite a homespun philosopher, and often applies the gentle philosophy of Mt. Idy to current problems. One night I asked him what they did about juvenile delinquency in Mt. Idy.

"We put on a ballet for the kiddies at Snyder's Swamp," he replied. "The boys dress as kumquats and the girls are draped in creeping nussman. In the finale, they all circle the swamp and then dance into it. Bottom's all quicksand. Have to replace the whole cast every year—but we don't have any delinquency problems."

Small wonder, with his money and practical philosophy,

that Charley is at peace with the world. His wants are simple. Just give him the large income from his myriad enterprises, and a bottle of good Scotch, and he's happy. Once while in Atlantic City he was interviewed by a reporter at a swanky hotel overlooking the beach. The reporter was struck by Charley's obvious cheerfulness. "Mr. Weaver, you see good in everything," he observed.

"Yes, sir, that's my philosophy," Charley admitted. "Just look at the beauty of that ocean, with the waves breaking on the sand in the moonlight."

The reporter and Charley gazed silently at the sea, drinking in the beauty of the scene.

"Man," sighed Charlie. "Whatta chaser."

16. THE HEARST PAPERS' ROVING CORRESPONDENT ON HORS D'OEUVRES

I'VE BEEN ENGAGED in a few skirmishes in my day, including one called World War II, in which I was driven off the island of New Caledonia by the U.S. Navy, but I take a back seat in the combat department to Elsa Maxwell, a lady Don Quixote who goes about with a jeweled hat pin tilting with the windbags of the world.

Miss Maxwell, who has been around long enough to have had a date with Caruso interrupted by the San Francisco earthquake, and lists her vital measurements at 60-60-60, is renowned for her lavish parties and her Vesuvian temper. She would just as soon throw a chair or a plate as a party. In her appearances on our program she manages to wreak such havoc among her enemies that the NBC legal department is kept busy mopping up for weeks afterwards.

In her forays on the show she has confined herself to attacking only world institutions such as Elvis Presley, Jayne Mansfield and King Farouk. Lately, though, I've noticed she is taking on whole countries and has threatened to withdraw her seal of approval from France unless that nation mends its ways. Obviously, considering the proportions of Jayne, Farouk and France, Elsa is not one to be cowed by size.

I first met Elsa while I was doing a morning show on CBS and she appeared to be interviewed about a book she had just written. She was warped in, huffing angrily, and began dropping names with thuds that could be heard from coast to coast. Elsa drops enough names on the average show to fill a phone book the size of Bangor, Maine's, and she doesn't mind how hard she drops them.

I do not agree with everything she says but, as Voltaire said, she'll say it anyhow. However, the viewers have reveled in her Olympian wraths and scorns and it's done a lot to take up the slack in the legal profession. She has been with me in my two subsequent reincarnations on the TV tube and is showing no signs of wear and tear of running out of indignation or opponents.

I try to stop Elsa somewhere short of libel, but it isn't easy. I just get a few whispered words with her before she comes on, so there's no telling where her wayward conversation will lead us. So far it's stopped just short of Alcatraz.

One day, just before going on, she whispered, "Ask me about ——." She named a socially prominent woman. (All names have been changed to protect the guilty.) After we chatted a few minutes, I complied with her request and inquired about the woman whose name meant nothing to me. Elsa ignored me. A few more minutes of talk passed and again I inquired about the woman, as she had asked.

"Oh, all right," Elsa said, in apparent annoyance. "Since you *insist.*"

With that she proceeded to complain that she was having difficulty sleeping because the lady in question, who lived near her in the Waldorf Towers, kept her awake by her carryings on with a baron. That nearly did it. The lady, flanked by the baron and her lawyers, arrived at the network shortly afterwards and demanded to hear a recording of what was said. After listening to Elsa's blast, they shook their heads resignedly, departed and were not heard from again.

Elsa, whom George Bernard Shaw called "The Eighth Wonder of the World," is noted for the number and variety of the parties she throws. "To get fifty people to a cocktail party in New York, you have to invite a hundred," she once told me. "In Hollywood you invite twenty."

Although I look upon parties as surpassed only by bubonic plague and rock 'n' roll singers among the ills afflicting mankind, Elsa once lured me to one of her posh affairs at the Waldorf. I agreed to come when she said it would be an "intimate little group," and when I got there I discovered that to Elsa an intimate little group is three hundred people. One by one she introduced me to her assortment of dukes, countesses and earls. Since the only earl I had ever known was my Uncle Earl in Canton, Ohio, and I wouldn't know the Aly Khan from Genghis Khan, I wasn't sure how to address Elsa's titled friends. Finally she introduced me to the Duchess of Argyll. "I wear your husband's socks," I told her, relieved that I had finally found common ground with someone.

I also met the Duchess of Westminster but was stuck for a conversational opener. I couldn't tell her I'd seen her husband's cathedral. Fortunately she broke the ice. She leaned over and said, "Mr. Pawh, awnt you in television?" I admitted I was, expecting a discourse on the cultural values of the medium. "Could you tell me," said she, "how I cawn get on the Sixty-four Thousand Dollar Question?" Later I told this story to Harriet Van Horne, the TV critic, who said she had a similar experience with the Duke of Windsor. They met at a party and the Duke asked if she didn't have something to do with television. Harriet said that she wrote a column about it. "Then cawn you tell me," asked the former monarch of England, "is the Roller Derby fixed?"

At the party I also met William Paley, Chairman of the Board of CBS, whom I had never been able to find in a year of working at his network and who I suspected had an unlisted floor. I watched in awe as he and Elsa executed a nimble Latin dance.

"I'm no longer worried about the other networks," I told our audience in genuine admiration the next day. "If things get tough, Mr. Paley can cha cha cha them to death."

Elsa is so famous for her parties that I have always assumed she was born with the traditional silver spoon in her mouth, although now I suspect it was a silver monkey wrench. I was a little startled, in any case, to learn that she was born in Keokuk, Iowa, and was a spear bearer with an out-at-the-elbows Shakespearean troupe, a piano player in a New York nickelodeon, a song writer and a press agent for Monte Carlo before tossing her first party at the age of thirty-five. It's quite a thing, it seems to me, that Elsa, who was born poor, who never finished grammar school and who calls herself the "world's oldest and fattest mannequin," has wound up a world-famous authority on society. She remains very democratic and feels that one king is just as good as the next. She leans particularly toward deposed monarchs. I once pointed out to her that she seemed to prefer the company of former crowned heads to that of ruling sovereigns. "They need me more," she said stoutly.

"Elsa can forgive a person anything," Art Buchwald once said, "except if he doesn't have a title or money."

She is scornful of the nouveau riche and accepts only the oldveau riche. Elsa once told me on the program that she was a good friend of England's Keeper of the Privy Seal. "What I can't understand," I said, "is if they have a privy why seal it?"

Elsa's greatest interest is in the arts. She has been particularly interested in music since her birth in a theater while a road company prima donna was tussling with an aria in *Mignon*. Being born at an opera performance was appropriate if awkward, as her father was a music critic. "If you had to be born in the middle of an opera," he told her later, "you might have chosen something better than *Mignon*."

When she was sixteen months old she won a San Francisco beauty contest over four thousand other babies. She has captured no beauty prizes since but has a prize sense of humor about herself. Once while chatting with her on the show I mentioned that the seams of her stockings were crooked.

"I'm not wearing any," she chuckled. "Those are varicose veins."

Another time I noticed she had some notes tucked away in her ample bosom. To tease her I snatched at her neckline to show the concealed notes to the audience. Elsa jerked back and her bosom quaked ominously. "Be careful," I warned, "you might start an avalanche!"

Elsa has little regard for money and sometimes has no idea where her next caviar and champagne are coming from. She has no regular means of support, which once prompted Oscar Levant to call her "the oldest living woman on a scholarship," but she manages to get by handsomely. In New York she lives in a plush hotel suite where she likes to hold court sitting in her bed like a Roman empress and nibbling bonbons.

Elsa loves traveling and is the Tugboat Annie of the international yachting set. Whenever she lands in a new country she plants the flag and claims it in the name of Conrad Hilton. Always the crusader, Elsa is generous in her advice to countries she visits. Once, on a trip to South Africa, she persuaded the wine growers to put sneakers on the natives who since time immemorial had been trampling out the grapes barefooted. So if your wine ever tastes a little strange, don't blame the grapes; it may just have been a bad year for rubber.

She is always full of plans to visit new places and recently told me she had actually been invited on a projected flight to the moon. "Be sure to get a seat by the window," I advised her.

Elsa was once nice enough to name me as one of the five people she would choose if she were cast away on a desert island and had a choice. The others were Artur Rubinstein, Maria Callas, Noel Coward and a great scientist. "The scientist," she explained, "would be to figure out a way to get us off the island."

Although she is the Hearst papers' roving correspondent on the hors d'oeuvre circuit, she has probably seen more action than any correspondent since Richard Harding Davis.

In France a few years ago she lost a legal decision to King Farouk, the deposed sovereign of Egypt. Their ruckus started when he invited her to a party and she wired him: "I do not associate with clowns, monkeys or corrupt gangsters." "He screamed like a pig—what else," she says happily. The rotund ex-monarch also haled her into court where she says the worst part of the trial was sitting on the hard French benches. "My fanny was absolutely black," she confided to me and our seven million viewers. In addition to her numbed *derrière,* Elsa sustained a fine of $840.

Elsa's latest rhubarb also occurred in France, a country which seems strangely oblivious to the danger it is courting in arousing her ire. After a scuffle with a customs official at the Orly airport, over the amount of francs she was permitted to take out of the country, she was quoted as having trumpeted: "If things are like this I shall see to it that millions of American tourists shall abstain from visiting France."

Elsa tells me it is not true she threatened to urge American tourists to shun France. "This man made a grab for my purse," she explained. "I told him to keep his hands off. Then I said, 'I pity the poor tourists when they fall into the hands of a rude man like this.'" She did not, she protests, threaten to withdraw diplomatic recognition from France.

Elsa's forays with premiers, kings and countries have not yet led to actual war, but she did once fight a bull.

She mentioned one night on the show that she was going to Spain and I asked if she planned to fight a bull. Laughing at my little quip, she said she'd be glad to. "When I got to Madrid," she later told me, "they had a great reception for me. I asked them why they were making such a fuss. They said: 'Because you came to fight the bull.' They were serious. It was too late to back out."

The bull fight took place at a ranch outside Madrid. I don't know if the bull was fixed, but Elsa had the assistance of Luis Dominguin, one of the greatest bullfighters in the world. Elsa entered the bull ring swinging a cape and attired in the traditional bullfighter's costume. I suggested the moment of truth must have come when she tried to get into toreador pants.

"Was your suit padded?" I asked.

"No, but I am," she replied.

"What happened when the bull came out?" I inquired.

"Dominguin said: 'Address the bull,'" she said. "The bull just stood there eying me. He didn't look very mad. I yelled 'How do I address him?' 'You call out Toro,' Dominguin said. My Spanish isn't good so I just yelled: 'Here bully, bully, bully.'"

"Did he charge?" I inquired.

"Certainly," Elsa snorted. "He must have understood English. He made right for me. Dominguin helped me wave the cape. The bull barely missed us! Then Dominguin had me get down on one knee. The bull charged again but missed. That was the end of the fight. The only damage was to my toreador pants. They split when I got up off my knee."

Although Elsa does not hesitate to take on an opponent as large as King Farouk or a bull, she also is not loath to take on smaller fry. Once, at a charity affair, she was with Mrs. Winston Guest, an elegant socialite, when they spotted Jayne Mansfield's seven-year-old daughter, Jayne Marie, cuddling a puppy. Mrs. Guest reached out to pet the puppy, only to get bitten. By Jayne Marie, not the puppy!

Elsa decided to apply the old Mosaic admonition of an eye for an eye and a bite for a bite. Knowing that the agile Jayne Marie could outfoot her in a frontal attack, Elsa resorted to guile.

"Won't you come see Miss Maxwell, dear?" she asked in honeyed tones, crooking a finger at the wary tyke.

Jayne Marie skittered out of the room with the speed of a startled rabbit.

"She saw the gleam in my eye," Elsa confessed. "I was going to bite her right back."

17. HAPPINESS CAN BE CURED

THE FIRST TIME I met Jack Douglas, a reformed bongo drum player turned comedy writer, he was immersed in troubles. His house had just burned down, he had a psychosomatic throat ailment and he was involved in a lawsuit against Jimmy Durante and Garry Moore for whom he had been writing. To this assortment of afflictions was shortly to be added one more: me.

I was likewise involved in a multitude of troubles. Having replaced Jack Benny on radio I soon found myself involved in guerrilla warfare with my platoon of writers. They had departed the scene of the insurrection in a four-man huff and I was shopping for a new assortment of writers. This had led to the rendezvous with Douglas at Lucey's, a high-toned scallopine emporium near Paramount Studios in Hollywood.

At first glance he looked like an unlikely suspect for anything more cheerful than a suicide pact. He is a glum, craggy-faced man whose expression runs the gamut from mourning to despair. With his gloomy demeanor he could give sadness lessons to a bloodhound. On this occasion he was wearing a trench coat despite the fact that the day was so hot that even the Hollywood Chamber of Commerce would have welcomed frost. At first I was puzzled by this unorthodox hot weather attire, but Douglas seemed to see nothing unusual about it. I soon learned that he wore trench coats for all occasions, including world premières at Sky-High Malt Stands, and has done more for that piece of masculine rainy weather apparel than anything since spy pictures. He was also wearing a key chain so long it looked as though he planned to jump rope.

"You look like a gas truck with that chain," I said. "At least if lightning strikes you'll be grounded."

It became quickly apparent that I was not meeting with any ordinary writer. When I asked him to tell me a little about his background he volunteered the information that he had been a part-time smoking instructor in a boy's camp. He also admitted having been drummed out of the Boy Brownies for refusing to salute Gaylord Hauser. These confessions won him to me immediately. We reached an accord over two tranquilizers in a glass of water—he doesn't drink anything stronger than milk—and he furnished jokes for my succession of shows from the Jack Benny summer replacement to my present midnight marathon. Despite his sad expression Douglas turned out to be a very funny man. Although his is a wild, sick, far-out kind of humor, he is the most imaginative wit I have encountered in a long career strewn with jokes.

As we worked together I got to know Jack quite well, a rather confusing experience at best. His character is mercurial. There are times when he seems very sophisticated and looks like he *knows* what became of Sally. At other times he seems puzzled by the normal world around him and wears the bewildered expression of a little old lady who has just been slugged by Norman Vincent Peale.

When I first met him, Jack was living in Northridge, a posh but rustic suburb of Hollywood. He was building a new home to replace the one destroyed by fire. It was an attractive modern house with a swimming pool, a pool table in the living room and a hog barn occupied by an elaborate electric train set.

He explained the pool table in the living room by saying that it relaxed him.

"It's a good thing that bowling doesn't relax you," I observed.

I also asked why he kept his electric trains in the hog barn.

"I just like electric trains better than hogs," he assured me, with undeniable logic.

Despite this reflection on hogs, I soon learned that Douglas loves animals and, in fact, prefers them to people. On my first visit he invited me to swim in his pool which was filled with floating lumber and orange crates. He methodically threw the debris out of the pool to enable us to swim. When we finished he carefully threw it all back in. "If a squirrel or a rabbit should fall in," he said, "they deserve a fighting chance, don't they?"

Jack, like me, has a passion for privacy. He jealously guarded the boundaries of his rural domain, which was enclosed by a steel cyclone fence, and was sometimes accused of shooting a rifle at low-flying private airplanes. This charge he denied.

"It was a neighbor of mine who used to shoot at those planes," he told me. "He was a retired bass player who had turned chicken farmer. The planes used to scare his chickens so he got a rifle and would fire away if they came too low. He never bagged any . . . just winged a few Piper Cubs."

Actually Jack is not really warlike. I once asked him how it happened he wasn't in World War II. "I had no interest in going," he said. "I read the book and didn't like it."

Douglas's penchant for privacy became quickly apparent as you drove down the driveway to his house. First you passed a sign which said: DANGER—MAD DOGS. A short distance beyond was encountered a sign saying: BRIDGE OUT—SLOW TO 60. Finally, as you neared his house was one that said: HAVE YOU TELEPHONED THESE PEOPLE?

In a further effort to insure privacy, Jack began buying up the surrounding property until his two-acre place had grown to twenty-two acres. One canny lady neighbor, noting the abandon with which Douglas was snapping up the surrounding real estate, and learning he was an affluent writer, decided to hold out for a steep price. Douglas refused to buy. She decided to wage a war of nerves.

Encountering him one day she confided that she was planning to sell her place adjoining his to some people who planned to raise dogs. "That's wonderful," Jack exclaimed. "I love dogs!" Thwarted, the woman decided on stronger measures. The next time she saw Jack she announced: "The deal for my place with the people who wanted to raise dogs fell through. But I have a new prospect. They plan to raise guinea hens." Douglas was somewhat shaken by this announcement. He suspected the lady was bluffing. However, if she wasn't, he knew that guinea hens are the most noisy and odoriferous of fowl, and would make sorry neighbors indeed, particularly for someone who cherishes quiet. He settled the matter with one of his signs. Outside his property, just adjoining hers, he posted a large sign which read: NORTHRIDGE LION FARM. Real estate values promptly sagged.

Douglas's handsome new house was just a short distance from the site of the burned structure, and was adjoined by a beautiful pool. This posed what Jack considered a very serious problem: what to do with his original swimming pool, which was about fifty yards from his new house. "You can't just have it sitting there," he complained.

"If you don't want His and Her pools," I suggested in a burst of whimsy, "why don't you just fill up the other pool?" This I thought was a rather hilarious suggestion. However, Jack did just that. The next time I came to call I found the first pool filled with lumber, debris and dirt.

When his new house was completed, Jack threw a little party for three hundred guests to celebrate. His handsome new home was crawling with movie stars and other assorted Hollywood denizens. However, just as the festivities were getting under way, a deluge broke. The liquid which Californians sometimes loyally refer to as "white orange juice," but which is more commonly known as rain, came down in sheets. A catering company had brought a large tent, to shield the guests from the sun, but it proved inadequate against the deluge. The torrent came pelting down with such fury it defied all efforts to raise the tent any higher than Mickey Rooney. Miriam and I, along with the 298 other guests, took refuge in the house. It was as if everyone in Yankee Stadium had suddenly decided to make a phone call at once, and in the same booth. I had never before met so many celebrities—nor at such close range. I was elbowed by Lucille Ball, Lionel Barrymore ran over my foot in his wheel chair and Mitzi Gaynor kneed me in the groin. By the time the storm ended, the smog broke through the clouds and the hostilities ceased, the Douglases' new house *did* look like the Northridge Lion Farm. Their new rugs were covered with more ashes than Pompeii. "No one could move to get to an ash tray," Douglas lamented.

Jack became a comedy writer in the simplest way I ever heard. Bob Hope stopped him on the street one day and said: "Do you think you could write some jokes for me?" Jack wrote the jokes, Hope liked them, and he's been writing jokes ever since.

One New Year's Day he accompanied Hope to the Rose Bowl game where the comedian was to make an appearance between the halves. Gazing over the gathering of a hundred thousand, Jack was gripped by an uncontrollable urge. Grabbing the microphone from Hope he growled at the huge throng: "This is a stickup. Don't anyone move."

Before starting with Hope as a writer, Douglas was a performer. Born on Staten Island, he went into vaudeville at the tender age of fourteen as a drummer. "I lived in a town so small we didn't have a village idiot," he recalls. "We all took turns." He drifted to Hollywood where he danced in some movie musicals and even occasionally lifted his voice in song. One night he was summoned to the Coconut Grove to replace an errant singer named Bing Crosby who had been banished for using a gargle not recommended to soothe a vocalist's tonsils. Later Jack met a struggling vaudevillian named Bob Hope who had just landed a job in the Broadway musical *Red, Hot, and Blue.* Douglas borrowed Hope's vaudeville act and toured with it for a spell. Back in Hollywood he teamed up with Cliff Arquette, now better known as Charley Weaver, and another man in a comedy act called "The Three Public Enemies." Later he became a writer for such radio shows as Martin and Lewis, Red Skelton and Ozzie and Harriet, before swimming into my ken on the Jack Benny summer replacement.

When I moved East in 1953 Jack continued to write for me via the mails. Between our jokes and our problems, the correspondence was sort of a blend of "Dear Abby" and Joe Miller. When I got the present show on NBC, Jack joined me as the lone writer at the outset, and also occasionally lent his raffish talents to the show as a performer.

Jack was a pioneer among comedy writers. Long before the so-called "sick" comedians were heard of, Jack was writing jokes that even the Mayo Clinic couldn't cure. His macabre sense of humor delighted in jokes about his girl who took a wrong turn going to the ladies' room at the Radio City Music Hall and was kicked to death by the Rockettes, and funerals so cheap that the corpse had to ride up front with the driver.

Douglas's working methods are worth noting, as I'm afraid they won't be found in any of the standard books or courses on creative writing. Coming to the office he would remove his trench coat. This would reveal that he was wearing nothing underneath but trousers and sandals. He would then take large sheets of paper, scribble slogans on them, and hang them on the wall for inspiration. These bear sayings such as: GUIDED MISSILE RANGE—PARKING ONE HOUR, NO SOWING WILD OATS WHILE AIR CONDITIONING IS ON and PLEASE CLOSE DRAWBRIDGE AFTER USING CASTLE. With these signs for inspiration, he would put a long-playing classical record on his phonograph, turn up the volume to deafening, put in ear plugs and start writing. Getting Douglas started was not always easy. When he first joined me in New York he announced he needed shelves for his files. I got a carpenter to start putting in shelves. Soon a wild-eyed Douglas accosted me. "How do you expect me to work in this office?" he demanded. "Some idiot is in there hammering and sawing putting up shelves." During all this creative travail Jack would consume endless cups of coffee—so much, in fact, that one time in the steam room of the Luxor Baths I saw him percolate. Somehow, from this din and madness, emerged much wild but amusing material.

Although he suffers torment in creating his macabre jokes, he is a quick man with an ad lib and is ever ready with his stiletto. Once while we were talking in his office I turned to leave and cracked my knee on the sharp corner of his filing cabinet. The pain was excruciating and I hopped around groaning and cursing the file cabinet. He looked up dryly from his typewriter and asked, "Want a bullet to bite on, kid?"

One night on our show Jack was holding forth at some length and it came time for me to do a Norelco Shaver commercial. I held up the shaver, which looks remarkably like an ocarina, to go into the commercial, but Douglas kept on talking. Finally, looking at me holding up the shaver, he cracked: "Well, either sell it or play it."

My idyll with Jack began to unravel slightly when he turned author. For years he had nurtured a book which he had privately published and distributed to his friends including me. It was probably the first book in which whole chapters consisted of one sentence. Then, in 1959, a publisher brought out an expurgated edition under the title *My Brother Was an Only Child*, and it became a best-seller.

In his opus Jack introduced to American literature such characters as Tim Snopes, who was such a shell of his former self that if you put him to your ear you could hear the ocean; Toynbee Doob, who erected a statue of a pigeon in the park, which generals came from miles around to see; and Dudley Hartrampf, the man who named Philadelphia "the City of Brotherly Love" and was later drawn, quartered, hanged, stabbed, shot and burned at the stake there for double parking.

After he turned book author, I thought I noted a certain hauteur in Jack toward our television show. He plunged into writing a sequel called *Never Trust a Naked Bus Driver* and I suspected he was using his jolliest morsels for this saga rather than for the show. I chided him for this dereliction of duty, at which he took down his signs, seized his phonograph and moved to his apartment in a funk (a conveyance similar to a punt). I missed his unfriendly face, the thunder of the music on his phonograph and the friendly pop of his ear plugs as he removed them after a hard day's work. Earl Wilson, the columnist, sought to mediate our contretemps. I proposed lunch.

"Paar knows I don't eat lunch," Douglas said, when my message was conveyed to him.

This so wounded me that I stopped waving the olive branch.

"I'm surprised to learn he doesn't eat lunch," I told Earl. "He's been putting in a big expense account for lunches for years. Ah, well, better to know that he was just fibbing than that he had a tape worm, as I suspected."

Jack's assaults on the expense account had been discussed in awed whispers in the corridors of NBC, and accountants were said to blanch at the sight of them. On our return from one trip to Hollywood he submitted this expense account: $36, bongo drum rental; $3, Alcoholics Anonymous; $3286, new car; $75, lunch with Lillian Roth; 50 cents, map to movie stars' homes; $37, keys to movie stars' homes; $50, bail; $600, group alimony plan payment. Of course he was just kidding. I think. In any event, he got the inspiration for that expense account from his *real* expense account.

Jack has now abandoned writing and turned performer again as a night club comedian. He is a talented man and I wish him well. I understand he has a joke about me in his act. He tells the audience that I'm the kind of a guy who takes the menus from the Forum, the ultra-chic New York restaurant which features specialties like wild boar and peacock, and distributes them to the bums on the Bowery. I don't mind his telling jokes about me, but lately he's been doing it on *my* show.

One night during his act a button popped off his shirt. Jack got down on the floor and was crawling around looking for it. "I don't know what I'd do if I found it," he mused. "I'm single and I have no one to sew it on for me. I do have a Filipino house boy but he's bleary-eyed by the time he arrives in the morning. He drives to work. From Manila."

18.

WOMEN I CAN'T UNDERSTAND

UNDERSTANDING WOMEN has never been easy and it doesn't help any when you're completely surrounded by them all talking in different accents. I never thought, when I got my first "Dear John" letter at the age of six, that I would wind up spending most of my evenings with a glamorous assortment of ladies who are witty, wicked and never shut up. There are nights when I look at the ladies around me on my show and feel as frustrated as Phil Spitalny if his all-girl orchestra showed up without their instruments. A further complication, for someone who speaks no foreign language, and has trouble with English, is that the female guests on my show have such a variety of languages and accents they often sound like the complaint department at Berlitz.

The champion in the fractured English department is Genevieve, the petite French *chanteuse* with the scalloped hair-do, who contributes as much to Franco-American understanding with her personality as she subtracts with her accent. The ebullient songstress scrambles syntax even better than she does eggs, and she can whip up an omelette in the best Gallic tradition. Her English is not merely broken; it's absolutely shattered.

I first met Genevieve one summer night in 1957 when she came on as a singer. She sings charmingly, but I was more taken with her personality which rubs off on you and lingers like the aroma of *escargot*. Once having savored her effervescent spirit I largely dispensed with the singing and since then Genevieve has done everything on the show from commercials to reading the baseball scores in which she refers to errors as *faux pas* and boo-boos. Just as captivating as her accent are the quaint phrases born of her unfamiliarity with the English language. She once told me she had "crossed Greta Garbo on the street." Another time, while talking about an expected visit from her father, she said he was going to "take a fly from Paris." Her charming language mangling has so endeared her to television viewers that when a butter-fingered stagehand, carrying her backstage in *Can Can*, dropped her and broke her leg, it was the biggest blow to France of any drop since the franc was devalued.

Television transformed her into a star overnight, but Genevieve is still baffled by the medium. "Ohhh, Jacques, on zee television once mus' be teeny," she told me. "Ozzerwise one does not feet een the screen. Ah, but on zee stedge, one can be beeg. One can geev everyssing."

I tried to explain to her that while it is true that the TV screen does shrink you to about the size of Toulouse-Lautrec, it can swell your audience from a few hundreds to millions.

"But, Jacques," she said, turning her dark, gamin eyes on me. "On television you say: 'An' now Genevieve will seeing' and zen zat beeg meekraphone ees turning on me—bing, bang, boom—and Aye mus' make song. *Pas bien*. Ees very 'ard."

Despite her misgivings about the medium, TV has made Genevieve an important star. Born Ginette Auger, she was presiding over a small *bistro* called the Chez Geneviève in the Montmartre section of Paris when she was spotted by an eagle-eyed American agent named Barron Polan. She sang for her supper at smart New York night spots when she came on our show and uncorked her bubbly personality with a pop so loud it was heard across the country.

She lives alone in a smart apartment overlooking the East River with a terrace approximately as large as Kansas and a big canvas swimming pool. Although her contours are of a design calculated to give any robust male what she calls "chicken skin" (English translation: goose pimples), Genevieve is not married.

"Ah, Jacques, marriage eeze not, how you say, com-pateeble with show bizneez. *Oui.* Aye queet wen I get mareed. But my man mus' be in show bizneez, or somsing like artiste, maybe, you understan'? I weel no marry wiz grosair, or bizneez man, maybe who know nozing but yak, yak, yak. Aye want leetle house wiz a beeg gardain. Lots of animals all ovair and enough money to receive all bodies (everybody) Aye loaf."

The biggest passion in Genevieve's life is animals. She is devoted to animals of all kinds and keeps four parakeets and a French poodle named Poudi who was born in Brooklyn. She goes often to feed the squirrels and pigeons in Central Park and plots, one of these dark nights, to free the animals in the zoo there. "Aye 'ate to zee them behind bars," she says indignantly.

She is particularly fond of her parakeets who sometimes present a problem when she has to travel. On one occasion she went to Canada to appear in a club and took her birds along. All went well on the trip to Canada, but on the way back her plane stopped in Detroit and a dispute broke out with customs officials over the parakeets. Genevieve finally overwhelmed them with logic and a torrent of fractured English and was allowed to keep the birds and continue home to New York.

She told this story on the program one night. It had a plot as long and involved as a novel by Alexander Dumas and seemed to lack any noticeable point.

"Just what is the point of your story?" asked Hermione Gingold, when Genevieve had concluded.

"Aye tell you becoose if Aye do not stop in Detroit Aye 'ave no trooble with my birds," she said.

"Why didn't you," Hermione trilled, dropping octaves like beads, "just have them fly down and meet you?"

Hermione was once appearing in a show called *Sweet and Low* in London. "I thought I looked ravishing," she told me. "When I came out on the stage a little boy in the front row asked his muthaw: 'Mummy, what's that lady for?'

"I've nevah figured out an answer faw that question," Hermione admits.

Hermione, a name strange enough to adorn the flank of a Pullman car, is an actress as British as tea and crumpets or Beefeaters gin. Her British accent is so pronounced that if it were any more so she would have to use Douglas Fairbanks, Jr., as an interpreter. "I feel aws if I were bawn heah," she told me when I first met her. "I don't speak the lawnguage veddy well but I lawve it heah."

I first encountered this extraordinary lady when I was presiding over the CBS "Morning Show." Although she tells me she was sort of the Daniel Boone of British television, she had never ad libbed before that time. Since then no one has been able to get her to use a script.

Hermione is nothing if not frank in her ad libbing. She was once invited to a dinner honoring Joey Adams, the comedian. One by one the speakers paid lavish tributes to Joey as is the custom of these tribal gatherings. Finally the toastmaster called on Hermione, who wasn't quite sure why she was there. "I'm delighted to attend this dinner in honor of Joey Adams," she announced. "In fact, I'm delighted to go to any dinnah on Sunday night. It's my maid's night out and I'm a perfectly ghawstly cook." With that she sat down.

Hermione's untrammeled spirit appeals to me and we have become fast friends. She once startled a reporter who asked her what she did when she visited me by replying, "We bathe." What she meant, she finally had to explain to the confused reporter, was that when she visited at our house we went swimming.

When I first met her Hermione used to like a good cigar, but lately has given up smoking. "I gave up smoking cigars," she told me, "when someone told me it wasn't gentlemanly."

Hermione was once a guest on "Person to Person." Not long

afterwards she got a call from Noel Coward who was also going to be on the program. "I've just moved into your apartment building, deah," Coward said, "and I'm going to be awn 'Person to Person.' I don't hawv all my furniture yet. Would it be imposing to borrow a few pieces of yaw furniture so my apartment wouldn't look so bare?"

"But Noel, dawling," Hermione protested. "My furniture has already been on 'Person to Person.' "

Hermione is a dedicated quilter and often attends quilting sessions at Gypsy Rose Lee's. At one she startled the other lady quilters by suddenly gasping: "Goodness, I think I just embroidered a dirty word in Arabic!"

Hermione comes of quite a remarkable family. "Rudyard Kipling was a constant visitor to my grandmother's house in London," she recalls. "He not only read her several of his splendid poems but he also gave her an extremely jolly Indian scarf with which she afterwards hanged herself."

Hermione made her first stage appearance at the age of ten in London as a herald in a show called *Pinkie and the Fairies*. She began playing Shakespeare at the age of seventeen and made her Broadway debut in 1953 in a revue with a famous entrance line—"Not Miss *Rhine*gold . . . Miss *Gin*gold."

Hermione can say more with one devastating "rawllllly" than most people can in a ten-minute speech. One night as she took her seat at our show I said: "That's the same seat that Zsa Zsa sat in last night."

"Rawllly," she said. "Zsa Zsa *who?*"

Another time she found herself at odds with Elsa Maxwell. At the height of hostilities, I asked Hermione what she thought of Elsa. "Just another pretty face," she flipped off gaily.

Another night I wondered aloud how Genevieve achieved such a tousled hair-do. "I sometimes do mine the same way," Hermione said. "You just stick your head out the window when it's windy."

We have been planning to take our show to London, and Hermione has been supplying me with advice. "Don't just drop in at Buckingham Palace," she advises. "Phone first. Don't fritter away time trying to master the coinage. Ignore it. Either buy nothing that costs less than a pound, which is paper and can be folded, or be gracious and let the other fellow pick up the check. One of the great thrills London affords visiting Americans is the opportunity to get into a taxicab without lying down. And when in pubs, beware of flying darts at all times."

Pondering Hermione's advice, I am grateful for the guidance of someone as worldly-wise as she. "Hermione," I once said to her, "you have really lived completely, haven't you?"

"Completely," she caroled, "is hawdly the word."

When I first took over the "Tonight" show, I wanted to find unusual guests. I hit the jackpot my second night on the show with the appearance of Dody Goodman, a witty, worried-looking strawberry blonde who was once described as looking like "someone you avoid at the laundromat."

Dody had been a dancer in such shows as *Call Me Madam, Wonderful Town, High Button Shoes* and something called *My Darling Aida* in which she played a cooch dancer and wore a large black diamond in her navel.

However, she seemed more like a bird-brained housewife than a ballerina as she came into my office to talk about the possibility of being on the show. She wore a black skirt, demure, ruffled blouse with a black string tie, and spoke in a distracted manner that defied description. I greeted her and we began to chat. To answer a simple yes or no, she would twist her mouth into a knot, scratch the end of her nose and open her large blue eyes to the size of fried eggs. She began to tell me a long rambling story about a Cary Grant movie she and her mother had seen in her home town of Columbus, Ohio. The story had no perceptible point, but her Midwest twang and hesitant, naïve manner were highly amusing in a baffling sort of way.

"Look, honey," I finally interrupted. "Just answer me one question. Are you for real? Or are you putting it on?"

She twisted her mouth, patted the top of her pink hair, widened her eyes and said: "A little."

She was, it soon became apparent, indeed real, and the more she talked the more obvious it became that no one could have made up Dody Goodman. She came on the show my second night, and soon millions of TV viewers were asking each other whether this seemingly dumb blonde was actually real. Her hesitant delivery gave the impression that her picture tube was on but her sound wasn't. Dody never seemed to try to be funny; she just stumbled into it. The things she said really weren't particularly funny, but as she talked, fidgeting, fluttering her hands and smiling happily, she achieved a wackily endearing quality. It was not easy to explain her appeal.

"Ralph Edwards is funnier than Dody," one critic said. "Lassie is as gifted at acting. Dame Edith Sitwell has more sex appeal. But after a while Dody grows on you."

That she does. Dody is not dumb, by any means. She is terribly witty, in a droll way, with a natural sense of the ridiculous. She is a tireless talker and before long I began to feel like the announcer on the Dody Goodman Show. Also, in our nightly verbal banter I began to get the feeling that she was shooting with live ammunition. I had a catch phrase I used on the show: "Give them enough rope."

One night I said this and Dody cracked: "And I'll skip."

"You can," I said, "because my end is untied."

Eventually I decided it would be better for the show to use Dody less frequently. The newspapers said she had been fired, and the supposed firing got more play on front pages than when the Russians fired Sputnik into space. Actually Dody was not fired. She is still a frequent guest on the show, and we are good friends. However, I still don't understand her. One night on the show, about a week after New Year's, she said good night in these words: "Good night, and a Merry Christmas to all. I know it's too late to say that, but I just thought of it."

Another night in the dressing room she said to me: "You have a speck on your eyelash."

I couldn't see anything, but batted at my eyelashes to brush it away.

"You still didn't get it," she said, brushing at my left eye. I still couldn't see anything.

"Oh, mercy," she finally said, touching her forehead. "It's on *my* eyelash."

Dody has a little dog of which she is very proud. One night on the show I asked her what breed her dog was.

"He's a little m-u-t-t," she spelled out. "I spelled it in case he's watching."

Life sometimes seems like a giant conspiracy to frustrate Dody, or perhaps it's vice versa. Once, while shopping at Macy's, she found a wallet on the floor. She dutifully took it to the floorwalker and turned it in. "He opened the wallet to see who it belonged to," she told me. "It was mine."

Dody feels that her cockeyed outlook on life may be inherited since, according to her, everyone in her family is a little odd. When Dody first started on the show, which wasn't seen then in Columbus, her mother used to take the bus to Cincinnati to watch her daughter. "She'd always be so tired when she got there," Dody told me, "that she'd fall asleep and ride back home."

After Dody's success on the show, her family gave a party for her in Columbus. Mrs. Goodman danced with various young men. Finally she confided to one with a smile: "I'm Dody's mother."

"I know," the young man answered. "I'm her brother."

Another of my favorite ladies is Zsa Zsa Gabor, the Eloise of the black lingerie set. Zsa Zsa has become such a good friend that I can call her by her first Zsa. Zsa is like the girl next door—if you live next door to Tiffany's.

It is hard to tell which has more candlepower, Zsa Zsa's dazzling smile or her array of diamonds. The first time she came on the show I thought she was carrying a flashlight, but I found she had just become engaged. Her engagement ring looked so heavy I suspect she had to starch her finger to support it. I had to ask her to turn it down to dim so I could see to interview her.

Just before coming on the show Zsa Zsa asked me what I wanted her to do.

"Just be yourself," I told her.

That was my first mistake. She burbled on about her romances, interrupted the commercials and otherwise confused the National Broadcasting Company. Her performance was unbelievable, and, as Earl Wilson said, I unbelieved everything she said. No matter what she said, she said it with great vehemence.

"That's what I like about you," I said. "When you say something vague you're very definite about it."

I confessed to Zsa Zsa that when I first saw her on a little local show in Hollywood I wanted her right away.

"Dollink, nobody gets me right away," she said.

Gazing on this Hungarian Iron Butterfly I told her that I thought she was one of the three most beautiful women I'd ever seen.

"Please don't tell me who are the other two," she said. "I don't vant to hear about other beautiful voomen. It makes me veel too insecure."

Mama Gabor is a friend of mine, too, as are her other daughters, Magda and Eva. Once on our show Eva reported that Mama planned to sell her jewelry store in New York and move to Palm Springs but there were so many protests that she changed her mind. She didn't clarify whether the protests were from New York or Palm Springs. Mama raised all her daughters carefully.

"In school I was taught that money isn't haffrything and that happiness is also important," Zsa Zsa once told me. "As soon as Mama heard this she made me change schools."

Zsa Zsa got her start in television by accident when she was invited on a program on which a panel dispensed advice to viewers. One wife wrote in asking what a wife could do about a husband who was running around with other women.

"Zhoot him in the laig," counseled Zsa Zsa.

Another time the question asked her was: "My fiancé gave me a car, a mink coat and a stove. Is it proper for me to accept these gifts?"

"Uff gorse not," snorted Zsa Zsa. "Zend back the stove."

Since she is such an authority I asked Zsa Zsa what makes European men better lovers than American men.

She looked at me, batted her big beautiful eyes, and purred: "European voomen."

Zsa Zsa acquired her knowledge of men in the course of three marriages and innumerable romances. Husband number one was a Turkish diplomat, number two was Conrad Hilton, the hotel magnate. Next came George Sanders, the actor. She is presently unattached, although she admits she is looking. "The right man must be about forty," she says, "and he must be married before. If he is a bachelor who vonts him?"

Although Zsa Zsa specifies the age she wants in a prospective mate, she has never revealed her own age. Once a reporter broached this delicate question. "I didn't gum here to be insulted," she huffed.

I once asked Zsa Zsa if she thought love was important.

"Yas, I theenk luff is the most imbortant theeng in a vooman's life," she said throatily. "A vooman should keep on marrying and marrying until she finds luff."

19.

IT COULDA ONLY 'APPEN INA SALERNO

ONE DAY the phone rang in my Radio City office.

"This is the U.S. Immigration Service," the caller announced. "We've been watching 'The Jack Paar Show.' Where can we find this Guido Panzini? We want to check on his port of entry."

The U.S. government, it seemed, had been taken in along with millions of TV viewers in a cheerful masquerade by a supposed Italian golf pro from Salerno named Guido Panzini. Actually Panzini was Pat Harrington, Jr., a bright fast-talking young American of Irish descent who was a television time salesman at NBC. Although Pat had made a national audience laugh with his wild tales of golf games in Tanganyika, where he said he shot a 77 and four Mau Maus, and of his improbable life on an Italian submarine, the Immigration Service didn't think his impersonation was very funny.

"The immigration man asked when I arrived in this country," said Pat, who is slight and dark with horn-rimmed glasses and looks as though he might be Italian. "I told him an Italian submarine landed me near Freeport, Long Island, in World War II. I said I was supposed to blow up Mitchel Field but I met a nice Italian family and deserted, they made such good spaghetti. I did it all in Italian dialect. The man never laughed. He asked what ship I came on. If it was the *Santa Maria* I guess it would have been okay. I finally told him it was all a joke. I said I was born on the West Side of New York. He said: 'Then what are you doing here on the East Side?' He was pretty mad. I'm probably the only man who almost got himself deported for laughs. How would you like to try to get back into your own country on the Italian quota?"

The Panzini hoax, which lasted for several months on our show, was born in a succession of Manhattan restaurants where Pat and a fellow TV commercial salesman named Lynn Phillips used to relax from the ardors of peddling television time. Pat had picked up a number of dialects which he and Phillips used to use to amuse sales prospects or just themselves. One day in Toots Shor's they were standing at the bar near a CBS program director and heard him discussing the *Andrea Doria* collision which had just occurred.

Winking at Pat, Phillips introduced him to the CBS man. "This is Guido Panzini, a survivor of the *Andrea Doria*," Phillips said. "He was on the bridge when it happened."

The CBS man was greatly interested. "What was it like up there?" he asked.

"Was a dark," said Pat, shifting into his dialect. "Werry dark. But wen Captain Calamai ask a question an' somebody answer in Swidish, we know we were close."

Pat and Phillips had so much fun with their impromptu act they were soon expanding it. Guido became a golf pro from Salerno and described the course so vividly once to singer Dick Haymes that Haymes said he had played there himself—although actually there is no golf course in Salerno. For a long time Pat's Italian act caused as much trouble as fun. One night at a party a famous announcer got so mad when he learned he had been taken in by the fake Italian that he was going to punch Harrington.

"He gave up that idea," Phillips said, "when I told him that Pat was a former Golden Gloves boxer, which he was."

We heard about Pat's Italian impersonations, put him on the show, and he quickly became a TV favorite. In his first appearance, I asked him how he got to this country.

"Wassa captured in war," he said. "I learna English in war

when serving on Italian submarine. We come up behind American warships and watch recreation movies. One time we getta so intrasted in double feature we follow U.S. ship righta into Newport and getta captured."

He talked about his career as a golf pro and I asked him the most difficult course he had ever played.

"Tanganyika Contary club in Africa," he replied. "It goesa uppa side of Mount Kilimanjaro. Hardest hole issa third. Green there issa other side of pygmy village If you short witha two iron means pow!—blow gun dart inna chest."

Guido told of having a wife and three children in Salerno and I asked if there was ever any hanky-panky with a handsome Italian chap like himself loose in New York.

"Mebbe a lidla bit hanky," he said, "but definitely no panky."

Guido was so well received that he made numerous appearances on our show and took over the program for me when I went on vacation. He also became a frequent guest on "The Steve Allen Show." Then, when he was chosen as a regular on "The Danny Thomas Show," he gave up his sales job and moved to California to make a full-time career as an actor.

"For years you made a career out of practical jokes," I told him, "and now practical jokes have made a new career for you. What do you think about it?"

"It coulda only 'appen ina Salerno," he grinned.

Although Pat wasn't even a professional entertainer when he became a success in show business, he comes from a show-business family and had been around show people all his life.

Pat's father, Pat Harrington, Sr., was a comedian at a New York night spot called the Club 18 which flourished in the 1930s. Mayhem was the motif of the club and Harrington Senior and Jack White specialized in insulting the customers, particularly the more prominent ones. It was while being heckled by Harrington one night that Jack Benny uttered a famous line: "You wouldn't talk to me that way if I had my writers with me."

The Club 18 was across from 21, the ultra-smart restaurant. In the wee small hours, the Club 18 waiters, carrying out the garbage, would march right across the crowded floor, while Harrington howled: "There go the hors d'oeuvres for 21!"

"Dad was always bringing his famous customers home when I was a kid," Pat, Jr., told me. "I used to go to the bathroom in the morning and run into Bob Hope or Pat O'Brien or Bing Crosby."

Pat attended Fordham University in New York where he played the piano, boxed, learned to shoot golf in the low 70s and got his master's degree in political philosophy.

During World War II Pat served in the Air Force, stationed at Mitchel Field on Long Island. "I wasn't in any fighting," he said, "but that cross-town traffic was a bitch. I had responsibilities, though. I was the driving range officer. I straightened out a couple of generals. They were slicing. My war record wasn't very distinguished, but we won anyway, so it turned out all right."

After the war he got married, sired two sons named Pat and Mike, and got a job selling TV time at NBC. "At least I was selling time and not doing it," he said. "I was called a junior executive sales trainee. That meant I was to watch the salesmen and learn what not to do."

It was at NBC that Pat fell in with Lynn Phillips, also an incurable practical joker, and their union boded ill for the more normal members of the TV industry. One day at the Lambs Club they encountered an obscure unemployed actor who bore a striking resemblance to General David Sarnoff, the dignified Board Chairman of RCA, the parent company of NBC. "We enlisted him in a practical joke," Pat said. "We took him to Brooks and got him dressed up in the ultra-conservative style of General Sarnoff. The resemblance was amazing. Then we told him what to do. The next morning he sprang the joke. The sales department at NBC has a long corridor, with about twenty offices opening on it. Each salesman has an office and outside is a secretary's desk with a lamp. It looks like the lamp section at Gimbel's. I was in one of these offices. Just at ten-thirty that morning, when we were to gather for our regular daily sales meeting, this actor strolled in. He looked so much like General Sarnoff it scared me.

"He didn't say a word . . . just bowed politely to the secretaries and began walking through the department as if he were inspecting it. The top sales executives began popping out of their offices as if they were drawn by suction. General Sarnoff probably hadn't been in the sales department for years, if ever, and most of the salesmen had never seen him in person. You could hear a buzz preceding this actor as he strolled along, as the word was passed that it was General Sarnoff. Finally he got to my office, which was one of the last ones on the long corridor. He stopped and said, 'Young man, what's your name?' 'Pat Harrington, Jr.,' I said, very politely. 'What do you do?' he asked. 'I sell TV programs,' I told him. 'How are sales?' he asked. I leaned back in my chair and said, 'General, you just look out for the research, and I'll look after the sales!' He just bowed and went out."

For some strange reason, it was not long after this that Pat left NBC. He received an offer from a local New York station. Armed with the offer he went in to see his boss and tell him he wanted to leave the network by August 15th. After the meeting he met Lynn Phillips and told him his resignation had been accepted.

"Didn't they even make a counter-offer?" Phillips asked.

"Well, sort of," Pat said. "They said I could leave by August 1st."

After leaving NBC, Pat couldn't resist giving the network one last needle. Knowing that his former boss was attending a convention at Greenbrier and had the presidential suite there, he telephoned him, speaking in a thick Southern accent.

"This is Clem Clemons in Jim Hagerty's office," he announced. "Ah understand you all have the presidential suite at Greenbrier next week."

The puzzled executive acknowledged that this was true.

"Ah'm afraid there's been some misunderstandin'," the fake Clemons said. "Mistah Eisenhowa is goin' to be at Greenbrier at that time and we thought we had the suite reserved."

"It must be a mistake, all right," the network man agreed. "I'll be glad to give up the suite for the President."

"Not at all, not at all," Pat protested. "That's not Ike's way. But would you be willin' to share the suite with him?"

The fascinated executive protested mildly that he wouldn't want to bother the President.

"No bothaw at all," Pat said, genially. "Matta of fact, the President loves company. He has a little indoor puttin' green and would jest love to have someone to play with. Do you play golf?"

The executive enthusiastically admitted that he shot a pretty good game.

"Fahn, fahn," boomed Pat. "Do you all sleep with one or two blankets?"

"Do you mean we'll be sleeping in the same bed together?" the network executive asked weakly.

"Awv cawse," said Pat. "There's only one bed and Ike wouldn't discommode you all faw the world. He'd just want to make sho yow wife wouldn't mind eitha."

There was a strangled sound at the other end of the wire that told Pat his victim had realized he was the victim of a large practical joke.

"I think the part about his wife gave the gag away," Pat said. "He was swallowing it until then, but when I asked about his wife he figured someone was pulling his leg and it must be me."

Clem Clemons, like Guido Panzini, is another in Pat's gallery of characters with which he has been amusing himself and ribbing other people for years. Another is Charley Wedebush, a profane and unreconstructed mythical station owner from Fuller's Foot, Arkansas. "Mah station is WORT-TV," he says. "We gotta towah built by U.S. Steel. Knocks that signal out seven city blocks. In one direction that is. Only about two blocks in the other direction. That's uphill."

Pat has another character he uses in his elaborate ribbing. This one he calls Harry Walikonis, and he's an aggressive, roughhewn retailer. Once Phillips put Pat up to telephoning Polly Hornburg, a fashion designer whose smart clothes are sold in the most exclusive shops.

"Well, baby, I understand you want to branch out," boomed Pat in the rugged accents of Harry Walikonis. "What kind of junk do you make? I've got fifteen hundred outlets in eastern Pennsylvania."

The elegant Miss Hornburg asked coolly what kind of outlets he had.

"Whatta ya mean, what kinda outlets do I have," he blustered. "What do yuh think I am . . . a name dropper or somethin'? I got Bonwit's Bargain Exchange, Heimindinger's Hi-Class Specialties, Bergdorf's Hardware, and Swartz's Fashions and Fuel . . . all the classy joints. Listen, baby, I can get your junk into the three-inch nail bins. Treat me right and I'll get your publicity into the John L. Lewis Newsletter. And don't fergit, sister, I've got fifteen hundred outlets. I'll get you shelf barkers, store streamers, island displays, gondolas, syndicated and static bins and quick-seller checkup sheets for your impulse items, all in vivid two-tone color. Black and white. We'll move that junk of yours, honey. Please remember this, and don't you forget it."

This telephonic encounter with the bogus go-getter left Miss Hornburg somewhat unstrung. Phillips called her later to see if she had caught onto the joke. "How did you like my friend?" he inquired.

"He used an awful lot of four-letter words," the designer said.

"I hope you didn't insult him," Phillips said, tongue in cheek. "Don't forget, he has fifteen hundred outlets in eastern Pennsylvania."

"Yes," said Miss Hornburg wearily. "He mentioned that several times."

Now this sort of ribbing, which Pat did for fun for years, is getting him not only laughs but money on big television shows. However, his habit of assuming fictional characters backfired on him on one occasion.

Shortly after his Guido Panzini characterization had made a big hit, he was walking across 44th Street in New York when a policeman advanced on him with a big smile and asked: "What's your name?"

"My name is Pat Harrington, Jr.," Pat grinned, "but I know what you're thinking. Here, I'll give you my autograph."

With that he wrote, "All the best, Guido Panzini," and handed it to the cop.

"Don't give me any aliases," the cop growled. "I wancher real name. You're gettin' a summons for jaywalkin'."

20. THE MOST UNFORGIVABLE CHARACTER I'VE MET

OSCAR LEVANT, a devout hypochondriac who has carried on a lifelong romance with himself, has probably gotten more mileage out of being miserable than anyone since Job. Although he was a brilliant concert pianist, he is probably better known for his barbed wit and the number and variety of his ailments. It was Sigmund Freud who pioneered the exploration of the troubled mind, but it remained for Oscar to introduce the do-it-yourself system to psychiatry and to make neurosis as well known to the masses as measles, and much more popular.

Levant dislikes so many things it is difficult to remember them all, but unfortunately he has a retentive memory. He has parlayed a good memory and a bad disposition into fame. At a time when striving for togetherness is a national trend, Oscar is the leading apostle of apartness. He hates flowers, telephones, the number 13, the city of Pittsburgh, fresh air, barbers, hummingbirds, Disneyland, cheerfulness and exercise. "My only exercise," he told me, "is groveling, brooding and mulling." He also dislikes practically all people, including me. One of the few people he admires is Oscar, although he concedes his devotion to himself is not widely shared. "There are two schools of thought about me," he admits. "People either dislike me or hate me."

All of the foregoing may not be ideal qualifications for

a Scoutmaster or a member of Moral Rearmament, but they make for a sprightly television guest which Oscar was on our show when we did it from Hollywood. I had hardly checked into a hotel in Beverly Hills when a phone rang and it was Oscar. "I never talk on the phone," he said in a querulous, high-pitched voice. "If you want me on your show you'll have to come see me. I can't stand telephones."

"But you called *me*," I protested.

"I know, but I hate telephones," he complained. "You'll have to come see me."

Ordinarily I don't meet ahead of time with people who are going to appear on the show, but it was obvious that in Oscar's case it would be a wise precaution, as with him living is just a sideline. All his life he has been fighting off a case of wellness. My visit with him turned out to be a two-hour discourse by Oscar on himself. It was like going to the zoo in mating season, and having only one animal turn up.

I agreed to meet him at his home in Beverly Hills. Oscar and his attractive wife, June, a frequent and unabashed sparring partner, live in a ten-room Spanish-style house on a fashionable street. The house, like Oscar, gives the air of falling apart, although not as ostentatiously as its owner.

When I rang the bell the door opened slightly and a maid asked nervously who I was. I said I was Jack Paar and that I had an appointment with Mr. Levant. She looked at me suspiciously, let me in and then locked the door and put up a heavy chain. From upstairs I heard Oscar shriek: "Who's down there?"

"It's Mr. Paar," the maid squeaked in fright.

"Who let him in?" Oscar demanded. "I want nobody in this house but the family."

He then shuffled in, shook hands limply, bared his teeth in a wolfish grin and collapsed into a chair which was also collapsing. "I've lost my voice," he gloomed, "and my memory is completely gone." He then proceeded to remember everything he'd done for the past thirty years. He also remembered to tell it all to me.

"I'm in the middle of a terrible emotional breakdown," he said. "It's my fifth in two years."

Although I had been warned of the precarious state of Oscar's health, I began to wonder whether Blue Cross would cover us if he collapsed on the show. "I may have a heart attack at any moment," he confided, clutching his side. As he rambled on it was plain to see that Oscar's pessimistic diagnosis of his health was not exaggerated. He slumped in his chair like a deflated balloon, his rumpled blue suit hanging loosely on his sagging figure, his sallow, moody features giving him the appearance of a dissipated satyr. His full lips looked as if they might have developed from kissing the mirror. "I'm an epic in bloat," he remarked. Although I myself feel I have achieved certain heights in the field of self-disparagement, Oscar made me feel as positive as Norman Vincent Peale. "Ralph Edwards wanted to have me on 'This Is Your Life,'" he said, "but he couldn't find a single friend of mine."

Oscar puffed gloomily on cigarettes or gulped cups of black coffee of which he drinks about sixty a day. "I tried drinking liquor once," he said. "I drank steadily for an entire year but it didn't take." He prefers sleeping pills, which he devours like popcorn.

Pacing nervously around the room, Levant spoke of the old days in New York before he became famous. "I was a penthouse beachcomber," he recalled. "Everything I touched turned to pennies." During this time he lived in the apartment of George and Ira Gershwin which he calls "the Penn Station of talent." He dropped in one night and remained nearly a year. At the end of that time, after finishing dinner one evening, Oscar jumped up, blurted, "Forgive me for eating and running," and disappeared.

During this time of doldrums Oscar also stayed with George Kaufman, the playwright. After one visit Mrs. Kaufman told him, "I thought you'd be embarrassed about the servants, so I tipped them each three dollars and said it was from you."

"Why didn't you make it five?" he demanded indignantly. "I don't want them thinking I'm a cheapskate."

While Oscar held forth, his three daughters, whom he secretly adores, drifted in and out of the room. "I haven't spoken to my three children in weeks," he declared. "Have I?" he demanded of one of the girls. "Whatever you say, Daddy," she smiled sweetly. "It gives them good reason to hate me," he sneered. "It's very therapeutic."

Oscar's lengthy discourse convinced me that his awesome reputation as a tireless talker was well earned. "A conversation with Oscar," Leo Durocher had said, "is like trying to argue with four umpires at once." Once Aaron Copland, the composer, after listening to Levant for hours, got up to leave. "Why, Aaron," Oscar cried in dismay. "You're developing into an egomaniac. You used to be able to listen to me all night." Another time, after Oscar had harangued for an hour, Paul Stewart, the actor, told a brief anecdote. "If there's anything I can't stand," Oscar said, as he strode out, "it's a monologuist."

Oscar's reminiscences to me were the longest sustained vocal display since Fidel Castro's last fireside chat. His wife June slipped in occasionally to refuel our coffee cups. She, like Oscar, has her own local TV show in Los Angeles. "We're the only couple with His and Her TV shows," she said proudly.

Years of listening to Oscar have wrought a considerable metamorphosis in his wife. "The first five years I was married to Oscar I never opened my mouth," she said. "The next five years I tried to break through. Now they can't shut me up."

Although Oscar is a fearsome talker, he sometimes lapses into unaccountable silences on his show. One night, after he had played a number on the piano, his guest, pugilist Art Aragon, was brought on. Oscar slumped in his chair and seemed to fall asleep. "Dear, your guest is here," June said quietly. Oscar sighed and his raccoonlike eyes remained closed. "Wake me up when he leaves," he mumbled.

The Levant marriage has been a stormy one and both nuptial partners have used their respective TV shows to air their domestic difficulties. On one program Oscar accused June of breaking his rib. "She hit me with a shoe," he charged.

"I didn't hit him," June retorted on her show. "I just gave him a little push. He's a hypochondriac anyway. He's gotten too big for one woman. I have decided to give him to the world."

After Oscar had talked for hours, I was still trying to say a few words about what I thought we should talk about on the program. My frustrated efforts to penetrate Oscar's sound barrier reminded me of the occasion when George Solotaire, the ticket broker, sat with Levant at Toots Shor's and then left to join a friend at another table.

"What were you and Oscar talking about?" the friend asked Solotaire. "You don't talk with Oscar," Solotaire said. "You just punctuate him with grunts."

Oscar's admiration for himself is equaled only by his dislike for other people, and he revels in insult.

"I'm the verbal vampire of television," he told his friend Maurice Zolotow. Groucho Marx, another master of the insult, has refused to go on Levant's show. "I understand Groucho's hesitance," Oscar says. "I once refused to go with George Bernard Shaw for the same reason."

Oscar was at his most insulting when he finally appeared on our show. He shuffled on stage, sat down like an accordion inhaling and began aiming jibes at everyone in sight including me. "I'd like to welcome you tonight," he announced, "on behalf of the mentally deranged of Southern California and the out-patients of all the mental hygiene clinics." He then declared that he was a graduate of several of these institutions. "One of these nights," he promised, "I'm going to come in white tie and strait jacket." I noticed that his hands were trembling. "What is this?" he growled. "And I'm supposed to do surgery."

As he talked Oscar clutched his heart, gulped coffee and complained about the world in general, particularly people. "I'm like Ike," he said. "Once I make up my mind I'm full of indecision." He poked fun at Eddie Fisher marrying Elizabeth Taylor. "How high can you stoop?" he asked.

Oscar seemed to take particular glee in insulting people from our show. "I took Elsa Maxwell to a masquerade party once," he said, "and when I tore off her mask I found I'd beheaded her." He declared that Zsa Zsa Gabor had "discovered the secret of perpetual middle age" and that she was "doing social work among the very rich." I reminded Oscar that Zsa Zsa had said that Oscar was brilliant but that "there is a fine line between genius and insanity." "I've managed to overcome that fine line," he growled.

I mentioned Dinah Shore, who is renowned for her wholesome sweetness.

"I never watch her," Oscar said. "Doctor's orders."

"Doctor's orders?" I echoed, thinking warily of his hypochondria.

"Yeah," he fanged. "I'm too diabetic."

He also told of the time he and his wife were guests at a large formal dinner at the White House. As they were saying good night to President and Mrs. Truman, Oscar turned to June and said in a resigned voice, "Now we have to have *them* over to dinner."

Oscar also needled me about what he called my air of humility.

"I'm no more humble," I replied, "than my talents require."

At one point I called him "dear friend." Then, remembering his aversion to friendship, I added: "Does that offend you?"

"You're getting close," he said.

Despite the verbal carnage wreaked by Oscar, critics hailed his appearance on the show as one of the highlights of the year and I invited him back for a return bout.

Because of his aversion to the telephone, he came to see me in my suite at the Beverly Hilton and found me watching his local TV show which he had taped earlier. "How can you watch it?" he demanded. "I can't stand it. Turn it off. I feel ill."

He slumped in a chair while I plied him with coffee and sympathy and he continued to demand noisily that I turn off his program. Suddenly I discovered why. While I sympathetically poured coffee for the live Oscar, the taped Oscar on my TV screen was insulting me!

The next day he called and said he would be unable to come on the show unless I would send him some sleeping pills. "My wife won't give me any," he whispered. Accordingly, I dispatched my Operative 5 (he's named after one of my old Neilsen ratings) with two Nembutal tablets in an envelope. He rang the bell at Oscar's house, a hand reached out and snatched the envelope, and the door slammed.

My emissary had scarcely returned and explained this to me than the phone rang. It was Oscar. "Your friend didn't come in the house," he complained. "We have an old gypsy tradition at our house that no one is ever turned away at the threshold. He must come back."

I sent the confused operative back to comply with the hospitality of Oscar's old gypsy tradition. Oscar greeted him quietly and led him into the living room. "Now you have crossed the threshold," Levant said, grandly. "It's been a pleasure. Good-by."

21. THE AMBASSADOR OF GRAND FENWICK

When I first arrived in Hollywood, a refugee from the jungles of the South Pacific, I was feeling the effects of being away from civilization too long. Finding myself suddenly and unaccountably under contract to a film studio, I became momentarily dazzled by the doings of movie stars. Every morning I would snatch the newspapers and turn anxiously to the movie columns to peruse the fascinating activities of the movie colony as chronicled by Louella Parsons, Hedda Hopper, *Variety* and other repositories of such trivia. I wonder, I would say to myself as I feverishly opened the paper, what Veronica Lake has done *now?* Being particularly interested in humor, I read with awe and envy the gay bon mots and merry quips tossed off at Ciro's, the Mocambo and other such gathering places by such finished *bon vivants* as Johnny Weissmuller, Greer Garson, Turhan Bey, Darryl Zanuck, Jennifer Jones, Gene Autry, Betty Grable and Broderick Crawford. The flash of wit at these gay soirees sounded more blinding than the glare of jewelry on the ladies there, and I longed to sometime attend one and hear for myself the gems of humor that fell from the lips of the filmland luminaries. Little did I know.

In a burst of naïveté I dashed off a few nifties of my own and innocently sent them to *Variety* and the *Hollywood Reporter*, two publications read more faithfully in Hollywood than the Koran is in Mecca. I then sat back to see my quips immortalized in print. In a moment of confidence, I told a friend of mine what I had done.

"That's terrible," he said. "You don't understand. That just isn't done."

"But I see jokes by other people in the columns," I protested. "They all seem to say them in night clubs. But I never go to night clubs, so I mailed mine in."

"A lot of them never go to night clubs either," my friend replied. "Most of them never even said those things. Their press agents make up those jokes, or steal them somewhere, and send them to the columns attributed to their clients. That keeps their clients' names before the producers and the studios, and makes them sound smart. If you're going to be an actor here, you'd better get yourself a press agent."

Since I was languishing in utter anonymity at RKO at the time, I accepted this counsel and secured myself a press agent. I'll call him Jack Needleman, as I understand the courts are quite crowded and I don't want to add to the jam. I outfitted Needleman with a fresh supply of my finest jokes with which to ply the columnists. Then I sat anxiously back to await the results. I could see my latest quip being bandied about on the lips of big producers as they gathered in the studio commissaries to complain about their income taxes.

Soon my jokes began to appear in the columns, but not my name. They seemed to have gotten scrambled on Needleman's desk, and began to bob up in the column attributed to his other clients. I would fume as I picked up Louella Parsons's column and read: "All Hollywood Is Talking About: Pinky Lee's joke about the longshoreman who was such a sissy he would only unload ribbon." Or I would spot in Earl Wilson's column: "Wish I'd Said That: 'Sonny Tufts says that in the Squibb Building they don't have elevators. They just squeeze you to the top.'" After this happened several times, I phoned Needleman to register a protest.

"I see my jokes in the paper, all right," I complained, "but they're all attributed to your other clients."

"Don't worry, baby," Needleman soothed me. "Those things

happen with columnists. Sometimes they switch the names on the jokes around. It will all straighten out in a day or two, kid."

Reassured, I continued to pore through the columns, waiting for my jokes to appear and alert Hollywood to what a debonair wit it had in its midst, hiding under a cloak of anonymity at RKO. Then it happened! I picked up *Variety* and read: "Jack Needleman says police raided a Hollywood restaurant where alphabet soup was being served with vulgar words. The suspects didn't have a chance to stir away the evidence."

It was *my* joke. And my press agent. Such was my introduction to press agents. It was also my farewell. I've never had one since. However, I've met some with magnificent imaginations.

In the fall of 1959, as Washington social circles prepared for a busy season, Embassy Row buzzed with a lively bit of news. A new embassy was opening, representing the Duchy of Grand Fenwick. Following this formal announcement in the capital's newspapers, the National Geographic Society received several calls from other embassies, asking for details on Grand Fenwick. The callers confessed ignorance as to the facts about the duchy, but added apologetically that it was difficult to keep up with things with so many small new nations being formed.

The mystery over Grand Fenwick was explained a few days later with the formal announcement that an ambassador had been appointed to represent the duchy. "In the first major step in cementing the newly established relations between her small country and the United States," the engraved announcement read, "H. R. H. the Grand Duchess, Gloriana XII, ruler of the Duchy of Grand Fenwick, has appointed His Excellency Viscount James Sterling Moran as her first Ambassador to this country." In her formal message announcing the Viscount's appointment, Gloriana XII paid tribute to his "years of unselfish devotion to the Fenwickian cause." "As an American of Fenwickian descent," Her Highness said, "the new Ambassador combines the courtliness which has long been the mark of the Fenwicks with the energetic zeal of his Virginia forbears."

The grand duchess's announcement reached me in Florida where I was taking my ease at the beautiful Key Biscayne Hotel. I was momentarily baffled by this intoxicating breath from the heady Washington diplomatic scene to which I am, to put it mildly, a stranger. Then it came to me. Between the lines of the engraved announcement, I recognized His Excellency, Viscount James Sterling Moran, as none other than Jim Moran, the large, pink-bearded press agent who has spent a merry lifetime spoofing the citizenry for excitement and profit. It was quite a start, I must confess, to learn that ambassadorial rank had been conferred upon the man who first gained fame by finding a needle in a haystack, selling a refrigerator to an Eskimo and hatching an ostrich egg by sitting on it for seventeen days in Hollywood. What, I wondered, was he up to this time?

Whatever it was, Jim was doing it up with his customary aplomb. The newspapers began to sprout stories of the doings of the new diplomatic figure. He opened the Fenkwickian embassy in the Shoreham Hotel, the duchy's flag fluttering proudly above the swank hostelry. He paid formal respects to the eighty-three other ambassadors in the capital, and had tea with the dean of the diplomatic corps, Ambassador Sevilla Sacasa of Nicaragua. He was at the airport with a band playing the national anthem of Grand Fenwick to greet Alida, the Marquise of Navarone, lady in waiting to Gloriana XII, when she arrived in Washington. Together with the beautiful marquise, he cut a wide swath through capital social circles, a commanding figure in powder-blue uniform with silver trimming and a broad silver sash. He also was host to a dinner attended by Mrs. Gwen Cafritz, noted capital hostess, movie czar Eric Johnston, and a large slice of official and social Washington.

Jim's sudden social and diplomatic triumph, I was relieved

to learn, did not go to his head. "I hasten to write to you," he said in a note on gold-crested ambassadorial stationery, "lest you get the mistaken impression that my sudden ascension to high rank might have a tendency to separate me socially from an old friend. Although I am now known by my formal title of viscount, you may still address me as Jim, the democratic diminutive of my given name."

While just plain Jim was thus reassuring me of his democratic instincts, he began encountering a note of skepticism on the Washington scene. This note of doubt crept into proceedings at a press conference where he received the capital press corps attired in a uniform of white with gold piping, and a gold medal of office around his neck.

"Grand Fenwick has an area of fifteen and three-quarters square miles," he told the press, "and is totally inaccessible. The population is six thousand and forty-four, or six thousand and forty-two with the marquise and me both here."

"What does the marquise have to do with Grand Fenwick?" a reporter asked.

"The marquise was orphaned in childhood when her parents were killed on a tiger hunt," Moran explained. "The hunt," he added gravely, "also marked the demise of Count Leopold of Bosnia-Herzegovina, consort of the ruler of Grand Fenwick."

"Where is Gloriana XII?" a newsman asked. "I thought she was supposed to be here?"

"She is, unfortunately, indisposed," the ambassador replied. "However, she has asked that her regards be extended to your President. Also to Mrs. Coolidge."

Although the viscount had a ready answer for all the reporters' questions, it soon became plain that the U. S. government did not plan to recognize Grand Fenwick and, in fact, was about to declare its emissary *persona non grata.*

"A man from the government called and asked me where Grand Fenwick was," Moran told me. "I told him it was in the French Alps, bordering France, Switzerland, Italy, Germany and Poland."

"Poland!" the man echoed.

"Of course," Jim replied, blandly. "Even the United States is not in one piece, is it? With the inclusion of Hawaii, it now extends several thousand miles into the Pacific."

In the face of this logic, the government man hung up. However, Jim decided he had carried his elaborate masquerade far enough, and hastily departed the capital diplomatic scene.

"What was all that hanky-panky about?" I asked when I next encountered the unfrocked ambassador, still attired in a dark-blue uniform with gold epaulets, which contrasted strikingly with his electric-blue eyes and pink beard.

"I admit that Grand Fenwick is a mythical country," he conceded, "but I am a real ambassador." Jim confessed that his ambassadorial tenure was a scheme to promote a motion picture called *The Mouse That Roared,* about a tiny country which declared war on the United States so it could be defeated and receive the benefits of a country conquered by Americans.

"You certainly look the part of an ambassador," I said, eying his gaudy uniform.

"Of course," he agreed. "Everything was done with the utmost care. We had our own stamps printed, and our own flag and national anthem. We made our own diplomatic license plates. These epaulets are from the court of Franz Josef of Austria-Hungary. I even had especially designed ambassadorial underwear. These may seem like details, but they had the psychological effect of making me feel like a real ambassador."

I observed that he was wearing so many medals he was in danger of getting stoop-shouldered.

"This one is for listening," he said, displaying a gold decoration. "It's the hardest to come by. If you've ever listened to the conversation at a Washington cocktail party, you'd know what I mean. These others are for finger painting, flower arranging, game fishing with a cork float and lute playing. The lute, as you undoubtedly know, is Grand Fenwick's national instrument."

Jim Moran has been ribbing people, including me, for years, and making a handsome living at it. Although his formal calling is press agentry, he is one of the most imaginative and versatile men I've ever met. He has a thriving public relations firm on New York's Madison Avenue, but refuses to go near it. His expansive schemes are dreamed up while reclining in bed in his large Manhattan apartment, sometimes reaching out to whirl a Hindu prayer wheel. He has written a book, entitled *Miserable,* about a dinosaur. He is a student of animal life. He plays the classical guitar, and has played Bach and Chopin on our show. He has composed a song called "George Washington Bridge" which consists of 289 verses, all identical. "I started with a lot of verses," he recalled, "but when I cut away the verbal fat there was only one left. I liked it so much, though, that I used it over and over again." Jim once sang his song on our show. Although there was a slight sense of monotony, hearing the phrase "George Washington Bridge" repeated 289 times, more than five thousand people wrote in when he offered free copies. This seems to me to indicate either that Jim's song has an appeal not readily apparent from listening to it, or that George Washington is more revered than we realize.

Jim is also an accomplished inventor. One of his latest inventions is the "belly buzzer." This boon to the obese consists of an elastic belt with a bell attached. "If the wearer relaxes his abdominal muscles," he explains, "the resultant sag rings the bell, reminding him to draw his stomach in."

Jim has strong opinions on the dominance of mind over matter. One night he expounded to me that it is possible to concentrate on a simple piece of matter, such as water, and by the intensity of mental vibrations to agitate the molecules in the water to such an extent that it comes to a boil.

"Okay. Let's try it," I said to him. "I've got a glass of water right here."

Jim fixed the glass of water with a gaze as piercing as a three-time loser at Alcoholics Anonymous staring at a double martini. Nothing happened and I sensed the audience getting restive.

"Hurry up," I suggested.

"How can I bring this water to a boil," he demanded, "if you keep interrupting my concentration?"

"Since we only have an hour and three-quarters on this show I think we'd better conclude this experiment later," I finally said. "Just tell me this: did you ever get water to boil by concentrating on it?"

"I never quite got it to a boil," he admitted, "but I did get it up to room temperature."

There is always a method in Jim's seeming madness, and it's a lively game, when he comes on the show with some outlandish new scheme, to figure out where in the enterprise the commercial tie-up is buried. No matter how seemingly innocent and funny the undertaking may be, with Jim you can be sure there's a gimmick hidden away some place in the scheme, and that he is being handsomely rewarded for his fertile flight of imagination. One night he announced he was setting out on a nationwide search to find the "happiest girl in America." He described in detail his plans for the great search.

"But why do you want to find the happiest girl in America?" I asked, walking into his trap.

"We want to find her," he beamed, "because she'll be happy as a lark." (Thus revealing that the Moran client, in this instance, was the Studebaker Lark automobile.)

He departed on his search, getting interviews galore around the country about his quest, and always managing to get the name of the Lark into the story somewhere. He met his comeuppance in Minneapolis, however, when the *Tribune* ran this story about him:

"Jim Moran is a world-renowned rambler. In his many travels as a press agent, he has been known to ford a river or brave localities where the mercury knows no bounds in order to plant a sponsor's name. Moran is well known in Cadillac and Pontiac, Mich. On the other hand, he has never been in Buyck or Austin, Minn. He has pulled many a dodge, but in general he is known in the trade as being solid as Plymouth Rock. Moran has a beard like Lincoln that gives people the willies. He is built in somewhat Goliath proportions and has the eye of an explorer like DeSoto. Moran was in Minneapolis promoting a contest to find 'The Happiest Girl in America.' The winner will receive a screen test and a new automobile, the maker of which is his sponsor."

Jim is an avid kite flier. "There is something psychologically quite wonderful," he says, "to be hooked to something flying in the air. It must be primal. Alexander Graham Bell wrote a great deal about kites. Franklin flew them, of course. Kite flying is very popular with old and young in the Orient."

Some years ago, while delving into kite lore, Moran made the acquaintance of the man in charge of the wind tunnel at Langley Field, Virginia. Working with the expert on aerodynamics, he developed a 100-square-foot kite that could carry up to 125 pounds. Armed with this unique secret, he set to brooding about some commercial application which would fit the usual Moran pattern of affording him not only fun but money.

"One day it hit me," he recalls. "I would send midgets aloft, bearing advertising slogans. I would fly the kites from Central Park and maneuver the air-borne midgets past the upper stories of the fashionable hotels fronting on the park. Although the audience we would reach with such an advertising campaign would, of course, not be large, it would be an exclusive one. Such a campaign would not only be good business but a boon to midgets, who suffer from spotty employment opportunities. It would insure midgets working on windy days. I called my plan the 'Midget Employment Stabilization Board.' My objective was eventually to get all midgets aloft on windy days."

Despite its laudable aim, Moran's midget-launching program encountered technical difficulties.

"I got three midgets and had them insured by Lloyd's of London," Jim said. "Then I began my experiments in New Jersey. I had ten men to a kite—thirty in all in my ground crew. We got the midgets up to fifty feet in our first trials. However, they began to spin in the wind, and a spinning midget is an unhappy midget."

Like the Wright brothers before him, Moran refused to be daunted by such technical problems. He equipped his diminutive kite pilots with rudders, strapped to their waists, which eliminated their tendency to spin in a stiff breeze.

"Finally came the big day," Jim said. "My ground crew and I deployed in Central Park near a baseball diamond where a game was in progress. The outlook for a successful launching was excellent. Visibility was good and there was a brisk wind from the northwest—splendid midget-launching conditions. I equipped each of my midgets with a sign advertising the merits of a fine product. The ground crew was in readiness around the launching platform, and I was about to begin the countdown. Suddenly the police swept down and halted me."

"Whatta you think you're doin'?" a policeman demanded of Moran.

"I am engaged in an advertising campaign," Jim answered with dignity, "which happens to involve the flying of these midgets by kite."

"Well, you can't fly no midgets by kites here," the cop replied.

Jim, however, was prepared for just such official opposition.

"Could you show me," he said firmly, "where there is any law in the statute books which prohibits flying midgets from kites in Central Park?"

The cop looked frustrated for a moment, but he too was equal to the challenge.

"Maybe there's no law against flyin' midgets," he conceded, "but what if one of them midgets falls and hits a baseball player. Droppin' a midget on a baseball player could be manslaughter."

That was the end of Jim's "Midget Employment Stabilization Board." Once more the altruistic plans of the visionary had been stifled by bureaucratic red tape.

The last time I saw Jim he was heading for Africa for a safari. Once before he had journeyed to the Dark Continent on one of his schemes. A fraternal club in this country had disbanded leaving unclaimed ten thousand handsome blue satin and velvet tunics ordered for ceremonials. Jim picked up the surplus cloaks at a bargain and headed for Africa with visions of selling his gaudy robes to the natives at a handsome profit. However, although he had been able to sell a refrigerator to an Eskimo, the wily Africans spurned Jim and his ceremonial robes. He is still trying to unload them, although he says he has given up on Africa as a sales territory. "This time I'm just going over for fun," he told me. "I have no commercial plans afoot for this trip."

That will be the day.

22.

THE UNHAPPY MEDIUM

In my Radio City office, a cozy hideaway between a broom closet and a ladies' powder room, is a sign which says: GOD NEVER MEANT FOR PICTURES TO BE SENT THROUGH THE AIR. There are times when I'm inclined to agree.

One night we had a joke on our show. A small boy, so the joke went, was watching "Meet the Press." He turned to his father and said: "This is a terrible quiz show. Everyone knows the answers." The audience chuckled appreciatively. Shortly afterwards that joke came true. On some quiz shows, it developed, everyone *did* know the answers. The joke was on the public.

Suddenly revelations of all sorts of shenanigans came tumbling out. The box with the 21-inch screen, it turned out, held more surprises than Pandora's fabled box. In no time the viewing public was rump-deep in confessions and disillusion. So many things on TV, it developed, were not what they seemed. That attractive contestant, sweating out the questions in an isolation booth, had been given the answers and coached in registering anguish. The bank vault, which sounded so honest and secure, had more keys than Phi Beta Kappa. The beautiful white icing, which looked so inviting on the cake commercial, was actually lather shave. The rock 'n' roll songs, assaulting our ears, were being played because the disk jockeys were getting payola bribes from record companies to play them. Where, the public asked itself, would it all end? If Charles Van Doren was rigged, how about Mamie Van Doren, the busty blonde actress? Were her ample curves all that met the eye, or had she too been fixed? What could anyone believe any more? Surveying the damage, a friend of mine summed it up by saying: "Television is not a happy medium."

The scandal set off by the disclosure that some quiz shows were fixed had world-wide repercussions. President Eisenhower deplored the situation. Moscow chuckled at our discomfort and called it all typical capitalist skulduggery. Clergymen thundered from the pulpits. Newspapers pointed with alarm. Critics called for Pay TV or a TV Czar. Television hastily set about cleaning its own house. NBC set up its own policing system. CBS dropped the big money quizzes. ABC, which had few quizzes but many Westerns, pondered giving saliva tests to prove its horses weren't doped. The people mostly just wondered how long all this had been going on, and how it could happen. How did it all get started?

As someone who was on the scene when the bomb went off, I think I can shed some light and considerable heat on the situation. For a time I thought I might be called to Washington to testify. After all, when I first started in radio I'd been a disk jockey. I served time on three national quiz shows. And I've probably done more commercials than anyone alive. Also, I have TV's most unrigged show. Not only do guests not know the answers; I don't know the questions!

However, since the Congressmen didn't see fit to call me as a witness, I'll tell all I know in this book. That way I'll not only save railroad fare to Washington, but maybe we can sell a few copies of the book to Congress as evidence.

Actually, my revelations aren't as hot as they might be. The trouble with my disclosures is that I'd been making them publicly long before Congress got into the act. For years on my various shows I'd made fun of quiz shows, ridiculed commercials, including many of my own, and generally kept my lawyers in a state of uneasiness bordering on panic with my remarks about the falsity of some aspects of TV. I not only bit the hand that fed me, but at times gnawed it up so high that a couple of my sponsors looked like the Venus di Milo.

"The international situation is getting calmer," I said several years ago. "Servicemen are beginning to lose again on quiz shows." In addition to giving the verbal hot foot to TV's hanky-panky on my shows, I put it in writing months before the quiz scandal reached full flower. In *Look* magazine of July 21, 1959, I wrote: "So much of what you see on television is phony. Announcers sing the praises of products they wouldn't have in the house. What seems to be a joke on a comedy show is often a plug for some product, with the writers paid off with a case of whiskey. That sweet little old lady who is an expert on paleontology may turn up on another show as an authority on Chaucer."

Months earlier I had written in a guest column for the Hearst papers: "The plugger is a guy I shy away from like the plague. He's got an ax to grind and if he grinds it he gets to keep the ax. It seems incredible a big name in show business would sell that name for a case of Scotch. This, perhaps, is a point of no consequence to the viewer. To me and my staff it's a question of honor, unlike the previous "Tonight" show where the payoff was a way of life nightly."

Having been in television since the days when it consisted mostly of puppets and wrestlers, I have been in a position to observe at first hand its faults and foibles, and have always honestly reported what I saw. Although I never liked quiz shows, and rarely missed an opportunity to say so even on the shows, I did a stretch on three of them. In 1950 I replaced Eddie Cantor on radio as emcee of "Take It or Leave It"—the predecessor of the rigged "$64,000 Question." The following year I did an NBC-TV quiz called "Up to Paar." Lastly I emceed "Bank on the Stars" on CBS-TV in 1953—a quiz featuring scenes from motion pictures.

These were all shows with modest budgets and the temptation to larceny was negligible. On "Up to Paar" the contestants got to scoop out of a barrel all the silver dollars they could carry. However, to temper their enthusiasm, I always told them we'd put a few fishhooks in with the silver dollars. On "Take It or Leave It" the top prize was $64. There was some reckless talk, before I took it over, of upping the top prize to $640. However, cooler heads prevailed and this spendthrift notion was vetoed. Devoid of big money prizes, quiz shows were pretty anemic fare.

Some time before I began handing out $64 prizes, "Stop the Music" burst on the radio air waves with Bert Parks dispensing noise, automobiles, mink coats, houses and trips to Paris. People had never heard of prizes of such value, and the show became a national sensation overnight. Other shows began popping up on every hand, passing out trips to Rome, London and Paris. Some little old lady, who went on a quiz show trying to win enough money to visit her sister in Vermont, would suddenly find herself being whisked to Paris. All at once the air was full of little old ladies, who didn't want to go there, all bound for Paris.

My modest little quiz, whose phrase "the $64 question" had passed into the language, soon passed from the scene. It couldn't compete with the big quizzes, passing out loot with the abandon of a dying tycoon with a guilty conscience. What concerned me more, though, was that the big money quiz shows began killing off some of the few good comedy shows. "Stop the Music," for instance, quickly outrated "The Fred Allen Show." Sardonically, Fred offered his own prize of a two-week cruise on the Weehawken Ferry, 4000 yards of dental floss (nearly new), 25,000 tons of dirt delivered to the front door, and 500 pounds of putty for every member of the family. Other comedians also fought back with humor against the well-heeled quizzes. Jane Ace did a sketch in which she won a lot of money on a mythical radio quiz when she correctly identified the inventor of the steam engine by asking the emcee: "What?" However, wit proved no match for money and the Allen show and other good comedy programs disappeared.

Eventually, though, the big prize quizzes on radio also sagged as the medium itself declined in popularity in the face of television's rapid growth. As TV grew, however, the big money quiz burgeoned anew, bigger and richer than ever, in the form of the "$64,000 Question" and "Challenge" and "Twenty-One." They brought overnight fame and fortune to people like Gino Prado, the little opera-loving Italian shoemaker; Billy Pearson, the colorful jockey and art expert; shy, scholarly Charles Van Doren; Gloria Lockerman, the little Negro spelling whiz, and Dr. Joyce Brothers, the pretty boxing expert.

Then the house that jackpots built collapsed, and the big money quiz shows became dead giveaways. Many of the contestants, whose apparent knowledge had impressed millions, admitted they were given the answers. Some producers had coached more people than Stanislavski. The bank supposedly guarding the questions turned out to have so many people in its vaults there was hardly any place to put the money.

The exposure spread to other aspects of TV including commercials. Living bras, it seemed, weren't alive at all. As panic set in, television began to lean over backwards in an orgy of confession. CBS announced that "Person to Person" was rehearsed, even though two of its male guests had appeared with their trouser zippers undone—something I considered a rather strong demonstration of spontaneity. Jack Benny confessed he was not thirty-nine. He was, he publicly admitted, forty-three. Roy Rogers acknowledged that Trigger is not one but four horses. It came out that Lassie is not a lady dog, as millions had thought, but a gentleman collie. Even the public was not above reproach. "What about people," Bob Hope asked, "who eat TV dinners while listening to the radio?"

Actually, the integrity of television, as of any medium of communication, is extremely important, and its faults cannot be condoned or laughed off. I could not agree with those who pardoned the fixed quiz shows by saying that "after all they were simply entertainment and all entertainment is only make-believe." I'm sure that no one would condone fixing the World Series on the grounds that after all it is "only entertainment."

I have also had some experiences with plugs—the mention of commercial products on a show sponsored by someone else. Although a good deal of sound and fury has been generated over this practice, and it has been made to sound like a cardinal sin, actually it is something that has gone on openly for years with the knowledge and even consent of both the networks and sponsors. The schlochmeisters (Yiddish for junk-masters) who arrange these plugs are well known and even rather famous in some instances, and their machinations while sometimes dubious have never been particularly furtive. This small and harried group sprang into being in the first blush of the big prize quiz shows. The shows wanted valuable swag such as mink coats, expensive automobiles and jewelry, and the new breed of loot procurers could scrounge it up in return for mention of the manufacturer's name. Some of them threw themselves into their new calling with such abandon that some programs were soon handing out such items as oil wells, airplanes, gold mines and even entire islands! The schlochmeisters also got their clients' names used in jokes on comedy shows.

I first learned of the wondrous ways of these loot merchants when I replaced Jack Benny on radio in the summer of 1947. We used a joke which happened to include the name of a commercial product and I was surprised the next day to receive a case of whiskey. I made inquiries and learned it was the custom, if a comedian did a joke about a product, to give him or his writers a case of liquor. Sometimes it was a gift certificate, or sometimes the actual product. I knew one comedian who did so many Mixmaster jokes he almost had to move out of his house to make way for the tidal wave of Mixmasters.

As far as I know, most if not all of the leading comedians used jokes about some commercial products, and they or their writers received the traditional case of whiskey or some similar token of thanks. Commercial products, of course, have been the subject of jokes from the days of Henry Ford's "tin lizzie," which spawned hundreds of quips, to Henry Ford Jr.'s Edsel, which also was the butt of numerous sallies. The difficulty in trying to censor plugs is that the mention of one commercial product may be a genuine joke, and of another simply a plug, and there's a very fine line between them. I can see a baffled network censor puzzling over this: "Slenderella is going to sponsor a new Western. It will be called Frontier Fat." Or this: "Can a girl who takes Nytol find happiness with a man who takes NoDoz?" Are they jokes, or plugs, or both? Actually, removing commercial products as a subject of jokes would remove one more in a dwindling field of subjects which can be used as a basis of humor, and there are few enough as it is.

The best criterion as to whether a commercial product can be used in a joke is whether the joke is funny. There is nothing wrong, in my opinion, with a joke about a product, if the joke is funny. However, plugging has been abused and many plugs are done blatantly on shows without the saving grace of humor. For that reason, when I took over the "Tonight" show on NBC I declared plugs out of bounds. We have done our best to keep plugs off the show, and when guests have managed to sneak them in they have not been asked back.

Another aspect of television which has been under fire, and no wonder, is the system of ratings. This, too, is something of which I have painful firsthand knowledge. Although programs and performers live and die by the rating systems, they are, in my opinion, as reliable as a fortuneteller in a Russian tea room. By means of the confusing and often conflicting rating systems, it is possible to prove almost anything—or almost nothing. Taking a sample as small as an agent's heart, these dream merchants project audiences into the tens of millions. One service rates the relative popularity of programs seen in about fifty million homes by a poll of a thousand persons! Another polls twelve hundred persons. Although the New York area alone has some five million TV homes, rating systems poll less than one one-hundredth of one per cent for their findings on what shows people are watching in that area!

Perhaps I'm unduly sensitive about TV ratings. As I am writing this chapter, the Nielsen system, which rates 135 nighttime programs nationally, rates my show as 135th among them. Yet the show has sponsors standing in line, has won numerous awards and is frequently described as the most discussed program in television. Perhaps, as Goodman Ace once suggested, people are so crazy about the show they won't get up to answer the phone when the rating service calls.

I have one final complaint about television: the audience. Although many people write me about the poor quality of television fare, the majority go right on looking at the worst things on TV. I hear and read endless complaints about Westerns and crime shows and soap operas, yet they keep going merrily along because they draw large audiences. The majority apparently would rather watch Lawrence Welk than Laurence Olivier. In television, as in government, the people usually get what they deserve. The worst fault of television, it seems to me, is giving the people what they want. The high-quality programs rarely fare as well with audiences as the trite and shoddy. Fred Astaire's program, which was months in the making, and which was hailed as one of the TV highlights of the year, drew a smaller audience than "Gunsmoke," which was on opposite it. The filmed program of Leonard Bernstein's widely acclaimed musical mission of friendship to Moscow attracted fewer viewers than the opposing "Lone Ranger." And the "Lone Ranger" was a repeat of an old episode!

In view of this evidence of the low estate of public taste, the amazing thing to me is not that there is so much wrong with television, but that it is as good as it is. Almost everything you can think of has been shown on television, from operas to Shaw, from Shakespeare to ballet. Within a few days, while I was writing this chapter, television presented the debuts of Laurence Olivier, Ingrid Bergman and Alec Guiness, and special programs from Fred Astaire and *Our Town* to Ibsen and Beethoven's *Fidelio.* Some of these things were seen by people who would ordinarily never be exposed to them in their lifetimes. Olivier's *Richard III,* for instance, was seen on television by an estimated forty million people—more than had seen the play in the more than three hundred and fifty years since Shakespeare wrote it. There is one more thing about this. It's all free.

I have never seen a bad TV show. I have knees that bend and wrists that turn, and if I see a show that doesn't interest me I quickly turn it off. The secret word in television viewing is selectivity. Too many viewers seem to use the glue invented by George S. Kaufman for gluing people to their TV sets. "It's awkward for showering and getting in and out of cabs," he admits, "but the set is always with the user and he needn't miss a thing." Viewers should miss more, in my opinion, and they would appreciate more the really fine things available on television through discriminating viewing.

In addition to the truly fine things on television, such as the classics, the opera and symphonies, are the few remaining live programs like ours which simply seek to entertain the viewer with some sprightly conversation and spontaneous fun. Our show is nothing pretentious, but it's freshly minted every day and alive and sometimes full of surprises. The audience reaction has been gratifying. One man wrote that he gets so interested in the show he doesn't realize he's not being entertained.

23. THE AUTHOR MEETS THE CRITICS

During the quiz exposé, I expressed sympathy on the air for Charles Van Doren, the young college professor who admitted he won $129,000 on a program on which he had been given the answers.

Without minimizing his mistakes, I said it was sad he was bearing the brunt of the scandal while the producers who did the actual fixing seemed to be escaping relatively unscathed. This was based on the fact that the producers of that particular show quietly made off with a fortune in return for the dead horse they had sold NBC in the form of their fixed shows, while Van Doren was fired from his jobs by both the network and Columbia University. My remarks brought a warm response from viewers but catcalls from various newspapers.

Dave Garroway, from whose "Today" program Van Doren was fired by the network, also made a similar plea on his show for compassion for his former associate. Dave was so moved in discussing his friend that he broke down and wept. The newspapers greeted this display with gleeful skepticism, pointing out that Garroway's show was taped the previous day and that he could have edited out his breakdown on the air. If he had edited it out, of course, they could have accused him of fixing his own show and censoring his own sentiments.

The comments which Dave and I made about Van Doren

and the role of the newspapers in the quiz disclosures prompted a reply from TV columnist John Crosby who wrote a column comparing the broadcasting industry unfavorably with publishing. "In radio and television," he wrote, "stars like Garroway and Paar live under the immediate and intimate control of their advertisers. They are so accustomed to doing what they are told that it's inconceivable to them that we don't run our business that way. The newspaper tradition is freedom to observe and report the facts as they are. It's the tradition of freedom that people like Garroway and Paar can't understand because they've never had any."

I know John Crosby and he's a nice man. I admire him as a perceptive critic. I have heard that he likes dogs and children, and that he occasionally helps old ladies across the street. But he couldn't be more spectacularly wrong than in the opinions quoted above. To say that I live under the control of advertisers, and that I couldn't understand freedom because I've never had any, strikes me as the most resounding piece of misinformation I've read in a newspaper since the *Chicago Tribune* announced the election of Dewey. I've been called a variety of uncomplimentary things by critics at one time or another, some of them true, but controlled by sponsors, networks or anyone else, I'm not. John could have questioned my ancestry, impugned my morals or deprecated my talent, without my raising a dissenting voice. But when he says that I'm accustomed to doing what I'm told, those are fighting words.

Having thumbed my nose at some rather formidable forces, including the U. S. Army, I have never felt any great awe for the manufacturers of denture fasteners or jockey shorts. I've never been under the control of any advertiser or network and, in fact, have been so free as to be positively abandoned. My present show is not only not controlled; it's not even prepared. I await the day when John Crosby or any other newspaper columnist pokes public fun at his bosses as I have at William Paley of CBS or Robert Sarnoff of NBC. I won't hold my breath until some columnist chides the advertising in his own newspaper, the way I have scoffed at commercials on my own show.

I have no special brief for sponsors. They are in business to sell their wares, and some of them have not been above fudging a bit on their claims, throwing their weight around or devising commercials capable of driving viewers to the brink of madness. However, their control over program content, or over individual performers, is not very prevalent and is steadily diminishing. I've worked for a long line of sponsors, beginning with the legendary George Washington Hill, who was reported to chuck ash trays and other ammunition at his minions, and none of them exercised any control over me other than how I did their commercials, and they didn't always do that. I know this is true of many other performers, including Dave Garroway.

I must say there were a few times when advertising men tried to exercise a little control, but after a brief scuffle they always capitulated. An agency man once handed me a comedy script I didn't like and ordered me to read it to an audience. Instead I tossed it into the audience and ad libbed for ten minutes on how bad the script was. I mentioned earlier the incident at CBS where an agency man asked me to read some lipstick copy which I felt was phony and unbelievable. I refused. The sponsor quit the show, but he didn't control me. The network then asked me to mingle with agency and client people at lunch and cocktails as a means of attracting sponsors, but I refused this too. I maintained my job was to do the best show I could, and their job was to sell it. They then menaced me with the name of William Paley, Board Chairman of CBS, a name calculated to make the timid TV performer, conjured up by John Crosby, jump to attention. I merely suggested on the air that Mr. Paley try getting up at 4:00 A.M., as I was doing, and do a three-hour show every weekday morning, if he thought it was easy. That was the last I heard of the plan for me to lure sponsors over the martinis.

On my present show, which I believe has more sponsors

than any other network program in television, I have never met most of the sponsors—let alone been subject to any control by them. Our sponsors pay nine thousand dollars a minute to put their commercials on the show. They have nothing whatever to say about the program itself, and none has ever so much as offered a suggestion. Also, they often take our advice on the handling of a commercial, rather than the other way around. If something does go wrong, as it did the night that a film of Dody Goodman in a bathing suit was shown while I was extolling the wonders of Prestone Anti-Freeze, the sponsor usually accepts it with good humor. An exception was the night when things went awry on a commercial for Cooper's jockey shorts. I began reading it seriously but there was an unintentional *double entendre* in the copy and the audience began laughing. I broke up in laughter and the audience laughed harder. It was quite a shambles. That night the company canceled their contract. By Monday, when sales reports began coming in from around the country, they canceled their cancellation.

Our show isn't typical of most television shows, since we have multiple sponsorship, but even on programs with a single sponsor there is relatively little client control in most instances. There are several reasons for this. Sponsor control of program content was widespread in radio where it started because most big network radio shows were produced by advertising agencies. The heavy hand of the sponsor can be detected in the commercial flavor of the titles of many of the early radio shows: the "A & P Gypsies," "Fleischmann's Yeast Hour," the "Sal Hepatica Review," the "Clicquot Club Eskimos" and the "Hellman's Salad Bowl Review." Perusing the newspaper program listings in those days was like reading a shopping list, and much of the fare was no bargain.

With the growth of television, however, the infinitely greater cost and difficulty of producing shows, and the increase in the number of filmed-over live programs, largely shunted advertising agencies out of the role of producers. The majority of nighttime programs now are filmed shows produced by independent producers or talent agencies. What the sponsor of these shows buys is a half-hour film into which he inserts his filmed commercials. He has little or nothing to say about the entertainment content of the film. After all, how can a manufacturer of toothpaste or cigarettes control people like Matt Dillon or Peter Gunn?

I would like to add a few final words on television itself. No one, from Congress to Crosby, has ever scoffed more at the shortcomings of television than I have. Yet its many good qualities must also be acknowledged. The networks canceled millions of dollars' worth of programs to give extensive coverage to the visit of Russian Premier Khrushchev. And, although often accused of scrambling for dollars, television gave $271 million worth of free air time to charitable campaigns in 1958.

Since John Crosby and other columnists have compared broadcasting unfavorably with publishing, I would like to note a few opinions on newspapers and magazines.

In a long association with publications, from furtively reading *Ballyhoo* as a youth to being on the cover of *Time,* I've noticed that magazines and newspapers also have their faults and foibles in abundance. They, like television, have their Achilles' heels, several of whom I've met. They, even as you and I, sometimes go about their business in the manner of Keystone cops, and occasionally trip, stumble or fall flat on their faces.

A classic example occurred right in the wake of the TV exposé. Two reporters for a New York newspaper wrote a ringing denunciation of the sins of others in a series titled "The Shame of New York" in *The Nation* magazine. Their disclosures were so hot, one of them said on a TV show, that a high city official had offered to bribe them to stop their investigation. This story got a big play in the press until the reporter admitted he made the bribe story up out of whole cloth. Both reporters were fired by their paper. The reporter who admitted the lie explained it by saying he "got carried away." I know the feeling well. I sometimes get carried away myself. However, it demonstrates to the publishing fraternity the wisdom of the old saying that those who live in glass houses shouldn't throw stones at those in isolation booths!

One characteristic of newspapers, I've noticed, is that they usually see the same event differently, depending on their individual points of view. For instance, here is how some leading publications might report Custer's massacre:

Wall Street Journal: "SIOUX LTD. UP 12 POINTS"

New York Mirror: "HAIR RAID"

Earl Wilson's column: "CUSTER'S WIDOW (38-26-36) MOURNS"

Variety: "CUSTER CLOSES OUT OF TOWN"

Pravda: "BIG RED VICTORY"

Sports Illustrated: "INDIANS WIN SERIES"

Woman's Wear Daily: "FEATHERS MAKE A COMEBACK"

Reader's Digest: "SITTING BULL REVEALS NEW CURE FOR DANDRUFF"

Washington Post: "CUSTER LOSES RURAL VOTE"

This sort of thing has been going on, I know, since they began cutting down perfectly good trees and making newspapers and magazines out of them, and comes under the heading of freedom of the press. I have no quarrel with magazines or newspapers giving their opinion on anything including me, but I have always felt that the subject of that opinion is entitled to a reply. If a newspaper or magazine can publicly criticize, or sometimes even misrepresent or misquote an individual, certainly the individual has the right to enter a dissenting opinion. As a practical matter, however, an individual usually lacks the means of replying. As a result, it has become customary for anyone from an actor to a politician to cower helplessly while a newspaper or group of them belabors him for his sins, real or imaginary.

Long ago I decided to do my frail bit to correct this. Having begun my career as an entertainer in a jungle, before an audience that was armed, I was not easily daunted even by

Dorothy Kilgallen, who will surely be our Princess if America ever becomes a monarchy. I felt if I hadn't got shot for some of those jokes, I had little to fear from the barbs of columnists or critics. In no time at all I found myself a knight with shining microphone, but without portfolio, defending the cause of actors against the jibes of critics.

I have already recounted in my experiences in Hollywood how I jousted with a theatrical trade paper for a slur against a distinguished elderly actor whom I didn't even know, and how my wife began hiding my typewriter, with which I had been peppering the paper's editor with angry letters. When I took issue with the paper my friends thought I had lost my mind and cooler heads counseled a cease-fire.

"You can't fight a newspaper," one friend cautioned. "They'll murder you."

"Why not?" I demanded. "The paper knocked a fine old gentleman. Why shouldn't I knock them right back?"

"They're entitled to knock someone if they want," my friend explained. "That's freedom of the press."

"That's why I knocked them right back," I pointed out. "That's freedom of speech."

Since I had no program to air my views on at the time, I was reduced to giving my low opinion of the theatrical paper by taking ads in a rival trade publication. This ceased when my unemployment insurance ran out, and I fulminated in private for a while.

In due time, however, I worked my way up from wrangling with one small theatrical trade paper to warring with some of the biggest publications and columnists in the country. This is not because I'm unduly warlike, or because when it comes to cultivating animosities I have a green thumb. It's just that when I read something that I know is false or slanted I can't resist saying so no matter how large or influential the publication or individual who said it.

It was probably inevitable that this feeling would sometime bring me into conflict with Walter Winchell, who is impatiently awaiting admission to the union as the 51st state. I have never seen eye-to-eye with Walter since the only way you can do that is to stoop to keyhole level. My lack of enthusiasm for the columnist, which began when he printed a falsehood about me, was suddenly reciprocated after Elsa Maxwell said on one of my programs that Winchell had never voted. Shrieking in a voice that sounded as if his underwear were too tight, he triumphantly produced a picture of himself at the polls. This proved he had voted at least once, and that it must have been an historic occasion to have been photographed for posterity. He demanded a retraction and trumpeted to the press that he was suing our sponsors for twenty-four million dollars. He also referred to me in his column as a "jerque." (Since I don't read French, I can't translate that little compliment. However, Walter always loses something in translation into English.)

Since Elsa was actually in error, I was glad to retract her statement on the air. In doing so, however, I told the audience that Winchell had once made a damaging false statement about me and had refused to retract it. In 1954 he printed in his column: "The comic Jack Paars have their pals depressed. She's the chawklit heiress." This implication that my wife and I were not getting along could not have been further from the truth and caused great distress to us and our child. Since I didn't know Winchell, I asked a friend to tell him that the item was false and to ask if he would correct it. This self-appointed General Manager of the world sent back word that he could not retract the item but that the source which gave him the wrong information would be "dead with him." That was consolation, indeed.

"The moral of this story," I told our viewers, "is: Time seems to have proved it is easier to speak the truth than to write it, and the only way to kill a lie is to pour truth on it. I have done that tonight. Mr. Winchell let his lie grow, and any farmer knows what makes things grow."

I have heard no more of his plan to sue me for twenty-four million dollars. Having made a career of spreading gossip, the role of injured innocent scarcely fits Winchell. He wraps himself in the American flag like a bathrobe. His orchids are poison ivy in a crackpot. He made his own hammock; now let him stand up in it.

Winchell and his fellow gossip-monger, Lee Mortimer, are leading examples of the indignation school of columnists. They are the angry old men of the keyhole. Whenever Winchell and Mortimer and their ilk are mounting their journalistic soap boxes to wax indignant, I always wonder at the motives that arouse such righteous indignation.

It always reminds me of a lady of easy virtue who lived in our town when I was a boy. It was well known that she was practicing the oldest profession but our elders took a tolerant view of her sins. Those were depression days, earning a living was a hard and chancy business, and the citizens were not quick to pass judgment on each other. After a busy career at her calling, the lady suddenly got religion. Like many converts, her zeal was boundless. She became the most virtuous lady in town. She also set herself up as a sort of self-elected censor of others. In her eyes, evil lurked around every corner. She saw a potential criminal in every small boy surreptitiously puffing a cubeb, and a future light lady in every girl who rolled her stockings and used lipstick. In her feverish imagination, she saw an amorous couple in every haystack. She had none of the understanding with which the people had treated her when she was a shady lady during the depression. I always think back to her when I see some columnist quivering indignantly over the public morals and acting as volunteer censor for the world. What were they doing, I wonder, during the depression?

For some reason, there seems to be a double standard as regards free speech between the press and broadcasting. Newspaper writers who speak out on controversial questions are looked on as fearless champions of free speech and heirs to Thomas Paine, while any TV performer who ventures an honest opinion on the air is considered a bumptious, uninformed oaf who should confine himself to reading someone else's jokes off a teleprompter. Almost any ink-stained lush who can't get his drinking companions to listen to him at the corner bar is greeted as an oracle when his words appear in some column. In newspapers, not just the editorial pages and Washington columnists comment on national and world affairs. Gossip columnists, sports writers and even comic strips are also not reluctant to sound off on issues of the day. Yet let a TV or radio performer speak out honestly and he is hooted by the journalistic corps.

Despite this perplexing double standard, I have never hesitated to speak out occasionally on controversial issues, even when I knew that my opinion would not be popular, at least with the press. This inevitably brought jeers from some papers, but encouragement from my viewers. The majority of people evidently still believe in the right to speak out frankly, whether it's on the air or in a column normally devoted to such earth-shaking matters as blessed events and divorces. People still believe apparently, even in these days of high living costs, that speech should still be free.

After one of my exchanges with Winchell, Dorothy Kilgallen or some other such guardian of the public weal, I received a letter from a housewife in Hartford which exemplifies the sort of support I have had from viewers in the matter of speaking out frankly on controversial matters. It said in part:

"Quite apart from whether one agrees with your sentiments, it is like a breath of fresh air to have any public figure make an unpopular remark spontaneously on the air. It seems odd that in a country which was born out of discord, contention and disagreement, one must look so far and so long to find anyone who really believes enough in the right of free speech to voice a unique opinion. No freedom can be handed down from parent to child—only the hope of freedom. Every generation must win it again, must insist upon it and must suffer for it."

I got another encouraging letter from a lady in Scarsdale, New York, enclosing an excellent piece of advice from an ancient Roman: *Nil carborundum illegitimo.* Translated, the Scarsdale lady tells me, this Latin saying means: "Don't let the bastards wear you down."

The lady need have no fears.

Despite my ruckuses with various columnists, I have never objected to criticism—only to untruths or distortions. I have often agreed with and profited by criticism, even of the harsh variety. In fact, Jack O'Brian, the TV columnist of the Hearst papers, and a tough and perceptive critic, once wrote: "Through the years of writing TV, drama, movie and music criticism, we remember no performer who has taken criticism so intelligently as has Jack Paar. He may cringe at a rough review but he never has even made passing mention of it after it got into print. Paar has the unique capacity to take the toughest criticism to heart and learn from it. He has fought with one or two publications but never on the basis of an opinion of his show, even when he was convinced the critics were 100 per cent wrong. He is accused of being 'nervous,' jittery and all the customary greasepainted traumas, but after fairly long observation of his reactions to criticism, we must admire him for his attitude. He learns from adverse notices."

Although I never mind adverse reviews of my work, like almost anyone I do resent being misquoted or misrepresented. Many a time, after seeing what I said appear quite differently in print, I have ruefully agreed with Phil Silvers who once sighed: "I've never won an interview yet." I once told an attractive young lady TV editor that I didn't have the drive, I didn't have it in my genes, to be a big star like Bop Hope or Jackie Gleason. I was a little startled the next day when it came out in her column that I "didn't have it in my *jeans* to be a big star."

There have been similar instances of facts getting somewhat scrambled by publications. Once, not long after we had completed our new red-barn house in Bronxville, *Life* magazine came up and shot a cover story there. We talked at length with the photographer and writer about the various problems of building it. We were quite surprised, therefore, when the layout appeared, to see our spanking new pride and joy referred to as a "converted barn."

I was telling Hugh Downs and some other friends about this and one of them explained that *Life* has to juggle the wording of captions to fit the space under the picture.

"I see," said Hugh, dryly. "All the news that fits, they print."

Another time, in commenting to a reporter on the total hours I worked on television, I pointed out that I "did more television than Gleason, Gobel, Steve Allen and Berle." This quotation came out in the paper that "I did more *for* television than Gleason, Gobel, Steve Allen and Berle"—a very different matter and one that caused me great embarrassment.

On another occasion *The New Yorker* magazine published a cartoon about me which I failed to understand. It showed two tired businessman types talking at a cocktail party. One was saying to the other: "I don't like Jack Paar any more than you do, but I can make contact with him as a human being."

Although I have always enjoyed *The New Yorker* cartoons, and would not mind in the least being ribbed by one, I had difficulty making contact with the point of this cartoon. I showed it to a number of friends, asking what it meant, but the point seemed to elude them too. Finally I described it to a nearly blind friend of mine who is one of the most famous *New Yorker* cartoonists and asked him what it meant. "I really don't know, either," confessed James Thurber.

Despite my occasional hostilities with magazines or newspapers, I have never had any real differences with television critics, most of whom I respect highly. A TV critic has an unusual role which Jackie Gleason once described as "being in the position of reporting an accident to a witness." The function of the drama or movie critic is a simple one: to inform his readers as to whether he thinks a specific play or movie is worth paying money to see. The job of a TV critic is entirely different. He is giving an opinion on a show which the viewer may have already seen, which may never be seen again, and which, in any event, was free. They occasionally comment on TV series, of course, but most of these assembly-line Westerns and private-eye dramas are of such a nature as to practically defy intelligent comment.

I do not think that TV critics exert much influence on the public, although they do seem to have considerable weight within the industry. Although most critics plump for the better things on the TV tube, viewers by the millions go right on staring at Westerns, quiz shows and soap operas. However, there is no doubt that certain influential critics are important in the TV industry—a group traditionally as steadfast as an insecure mambo dancer.

To have expressed this benevolent appraisal of critics is a heresy which may get me drummed out of the actors' union and have my credit card at Sardi's restaurant revoked. Most actors take a dim view of critics. "People who let drama critics pick their plays," Fred Allen once growled, "should first take a look at the critics' wives." I have noticed, though, that an actor's opinion of critics is usually highly influenced by the critics' opinions of the actor. Since the critics have generally been kind to me, I consider most of them models of clear thinking and proper deportment.

The only time I ever differed publicly with a TV critic was not over a performance of mine. In fact, it was just the reverse. A number of years ago, when a radio show of mine was replaced by a quiz show, John Crosby lamented that what he called "one of the most literate new comedians on radio" was replaced by a "routine quiz show." I was naturally sorry to have my show canceled, and appreciated John Crosby's encouraging words, but I pointed out publicly that the show which replaced me was, in all fairness, not a routine quiz show. I was quite right, as time has demonstrated. That quiz show, presided over by Groucho Marx, is still going strong at this writing after twelve years.

Although I find myself more often than not in agreement

with critics, I still maintain that the mantle of critic is not granted by Divine Right to publishers, and that television or any other field has the same right to criticize them. For instance, to turn the tables, this is how it might look if I were to criticize a newspaper in the same manner in which its critic treats television:

The headline story about Russia in last night's paper fell flat. Written by Clyde Forbush and edited by Herman Krine, the story moved through seventeen paragraphs in lackluster fashion. It was neither fresh nor original. Forbush split an infinitive in the opening paragraph and dangled a participle in paragraph six. It seemed to this reviewer that Forbush could use more seasoning—perhaps another year in journalism school.

Type was set in six point Gothic by Willard Semple. He made three mistakes.

The want ads also left something to be desired. It's always been the opinion of this reviewer that want ad type is far too small.

Although set in larger type, last night's editorial page drew a blank with this reviewer. When will editorial writers learn that the public is fed up with grade "B" opinions?

The political cartoon lacked punch. The letters to the editor lacked imagination and were placed at the bottom of the page—leaving the Alsop Brothers dangling from a one-column headline.

The newspaper as a whole had entirely too many ads.

The tender eyes of children reading the comics should not have to read in the same paper about wife beatings, infidelity and couples who switch mates.

And why don't they get some fresh news? Most of it sounds like reruns.

24. PAAR POURRI

For some reason I have never quite understood, I seem to have been mixed up most of my adult life with assorted Cubans. There have been times, in fact, when I've been surrounded with so many Cubans that life has seemed like one big cha cha cha.

This affinity for the citizens of the beautiful, fragrant and mixed-up island in the Caribbean started in the Army in World War II where I encountered Jose Melis, a talented conductor and pianist and a demon automobile driver. As I've already mentioned, Jose played at my wedding and has been making beautiful music at my various shows since, including my present midnight madness.

My association with Cuban musicians was compounded a few years later on the CBS "Morning Show" when as a sidekick I acquired Pupi Campo, an energetic rhumba purveyor. Pupi and I didn't always see eye to eye on maracca shaking and other vital show business matters and the last I heard he was suing me for impugning his talents. My association with Cuba and Cubans got as thick as the smoke from a good Havana cigar when we did our show from Havana and later when I interviewed Fidel Castro just a few days after he came to power.

We did the program in Havana in July, 1958, when Fulgencio Batista was still in power and Castro was fighting from the hills of the Sierra Maestra, and it was like performing in no man's land. There had been rumors that the Castro forces might try to kidnap me, as they had the famous Argentine racing driver, Juan Fangio, to call attention to their cause, and all of our party were a little jittery when we landed in Havana.

Genevieve and I saw a limousine we thought was for us so we got in and asked the driver in scrambled Spanish to take us to the Havana Hilton. On our arrival there, I discovered we had mistakenly gotten into the wrong car. The Batista government had assigned a car, driver and bodyguard to us, and they were left behind when we got into the wrong limousine and sped away.

The driver, I later learned, was a big, cheerful, bearlike man named Roberto Garcia. The bodyguard was a chunky, mustached, villainous-looking Cuban known only as Tito. When Genevieve and I missed them and disappeared, the nervous Tito evidently thought we had been kidnaped by Castro forces and that Garcia was a party to the plot by letting another car whisk us off. He crashed his revolver down on Roberto's head, knocking him unconscious, and hauled him off to jail. There he was held and questioned until it was established the whole incident was an innocent foul-up and we were safely at the hotel.

Tito never left my side after that. Even when I was swimming in the hotel pool, he would loll nearby with his .45 automatic in his lap, discreetly covered by a towel. Tito had one habit that puzzled me. He always wore dark sunglasses indoors, and took them off when he went out in the sun. Since he was assigned to protect me, I used to hope this strange habit wouldn't adversely affect his shooting eye.

Trying to do a televison show in a foreign land, with technical problems and a language barrier, is never exactly easy, and when you throw in a full-scale shooting revolution it does nothing to simplify things. Nothing seemed to go right. We had hoped to have Ernest Hemingway as a guest but he was tied up on a book. Later I learned he was *reading* it—not writing it. We also tried to get Errol Flynn but he was in the hills hiding from Batista's troops and an even larger army of process servers.

The show itself was the worst disaster in Havana since the sinking of the *Maine*. I was doing part of the show from the Tropicana night club, while Jose Melis was to conduct the seventy-eight-man Havana Symphony from the penthouse atop the Havana Hilton. To add to the confusion, the program was being relayed to a station at Guanabo, Cuba, from where it was rebroadcast via scatter system to Florida. From there it was transmitted via microwave relay to New York, whence it was rebroadcast again over the NBC network to the entire U.S. At least what was left of it was.

Things began falling apart on the show from the opening theme music. Since Jose was conducting the symphony at the Havana Hilton, we had a Cuban rhumba orchestra at the Tropicana to play the theme and other musical numbers there. They spoke no English but Jose had instructed them in Spanish on our American television signals: that when the stage manager made the motion "T" it was the signal to start the theme music; his finger drawn across his throat was the cut signal to stop the music.

The show started, the band struck up the theme and I walked out on the Tropicana stage to do my opening monologue. However, the music didn't stop. The rhumba band was blaring the theme furiously and gave no sign of stopping. I started my monologue, to give them a hint, but was drowned out by their melody. Our stage manager began frantically motioning the band leader to cut but he grinned back happily and kept right on playing.

"El stoppo del musico!" I yelled, but without any success.

The beaming rhumba artists apparently were enjoying their own music, and weren't going to give up easily. As they played on and on it looked as though the program was going to be an hour and three-quarters of theme music, with me making muffled sounds amid the din. I began waving at the band leader and drawing my finger across my throat, but I wasn't giving TV signals—I was threatening to cut his throat! After about nine choruses of the theme we finally got the band to subside, and I started the show. This was also a mistake.

"If you'll only not think of it as a show," I implored the audience, as everything began to go awry. "Just think of it as international bad relations. It's a lend-louse deal."

One of my guests was Gaspar Pumarejo, who was called "the Arthur Godfrey of Cuba," but since he spoke almost no English he wasn't much help. I couldn't seem to penetrate the language barrier, but at least we were shattering the sound barrier with the noise and the music. The audience was a noisy one except when I told a joke. Then there was complete silence. Most of the noise was coming from backstage. I could have sworn the stagehands were dancing the rhumba in the wings, if I hadn't heard them arguing heatedly in Spanish.

"More silenzio back there," I shouted over the din, "or you won't be amigos."

Finally I got some semblance of quiet and began talking with Cesar Romero. Just then we were drowned out by the wail of sirens outside. This, it turned out, was a police escort delivering Jose from the hotel where he had just finished conducting the symphony. What the audience needed by then was not the symphony but sympathy. The show was summed up, rather accurately, I'm afraid, by a New York paper which headlined its review: MUCHO MESSO.

Despite the difficulties of doing a show with a language barrier and in the midst of a revolution, I liked Cuba and its friendly people immensely and have visited there several times since. Because of this feeling for Cuba, when Fidel Castro finally overthrew the Batista government in January, 1959, I decided to fly down and try to get an interview with him. I was impressed by Castro—possibly because he is the only man I know who talks longer on television than I do.

Jim Bishop, the Hearst columnist and author, flew with me to Havana for the interview.

On landing in Cuba I discovered that Roberto Garcia, the burly chauffeur who was slugged and jailed when I mistakenly got into a wrong car, had fled to the hills, become a captain under Castro and had been a hero in the fighting. He had, we learned, made a makeshift tank out of an International Harvester tractor to capture an important bridge held by Batista forces. At the controls of his do-it-yourself tank, Roberto rumbled up to the bridge calling on its defenders to surrender. Out of the nearby trees stepped several bearded soldiers who announced: "We're Castro troops. We took the bridge two days ago."

Despite this typically Cuban incident, Roberto was a real hero in the fighting and a highly respected officer with Castro's forces. He was now in Havana looking for Tito, my erstwhile bodyguard who had slugged and jailed him. Tito, no fool, had suddenly remembered an urgent appointment and had put on his sunglasses and departed for a friendlier atmosphere.

Havana was in a fever of excitement when Jim Bishop and I arrived. We moved into the Havana Hilton, where Castro had his headquarters, and began trying to get an interview with him.

All was chaotic, but I never saw better disciplined soldiers than Castro's green-clad *barbudos*, their luxuriant, unkempt beards reminding me of busted sofas. The only exception to this impression was Raoul Castro, whose short, scraggly beard made him look like a bus boy at the Last Supper. Although the beautiful, thirty-story hotel was swarming with these soldiers, I never saw one so much as chip an ash tray.

When the tall, bearded Fidel Castro would stride into the lobby, crowds would swarm around him almost reverently, and reach out to touch him or pluck his sleeve. He would come to the hotel for dinner, usually shortly after midnight, and eat in the kitchen with the help there. No problem seemed too small to escape his personal attention. While we were there the hotel fired two employees. They appealed to Castro and he called a meeting to investigate the action. Castro listened patiently while each side heatedly argued its case. Then he handed down his decision. The employees were rehired. During all this varied activity, he kept in touch with the country with frequent rambling speeches. Television sets were being set up in the squares of towns all over Cuba, and the revolutionary leader, looking like an El Greco apostle, would harangue the people sometimes as long as five hours at a time.

Jim and I were ensconced in a magnificent suite on the twenty-second floor of the hotel, just below Castro's, and busied ourselves trying to fight our way through the confusion and crowds around him to arrange our interviews. The tumult and excitement around the hotel were tremendous, and all night long we could hear the heavy clump of his soldier's boots on the marble floors directly overhead. After three days of this confused frustration, Jim, who has a fiery Irish temper, got angry at the delay and flew back to the United States.

He had scarcely left when I got a call at two o'clock in the morning that Dr. Castro was on his way down to my suite for an interview.

It happened so suddenly, when it finally came about, that I was momentarily at a loss for words as the rebel chief walked into my big suite, trailed by a group of his armed *barbudos*, many of them just youngsters from the hill country.

"Dr. Castro, you are a good neighbor," I finally blurted as we shook hands. "My suite here is just below you, and you haven't been down once to borrow sugar."

The Cuban leader smiled and shrugged as if to say: crazy Americano.

Since I speak only fractured Spanish, and Dr. Castro's English leaves something to be desired, I found myself in our interview sounding like Tarzan addressing Jane. He was wearing a rumpled, green military uniform and cap, and puffed on a big Havana cigar as we talked.

I told him that he and his soldiers had been clumping

about in their boots on the marble floors just over my bedroom. "Please don't drop your shoes tonight," I asked.

Castro said he was not a Communist, that he liked and admired Americans, and that the people of Cuba were united behind him in his determination to punish those who had led the Batista tyranny. "To understand tyranny," he said, "it is necessary to live under tyranny."

I told him that I had visited La Cabana Fortress, Camp Columbia, from which Batista had fled, and the former dictator's magnificent home.

"You want to buy?" he asked, brightening noticeably. "We sell for two million dollars. You have two million dollars?"

Castro seemed tired and his voice was hoarse from his marathon-length speeches to the Cuban people. Glancing at the armed soldiers around us, I remarked on their beards and suggested that I'd like to have the Norelco shaver concession in Havana when they decided to shave them off.

I asked him about his nine-year-old son, Fidelito, and he told me of how the boy had been the means of the Cuban people expressing their support for his father while he was still fighting in the mountains. Although he had many followers in Havana even then, Castro said, they were for him in secret as any open display would invite arrest or even death at the hands of the Batista regime. On one occasion, however, little Fidelito entered a swimming race. "There were many youngsters in the race," Castro said, "but the crowd all began to yell: Fidel! Fidel! They were actually demonstrating their support for me, by shouting the Castro name, but there was nothing the Batista police could do. After all, they were just cheering for a little boy in a swimming race."

One time later, Randy went swimming with young Fidelito at our hotel pool.

When it came time for them to leave the pool, his nurse called to Fidelito in Spanish to get out. However, he was enjoying his swim and made no move to obey. Then the life guard asked him in English to get out. Stubborn as his father, the nine-year-old youngster kept right on splashing around in the water. I decided to try a little of my fractured Spanish on him.

"Adios to aqua!" I yelled.

He hopped out.

On one trip to Cuba, Miriam, Randy and I decided we wanted to go to a typical Cuban restaurant. We didn't want to go to any of the tourist type places so we enlisted a cousin of Jose Melis to act as our guide. He took us to an obscure little restaurant in the old section of Havana where we planned to invite heartburn by sampling various fiery Cuban dishes.

Our guide had to go on to another date so we found ourselves minus an interpreter in the restaurant which had only Spanish-speaking waiters. By a combination of fractured Spanish, acquired watching old Cesar Romero and Leo Carillo movies, and much violent gesturing, I managed to get us a martini and a lethal combination of black beans, onions and rice served by a waiter who must have operated a flame thrower under the Machado regime.

Finally came dessert. I was linguistically exhausted, and willing to retire on my laurels of having successfully ordered our main course, but Randy insisted on dessert. I finally consented on the condition that it be something simple like ice cream. With a sigh I summoned our waiter and resumed my arm-waving.

"El cremo . . ." I tried. "La cremola? . . . el bovino? . . . la chilly cremo? . . . el mucho cremo?"

Suddenly the waiter's swarthy face broke into a big grin.

"Sí, sí, Señor," he beamed. *"Helado."*

From his smile of recognition I decided I'd hit the right category. Now for a flavor. Chocolate seemed the simplest, so I began to try to order that in my scrambled Spanish.

"El chocolate?" I said. "El browno? . . . tres chocolate? . . . une darko?"

The waiter broke into another smile of recognition.

"Ah, sí, sí. Helado de chocolate. Sí."

"No, Papa!" wailed Randy, as the man headed for the kitchen. "I want peppermint stick!"

Although I enjoy participating in sports like swimming and fishing, I could never understand people who merely watch sports or, worse yet, just read about them. I can't comprehend how someone can sit in front of a TV set watching two boxers batting each other in the sinuses, in between commercials on the importance of being well groomed, and then spend hours reading on the sports pages about what they saw. To me the sports page is just something you flip past to get to the financial page or the obituaries, and Mickey Mantle is just a guy who shaves on television instead of in his own bathroom like anyone else. The last sports figure I worked up any real enthusiasm for was Esther Williams.

I'll never forget the day that Tom Cochran, my associate producer, rushed up to me and said: "I think I can get Larsen as a guest on the show."

"He sounds very interesting," I said. "He's a very well-informed, articulate man and his book helped shape the concept of modern Republicanism. I saw him on 'Meet the Press' and he was excellent. I think he'd make a very good guest."

"I don't mean Arthur Larsen," Tommy groaned. "I mean Don Larsen. He just pitched the first no-hit, no-run game in World Series history!"

Despite my ignorance of such athletic lore, and my lack of enthusiasm for reading the major league fielding averages, or sitting for three hours in the rain while twenty-two mud-coated figures butt heads on the football field, I love outdoor life and actually participating in sports. The very day I was writing this chapter at Key Biscayne, Florida, I went swimming, sank a fifty-foot hole in one on a pitch and putt golf course and caught a seven-foot swordfish.

The most ambitious outdoor endeavor I ever undertook also took place at Key Biscayne. I was sitting around the pool of the beautiful Key Biscayne Hotel one day with Tom Ferris, a genial publicity man with a hot-rod imagination. As an illustration of his imagination, Tom was once hired to publicize J. Meyer Schine, the hotel tycoon. He proposed that Schine buy a race horse and name it "Harvest Moon." "Then we can send out pictures of you on the horse to the papers," he explained to the hotel man. "The caption would be: Schine on Harvest Moon."

On this occasion, one daiquiri led to another and pretty soon Ferris asked: "How'd you like to water ski behind a blimp?"

"We'd better not have any more daiquiris in this hot sun," I said. "I think I'm beginning to hear things."

Tom assured me that he had indeed mentioned water skiing behind a blimp, and that it was entirely possible.

"But I've never even water skied behind an outboard motorboat," I protested.

"All the more reason to do it behind a blimp," said Tom, expansively. "Start big."

The evening grew a little hazy after that and, between the daiquiris and feeling sure that Tom couldn't get a blimp, I apparently agreed to the skiing stunt. The next morning I was sitting in front of our villa trying to regain my health when it suddenly turned dark. I sat up in alarm, thinking it must be an eclipse of the sun. I looked up and there, hovering above and blotting out the sun, was a blimp. With horror I recalled my rash promise of the night before. I began to quickly think of ways of getting out of it when Tom appeared beaming cheerfully and flanked by reporters and cameramen. He even had a newsreel man. I was trapped!

Cursing under my breath, I let them strap the skis to my feet with all the enthusiasm of a man being strapped into an electric chair. My legs reacted like limp spaghetti that someone had tied knots in for knees. However, after several false starts, during which I gargled part of Biscayne Bay, I struggled upright and to my wonderment stayed that way while

I was towed along behind the blimp hundreds of feet above me.

I felt pretty good about my accomplishment, when it was all over, and had no nervous reaction until the next day when I returned to the scene of my triumph. Tom took me back over Biscayne Bay in the blimp to retrace the course I had negotiated the previous day. I was looking down through the clear waters I had skied over the day before when I saw several shadowy shapes moving ominously beneath the surface.

"What are those?" I asked Tom.

"Oh, them," said Ferris, peering down on the water I had been wallowing in the day before. "Those are sharks."

"Sharks!" I yelled, as if one had just bitten me. "You let me water ski where those sharks are!"

"You were safe," Tom said, with a nonchalance I couldn't share. "I have a theory that sharks only attack if you're wounded, or if you're wearing something shiny. That's why I had you take your ring off."

Coming back to Hollywood to do our show in November of 1958 I found everything changed. When I had slunk out of town a few years before, and headed East in my station wagon to try to find a job in television, I was broke and discouraged. Everything seemed to have gone wrong in Hollywood, and even my footprints in the forecourt at Grauman's Chinese Theater seemed headed in the wrong direction.

Now, with a hit television show, everything was different, although it is an old, old story. We were ensconced as guests of the exclusive Beverly Hilton Hotel, an edifice so swank that the fire ax in the hall outside our suite said: "In case of fire—break crystal." "This is a nice place to visit," Paul Keyes, my head writer, sighed as he surveyed the posh hostelry, "but I wouldn't want to *pay* here."

When Miriam and I got to our suite there were so many telephone messages from old friends that A T & T stock must have jumped several points. I registered as Gunther Badue, to escape old friends I had never met, and took stock of our beautiful suite. We were so amply supplied with liquor that I had enough to endow Charley Weaver for a year.

The maids at the hotel were terribly efficient. If you wanted one to come in and fix up your room all you had to do was put up the sign saying: "Please Do Not Disturb." Every time I stepped out of the shower, it seemed, a maid would barge in. I spent half my time grabbing towels and ducking back behind doors. If anyone ever asks those maids what Jack Paar is really like, they'll say he's a nude man who's always stooped over looking surprised and clutching a towel. I appreciated the wonderful service, but I hope by the next time I visit the Beverly Hilton they will have found the mystery guest they seemed to be looking for.

We had hardly gotten settled in the hotel than people began calling wanting to entertain us. Miriam and I were invited to several typical Hollywood parties. Almost everyone was dressed in formal slacks. Of course there were a few nonconformists like the Western TV star who came in Italian Bermuda shorts. He was wearing a holster for a loaf of garlic bread.

Hollywood itself was considerably changed from when we had lived there, and the smog was much worse. However, the papers were full of stories that the California Chamber of Commerce was working on a solution for the whole problem—medicated smog.

Another new development since we'd been away was the great Freeway System which was already overcrowded. Lots of people were meeting the problem by driving the little new foreign sports cars. Some of them were so small that the drivers had to be fitted for the car by an operation to put hinges on their shins. There was one advantage to the jammed Freeway. If you ran out of gas you could still go twenty-five miles on the group plan.

As we drove around we saw that Hollywood still had its variety of strange religions and cults. People seemingly would join anything. We had an interoffice memo blow out the window and by noon we had thirty-five followers. Driving through the canyons we'd see painted on the rocks: "Where will YOU spend eternity?" The answer, in view of the jammed traffic, seemed plain: On the Hollywood Freeway!

Hollywood seemed as preoccupied as ever with dying. Forest Lawn Cemetery was as popular as always and seemed a sort of Disneyland for shut-ins. One cemetery advertised "Foreverness," which seemed to be horizontal togetherness.

I got a kick out of just driving around Hollywood, past Twentieth-Century Fox and RKO studios where I used to work or, rather, where I was under contract and used *not* to work. Now RKO was owned by Desi and Lucy Arnaz, and all the old lots which used to turn out movies were busy making films for television. There was even a budding new business aging movies for use on television. The television stars were the big attraction now, and movie stars weren't as important as they used to be. I saw one newsstand that was even selling maps of where the movie stars *used* to live.

Whether working in TV or movies, however, actors had remained the same. Although they make their living speaking in pear-shaped tones on the screen, most of them can't even lift a conversation let alone carry one. If paid by the word for ad libbing, these worthies would be in the poorhouse instead of before cameras.

I knew from past experience the difficulty of conducting interviews with actors. I would ask, "Tell me about your last picture," and they would reply, "It was fun." Western or Biblical epic, the answer was always the same: "It was fun." Although they could be seen gunning down outlaws or brandishing cutlasses at pirates on the screen, these actors were overcome by timidity at the prospect of a little light conversation.

As soon as word got around that we were in town looking for talkers, it started the biggest exodus from the film capital since they struck real estate at Palm Springs. My scouts began scouring the Brown Derby and other gathering places of supposed filmland wits, but most of them remembered dates elsewhere. I tried to enlist the aid of Leo Durocher, then an NBC executive whose duties included snaffling talent for the network, but he vanished as completely as if he'd been thrown out by an umpire. Bob Hope, Groucho Marx, Dennis Day and Oscar Levant heeded my call, but other stars proved elusive. We rushed nine-year-old Evelyn Rudie of Eloise fame into the breach, but still we needed additional reinforcements. I finally wound up sending an SOS to New York for Charley Weaver, Genevieve and other accomplished word warriors. Importing actors to Hollywood would seem to be like bringing ham to Hormel, but we had to do it.

The next time we went to Hollywood everything was different. The great Hollywood wits—Jack Benny, Red Skelton, George Burns, Jerry Lewis and others—all came on our show. Good conversation sparkled like champagne, and we had Mickey Rooney for a chaser.

The biggest new thing since I'd left Hollywood was Disneyland, and Randy, of course, was dying to see it. Disneyland is such a big thing to Californians, I discovered, that when you cross the border you have to raise your right hand and take an oath that you believe in Walt Disney. The only non-believer I encountered was Oscar Levant who wouldn't visit Disneyland because he said he had his own hallucinations.

I took Randy and it was some experience. You can have a wonderful time there with a child and $42. Fortunately the Bank of America has opened a branch there so you can finance an afternoon. At Disneyland there is absolutely no waste; you have to have a ticket for everything. At one point Randy fell down and a man said she'd have to have three blue tickets to get up.

Disneyland is so important there is talk it will be admitted to the Union as a new state. The flag would then contain fifty stars and one dollar sign. Randy and I were goggle-eyed as we gazed over the wonders of what Walt Disney had wrought. It was a magnificent demonstration of what God could do if He had more imagination.

As I looked over the many attractions I remembered reading that when Walt Disney was in Switzerland making a movie he saw the Matterhorn and announced: "I want it." Well, he's got it and a lot more besides. Randy and I rode down his Matterhorn in a bobsled, and went underwater in a nuclear-powered submarine. It was fun, but I began to worry about the effect of such man-made extravagance on children's minds. The thing that set me thinking was that Randy said wistfully: "It's a nice place to visit, but I wouldn't want to *leave* there." I had to practically drag her away. I'm afraid that kids now will feel that you haven't really lived until you've seen a sunset at Disneyland. When they see the real Grand Canyon it will seem like just a big, purple hole in the ground. All these artificial Fantasylands and Tomorrowlands will give children the false idea that happiness can be found only in aluminum.

To restore a sense of reality, I think Walt Disney should have a Hardluckland. There the visitor could have the experience of falling in love and getting his first "Dear John" letter; the adventure of receiving his draft and induction notices; the sensation of falling behind in his car payments; the surprise of learning that his brother-in-law and his five children are arriving to spend the vacation with him; or the shock of learning that his father is secretly in love with his aunt.

25. BLOOD OVER THE DAM

I HAVE BEEN told that any book should have a rousing finish, and I seem to have acquired one. While this saga was already on the presses an incident occurred which seems so typical of my life that it makes an appropriate ending to round one of my autobiography.

On the show of February 10, 1960, I read a little anecdote given me by a friend. He had got it from his thirteen-year-old niece, whose teacher had read it to her junior high school class. They had enjoyed it so much that the teacher had given each class member a copy.

Although it was a rather ancient story, I thought it was amusing and decided to tell it on the show. I didn't consider it in bad taste. I have never approved of off-color stories, on or off the air. On the show I have always tried to have our lady guests avoid low-cut gowns and wiggling behinds. I have frequently asked comedians to drop jokes which I considered risqué from their routines when they appeared on the program. I considered this story an innocent and funny one and told it on the air. The studio audience seemed to enjoy it hugely, and when I asked afterwards if anyone considered it in questionable taste, not one person did.

However, the network, without telling me, cut the portion where I told the story out of the tape, so it did not appear on the show when the tape was played later that evening.

This gave the public the impression that I had told a smutty story, something I did not consider to be true. I asked NBC to show the censored portion of the tape the next night, and to let the viewers decide whether it was in bad taste. The network refused to do this. Therefore I am printing the story here, exactly as I told it on the air, to let readers decide for themselves whether it is objectionable.

An English lady, while visiting Switzerland, was looking for a room, and she asked the schoolmaster if he could recommend any to her. He took her to see several rooms, and when everything was settled, the lady returned to her home to make the final preparations to move. When she arrived home, the thought suddenly occurred to her that she had not seen a "W.C." (water closet) around the place. So she immediately wrote a note to the schoolmaster asking him if there was a "W.C." around. The schoolmaster was a very poor student of English, so he asked the parish priest if he could help in the matter. Together they tried to discover the meaning of the letters "W.C." and the only solution they could find for the letters was a Wayside Chapel. The schoolmaster then wrote to the English lady the following note:

Dear Madam:

I take great pleasure in informing you that the "W.C." is situated nine miles from the house you occupy, in the center of a beautiful grove of pine trees surrounded by lovely grounds.

It is capable of holding 229 people and it is open on Sunday and Thursday only. As there are a great number of people and they are expected during the summer months, I would suggest that you come early; although there is plenty of standing room as a rule.

You will no doubt be glad to hear that a good number of people bring their lunch and make a day of it. While others who can afford to go by car arrive just in time. I would es-

pecially recommend that your Ladyship go on Thursday when there is a musical accompaniment.

It may interest you to know that my daughter was married in the "W.C." and it was there that she met her husband. I can remember the rush there was for seats. There were ten people to a seat usually occupied by one. It was wonderful to see the expressions on their faces.

The newest attraction is a bell donated by a wealthy resident of the district. It rings every time a person enters. A bazaar is to be held to provide plush seats for all the people, since they feel it is a long-felt need. My wife is rather delicate, so she can't attend regularly.

I shall be delighted to reserve the best seat for you if you wish, where you will be seen by all. For the children, there is a special time and place so that they will not disturb the elders. Hoping to have been of some service to you, I remain

Sincerely,
The Schoolmaster

That's the story that brought the NBC censor out brandishing his blue pencil. When I learned that the network had cut it out of the show without even telling me, I was angry and concerned. I felt the implication that I had told an objectionable story was harmful to me and the show. I also felt that the question of free speech was involved.

The network officials I protested to treated the whole matter lightly and seemed to consider it just a tempest in a water closet. They suggested I pass the incident off with a joke. Suddenly the censors were the ones with the sense of humor! However, I didn't think the principle involved was funny. I have never liked the idea of censorship and it had reached a ridiculous state a few days before when my ten-year-old daughter Randy, who sometimes appears with me on the show, was asked to sign a network form that she had never accepted payola! Now I had felt the heavy hand of the censor over a joke about a water closet, an innocent enough accommodation I thought was familiar to most people, even network censors.

The next night when I went on to do the show I was still angry. It was nearly midnight. In less than an hour it would be the birthday of Abraham Lincoln—the man who freed the slaves. So I emancipated myself from the program. I explained to the audience what had happened and told them how deeply I felt about the matter. Then I walked out of the studio and turned the program back to the censors. Having been fired a number of times by networks, I finally fired a network.

I must say I was amazed at the uproar caused by the midnight walk of Jack Paar. I was also heartened by the support of my position expressed by the public and even by some of the press. I would like to quote from something written at the time by the highly respected Jack Gould of *The New York Times*, since it seems to me to sum up my sentiments and the background of my leaving the show:

Mr. Paar is not the traditional trouper; he is a creation of television. If he began as a light humorist, his forte on his own show has been an outspokenness that has not alienated viewers weary of nice nellyism and self-appointed sacred cows who can dish out criticism but cannot take it.

In this regard let Mr. Paar be champion, other faults notwithstanding. During his farewell he assailed the Hearst press. More specifically, he castigated the type of yellow journalism that pontificates on morality and then over its front pages splashes lurid accounts of sexual goings-on brought out in a murder trial.

The Fourth Estate would be well advised to take heed and, in this instance, not dismiss Mr. Paar as a buffoon with inadequate reference; he is echoing a point of view widely held by responsible and sensible people.

These individuals are tired of seeing newspapers criticize television for excessive sex and violence when some journals pursue circulation and profits by the same means.

Innumerable figures in the theater, while recognizing that they must live in the public eye, fail to see why they must be made the butts of gossip items that are never checked before publication. And what particularly infuriates them is the Fourth Estate's position that it is a gentlemen's club. The responsible press, they note, does not lash out at irresponsible journalism as it does at irresponsible television.

And if an individual in the entertainment world wants to state his version of a particular situation before the public, what happens?

Many members of the press insist on the immature privilege of having the last word or they camouflage as a reportorial account what should be unmistakably labeled as an editorial, criticism or interpretation.

There appears every likelihood that one consequence of l'affaire Paar will be broader ventilation of the taboos of TV.

Those words of Jack Gould in *The New York Times* sum up very well my feelings that lay behind events leading up to my walking off the show. The comments of *The Times* and other papers and the support of my position expressed in thousands of letters, wires and phone calls, indicated again the deep concern of people for free speech. They were cheering evidence of the public's dislike of censorship and their belief in a man's right to say what he pleases, even if it is only to tell a joke.

Looking back on the incident, I'm sorry for my actions and I'm glad that NBC and I have kissed and made up. I regret that I walked off the show. Perhaps walked is hardly the word, as I wound up in Hong Kong, which is a terribly long way to go for a silk suit.

Such is life to date. It's been confusing, strenuous, rewarding at times, frustrating often and rarely dull. Looking back, my life so far seems like one long obstacle race, with me as its chief obstacle, and there are times when things are happening so fast I think maybe we should have made this a looseleaf book. The misadventures that befall me have a way of happening at the most inappropriate times. One time, just before going on "The Ed Sullivan Show," I sprayed my throat with what turned out to be a deodorant. This had the effect of making my vocal chords as frozen as Ed Sullivan's face, and he seemed to be wearing novocaine makeup. Another time I bent over in my dressing room to tie a shoelace, when my secretary burst in, nearly doorknobbing me to death.

Despite these occupational hazards, life has been full. I've entertained for President Eisenhower, measured the Miss Universe candidates, whose group measurements were 504-306-504, and even fired a network. Tomorrow the world!

Meeting the President was an especial thrill for me, since we were dress-alikes in World War II. The occasion was a big banquet in the capital and I entertained, along with Kathryn Grayson, the singer, and Conrad Nagel, the veteran actor. After the dinner we all got to meet and shake hands with the President. I'll never forget what he said to me. He shook hands warmly and said: "It's nice to meet you, Mr. Nagel."

Life has also been very good to me. Unlike most actors, I have something put away for a rainy day. I have a safety deposit box full of galoshes. I have a wonderful wife and daughter, and a pleasant home. I have some good friends and some enemies anyone could be proud of. I'm doing the kind of show I've always wanted to do—adult, honest and free and easy—and it's nice to have it a success. However, I never let applause go to my head. I always remember they applauded Lincoln the night he went to that theater. I've been up and down often enough not to be unduly impressed with success.

Once, after it had been on a year, NBC gave a big testimonial dinner for me at the Plaza Hotel in New York to celebrate the success of the show. It began at two o'clock in the morning, after the show, and raged until dawn. Some of the best-known people in show business made speeches saying what a big success I was. All through the speeches, though, I kept thinking that just a year before, and only a few blocks away, I'd been fired as a disk jockey on radio.

It's a tough struggle and there are times when I wonder if it's all worth it. One viewer wrote me that she kept the show on but with the sound off. She said it made a very good night light. It's depressing, after more than twenty years in show business, to be used as radar to the bathroom.